THE WINES OF AUSTRALIA

THE INFINITE IDEAS CLASSIC WINE LIBRARY

Editorial board: Sarah Jane Evans MW,
Richard Mayson and James Tidwell MS

There is something uniquely satisfying about a good wine book, preferably read with a glass of the said wine in hand. The Infinite Ideas Classic Wine Library is a series of wine books written by authors who are both knowledgeable and passionate about their subject. Each title in The Infinite Ideas Classic Wine Library covers a wine region, country or type and together the books are designed to form a comprehensive guide to the world of wine as well as an enjoyable read, appealing to wine professionals, wine lovers, tourists, armchair travellers and wine trade students alike. Other titles in the series include:

Port and the Douro, Richard Mayson
Sherry, Julian Jeffs
The wines of Austria, Stephen Brook
Côte d'Or: The wines and winemakers of the heart of Burgundy,
    Raymond Blake
The wines of Canada, Rod Phillips
Rosé: Understanding the pink wine revolution, Elizabeth Gabay MW
Amarone and the fine wines of Verona, Michael Garner
The wines of Greece, Konstantinos Lazarakis MW
Wines of the Languedoc, Rosemary George MW
The wines of northern Spain, Sarah Jane Evans MW
The wines of New Zealand, Rebecca Gibb MW
The wines of Bulgaria, Romania and Moldova, Caroline Gilby MW
Sake and the wines of Japan, Anthony Rose
The wines of Great Britain, Stephen Skelton MW
The wines of Chablis and the Grand Auxerrois, Rosemary George MW
The wines of Germany, Anne Krebiehl MW
The wines of Georgia, Lisa Granik MW
The wines of South Africa, Jim Clarke
The wines of Piemonte, David Way
The wines of Portugal, Richard Mayson
Wines of the Rhône, Matt Walls
The wines of Roussillon, Rosemary George MW
Fizz! Champagne and Sparkling Wines of the World, Anthony Rose

THE WINES OF
AUSTRALIA

Mark Davidson

infiniteideas

Born in London and raised in Sydney, Mark Davidson has over 40 years of experience in the hotel, restaurant and wine business, fifteen of those as a sommelier.

Mark lived in Vancouver, Canada, for more than 25 years. While also working hospitality, he established the Vancouver Wine Academy and taught wine classes to trade and consumers. In 2001 he was named Sommelier of the Year at the Vancouver Wine Festival and in 2014 he won the Spirited Industry Professional award.

As a Department Head and instructor with the International Sommelier Guild, Mark was instrumental in the ongoing development of the curriculum and has taught classes in Vancouver, Seattle, Portland, San Francisco, Los Angeles, San Diego and Las Vegas.

Mark is an annual judge at the TEXSOM International Wine Awards and has judged many other competitions in both Canada and the US. Since 2008, Mark has been Head of Education Development for Wine Australia in North America. He now lives in the United States.

First published in 2023 by
Infinite Ideas Limited
www.infideas.com

Wine Australia did not provide any investment or support for the research and writing of this book, and no Wine Australia personnel have reviewed its contents prior to publication. The research was personally funded by the author. The opinions expressed and producers recommended are the author's own. This book does not represent, or purport to represent, the position or opinions of Wine Australia.

A CIP catalogue record for this book is available from the British Library
ISBN 978–1–913022–05–1

Front cover photo © Cephas/Mick Rock

Interior photos: page 45 courtesy of Cirillo Wines; page 79 courtesy of Clonakilla Wines; page 111 courtesy of Small Fry Wines; page 141 courtesy of Wine Australia. All other photos by the author.

Maps copyright Wine Australia

CONTENTS

Maps

ACKNOWLEDGEMENTS

I do not come from a writing background, so this book stretched me in more ways than I care to admit, and took way longer to write than anticipated. COVID lockdowns and a full-time job contributed as did a degree of creative paralysis in the early stages. My family was very patient, particularly my wife Abbe who was encouraging and supportive but also not shy to dole out a few well-timed servings of impatience. There are many people who have provided guidance and advice, so many that I apologize in advance if I have missed you. I owe deep gratitude to James Tidwell MS for convincing me that I was the right person to undertake this project. To my editor, Rebecca Clare of Infinite Ideas, what can I say other than sorry for the workload and thank you for your astute commentary and patience. You are a gem.

Several colleagues at Wine Australia were very helpful in sourcing pertinent information and providing salient commentary especially Hannah Bently, Dr Liz Waters, Rachel Triggs and Angelica Crabb. I am beyond grateful for the engaging conversations with Australian wine writers Mike Bennie and Nick Ryan. Aside from being fun to drink wine with, they helped crystallize thoughts on many topics. A special thanks goes to Laura Jewel MW; bouncing thoughts and ideas with you inspires me as does your steady voice of reason.

The Australian wine community is, in general, incredibly accommodating with their time and enthusiasm for explaining what and how they do things, and several producers are mentioned at the end of the book in Appendix II: Mac Forbes, Steve Pannell, Prue and Stephen Henschke, Virginia Willcock, Vanya Cullen, Louisa Rose, Dylan Grigg, Michael Dhillon, Michael Hill-Smith MW, Stu Proud and Steve Flamsteed. A heartfelt thanks to all of you. James March is now at Rockford but when at Barossa Grape and Wine he was instrumental in connecting me with key Barossa producers and giving me access to a large number of excellent wines over the years. Phil Reedman MW, thank you for your insightful mentorship in my MW study years and for being a patient sounding board. A special thanks is due to Paul Henry: we may have lost contact, but you saw something in me that made you determined to hire me at Wine Australia, which brought me back into the Australian wine fold. And finally, to my dad, who passed in 2020. He introduced me to wine, showed our family what good food was and handed down his obsession with quality coffee. He remained a curious and voracious reader of books until the end. I think he would be proud that I finally wrote one.

PREFACE

My parents moved to Australia in 1967 on the Assisted Passage Migration Scheme. We were Ten-Pound Poms. My father worked in wine sales in the 1970s so wine was always on the dinner table and that was how I was introduced to the drink I would later make a career of. This led to a consistent pattern as a teenager of sneaking under the house and 'borrowing' unlabelled bottles from my father's not-so-secret stash. It turns out that they were really good bottles of McLaren Vale Shiraz, but I didn't know that at the time, my mates and I just thought that they tasted a whole lot better than Blackberry Nip, a cheap black-berry wine we occasionally got access to.

In my late teens and twenties I went through Culinary and Hotel Management school and started to travel and learn about wine from many parts of the world. Australian wine remained close to my heart and I tried to keep up to date even though I was living abroad.

In 2008 I was approached by Wine Australia to take on an educa-tion role in the United States. It morphed into a global role for a period of time and has now settled as a position overseeing North America. At the time of publishing, I am still in this position. Writing a book on Australian wine while being employed by an organization that pro-motes Australian wines might from the outset seem like a conflict. An understanding of my role should help to clarify this. Most of what I do involves engagement with key trade in overseas markets to help illumi-nate the regions and wines that make Australia a compelling proposi-tion. As my role requires me to represent the entirety of the Australian wine offer, I have had to remain neutral and impartial, with no bias towards any particular regions, styles or producers, and have worked diligently to avoid any such perception. Most of the wines I have presented over the past 15 years lean towards more premium, regionally expressive styles as the remit for my role has been to shift the perception of Australian wine and increase the premium paid for our wines globally.

This book ultimately serves as a guide to Australia's regions and wines. It is not a deep dive into Australian wine history, geography, climate and soil. The historical references, explanations of regional climate and soils are deliberately short to allow for more detailed discussion on regions, producers and wine styles.

Some sections were much more challenging to write than others. Knowing what we now know about how First Nations peoples were treated as the colonies were developing makes glorification of Australian history in general very difficult. But the history of wine production in Australia exists, and it is a compelling story of endeavour, vision, hardship and adaptation. First Nations involvement in grape growing and winemaking is new. I have tried to respectfully address this and explain how our industry is engaging and collaborating for the future in Chapter 1.

The first part of the book touches on key topics that will help lay a foundation for understanding how and why Australian wines look, feel and taste the way they do today. In the regional chapters I recommend producers and wines. This has been a daunting task in certain regions given how many excellent producers exist. Please note that this is not a catalogue of producers. They are my personal selections, choices I feel will help you understand that region and Australian wine as a whole. The breadth of wine styles in Australia is staggering and not well understood so at the end of the book I decided to include a list of specific wines to try: 101 wines that illuminate Australian wine today. If you try all the wines on the list you will have a very good chance of grasping fully the character, complexity and quality of Australian wine today.

PART 1
AUSTRALIAN WINE – AN OVERVIEW

1

HISTORY AND CULTURE

People first arrived on the Australian mainland by sea from Maritime Southeast Asia somewhere between 50,000 and 65,000 years ago. All parts of the continent were eventually occupied in one form or another – from the rainforests in the north to the deserts of the centre and beyond, to the islands of Tasmania and Bass Strait. The art, music and spiritual traditions of First Nations/Indigenous Australians are among the longest surviving in human history.

The first Torres Strait Islanders – ethnically and culturally distinct from the Aboriginal people – arrived from what is now Papua New Guinea around 2,500 years ago, and settled in the islands of the Torres Strait and the Cape York Peninsula, forming the northern tip of the Australian landmass.

The first Europeans exposed to Australia were Dutch. Navigator Willem Janszoon landed on Australia's northern coast in 1606, and later that year Spanish explorer Luís Vaz de Torres sailed through what is now called Torres Strait and associated islands. Twenty-nine other Dutch navigators explored the western and southern coasts in the seventeenth century and named the continent New Holland. There was no lasting attempt at establishment of a permanent settlement though. Most of the explorers of this period concluded that the apparent lack of water and fertile soil made the region unsuitable for colonization. Macassan trepangers (fishermen from the port town of Makassar in southern Sulawesi) visited Australia's northern coasts around 1720 in search of sea cucumbers, which were prized for their medicinal qualities. Other European explorers followed but it was Lieutenant James Cook who charted the east coast of Australia in 1770 and claimed it for Great

Britain. He returned to London with positive reports about the prospects of colonization at Botany Bay.

The First Fleet of British ships arrived at Botany Bay in January 1788 to establish a penal colony. This was the first colony on the Australian mainland. In the century that followed, the British established other colonies on the continent. European explorers also ventured into the interior. The Aboriginal populations were decimated by introduced disease and conflict. While current day recognition and reparations are ongoing, this part of Australian history remains a tragedy of immense proportions.

Transportation of British convicts to Australia was phased out from 1840 to 1868. Gold rushes and agricultural industries brought prosperity and this impacted grape growing and winemaking in many areas, a subject which is discussed in the regional chapters. Autonomous parliamentary democracies began to be established throughout the six British colonies from the mid-nineteenth century. The colonies voted by referendum to unite in a federation in 1901, and modern Australia came into being. Australia fought as part of the British Empire and later Commonwealth in the two world wars and was to become a long-standing ally of the United States when threatened by Imperial Japan during the Second World War. Trade with Asia increased and a post-war immigration programme received more than 6.5 million migrants from every continent. There has been consistent immigration of people from almost every country in the world since the end of the Second World War. The population as of December 2022 was 26.75 million people, 30 per cent of whom were born overseas.

THE HISTORY OF VITICULTURE IN AUSTRALIA

Grape vines are not native to Australia. Records indicate that the first vines arrived with the early European settlers on the First Fleet in 1788. The cuttings were collected in Rio de Janeiro and the Cape of Good Hope. Heat and humidity presented problems for these initial vines but in spite of this, vineyard planting and expansion continued in the area for the next several decades. There are limited records of viticulture and winemaking in these early years. A few dispatches here and there help piece together a picture of viticulture in ensuing years. In one dated 16 October 1791 Governor Phillip states that he had planted three acres of vineyard in the Government House grounds at Parramatta and that Phillip Schaffer, a German from Hessen had planted one acre of vines on his property on the north bank of Parramatta River, thus entitling him to be recorded as the first vigneron of Australia. In another, from December 1791, Governor Phillip wrote to his friend Sir Joseph Banks that 'from a few cuttings I brought from Rio and the Cape we now have many thousand young vines here [Parramatta and Norfolk Island].' Significant vineyards were eventually established near Parramatta in 1805 by Gregory Blaxland and near Camden in 1820 by William Macarthur. Scottish botanist James Busby became involved in viticulture around 1825 and in 1831 he went to Europe and collected 650 varieties. Of these, 362 survived the return journey and were planted in the Botanical Gardens in Sydney. Busby does not mention in detail which varieties did not survive, nor why. It is probably safe to assume that the long, arduous sea voyage played a big part in their demise. Busby does catalogue everything he brought in and planted in his journal, which was printed in 1833, by Stephens and Stokes.[1] A duplicate collection was planted at his Hunter Valley property and subsequent cuttings made their way to various parts of the country as the colonies expanded in New South Wales, Tasmania, Victoria and South Australia. Exactly where additional vine material went in the form of cuttings from this original collection is difficult to trace. Many of Australia's old vines are a direct result of the original Busby collection. Expertise in viticulture in the early days of colonization was scarce. As you explore regional history a pattern of planting a multitude of varieties recurs. It was, for the most part, a shotgun approach to planting: take what was available and see what did or did not work. There are now over 100 different varieties planted in Australia. For more details on these see Chapter 4.

The Hunter Valley was the first commercial region, with Dalwood Estate being established by George Wyndham in 1828. After a convoluted history and several ownership and name changes – Wyndham Estate being the most notable – the estate relaunched under the Dalwood name in 2018. By the 1840s viticulture had been established by Italians in Riverina, Swiss in Victoria, Dalmatians in Western

---

1 A facsimile reprint was published in 1979 by David Ell Press Pty Ltd. I mention this for those who wish to delve deeper but for the purpose of this book listing all the vine cuttings that did survive would only serve to confuse, as many of the names are obscure and possibly incorrect.

Australia, and Lutheran Germans in South Australia, particularly the Barossa and Clare Valleys. Commercial viticulture had been established in most states by 1850. Small amounts of wine were exported to the UK around this time. New South Wales wines were listed as being exhibited at the London Exhibition in 1851 but there is no mention of what the wines were or how they were viewed at the time. New South Wales wines were shown at the Paris Exhibition in 1855 and judged to be 'better than expected'. There is not a lot of information beyond documents that indicate the quantities of wines exported, but the fact is that there was interest in showing what was possible from 'the colony' and an eye for commercial possibilities.[2]

PHYLLOXERA IN AUSTRALIA

Phylloxera affected some states in the late 1870s and a few active pockets remain but it has not spread the length and breadth of Australian viticultural areas. This is due to a few factors. Australia has always had very strict interstate agricultural controls and quarantines. The damage caused by phylloxera in Europe was widely reported and South Australia Government Acts were set up from the late 1800s to protect the industry. The Vine Protection Act of 1874 prohibited the importation of vine material from other countries or from Australian states infested with phylloxera. The Phylloxera Act 1899 was established by the Phylloxera and Grape Industry Board of South Australia, now called Vinehealth Australia. Vinehealth Australia is a statutory authority dedicated to the protection of vineyards from phylloxera infestation. The National Phylloxera Management Protocol is the nationally agreed standard for minimizing the risk of spreading phylloxera. If anyone in Australia suspects their vineyard has phylloxera, they are legally obliged to report it to their state biosecurity department.[3]

---

2 Andrew Caillard MW is currently writing a very detailed book on the history of Australian wine (titled *The Australian Ark*). His contention is that Australia's wine history is more ambitious, more romantic, and more extraordinary than is generally known. There is no one better placed to pen a tome of this calibre and I am excited to see it completed. It is due to be published in 2023.

3 More information can be found at: https://vinehealth.com.au/rules/plans-and-policies/national-phylloxera-management-protocol-2/. Phylloxera is active in Australia and detailed information about infestation zones can be found on the Vinehealth website at: https://vinehealth.com.au/tools/maps/phylloxera-management-zones/

Vinehealth also categorizes areas according to the following:

- Phylloxera Infested Zone (PIZ) is known to have phylloxera.
- Phylloxera Interim Buffer Zone (PIBZ) means a zone of 5 kilometre radius around a new detection of phylloxera in Australia. This is officially notified by the Chief Plant Health Manager of the jurisdiction in which the detection has been made, as an interim measure pending declaration of a new or amended PIZ in that jurisdiction.
- Phylloxera Risk Zone (PRZ) means the phylloxera status is unknown (but never detected).
- Phylloxera Exclusion Zone (PEZ) known to be free from phylloxera.

Many areas in Australia remain phylloxera free and have very old, ungrafted vines (see Chapter 5 for more on Australia's old vines).

AUSTRALIA'S EXPORT SUCCESS

In 1950, 86 per cent of Australian grapes were used for fortified wine. By 1995, this had switched and over 90 per cent was being used for table wine production. Throughout the 1970s, exports had actually declined. Then came an export boom. In 1981, Australia, with a total of 8 million litres, was the eighteenth largest exporter of wine in the world. Just ten years later that total was 39 million litres making it sixth in the world in terms of exports. By 2007 this figure was 805 million litres, a staggering increase which was followed by a dramatic decrease due to changing tastes (see below). In the last 15 years, Australian wine has gone through boom and bust cycles. The emergence of the wine market in China was very profitable for exporters and saw tremendous growth over a 10 year period starting in 2010. This came to a grinding halt when a 200 per cent tariff on imports was imposed by the Chinese government in late December 2020. The tariff effectively put the brakes on approximately A$1.2 billion worth of wine exports. As of March 2023 the overall Australian wine export figure was 620 million litres on a rolling 12 month average.

Fortified wines in Australia

Fortified wines have been produced in Australia for long as the country has been making wine. Port and Sherry were very popular in the UK during the late 1800s and early 1900s. Given that Australia was a British colony this, to a degree, dictated what was planted and produced, and Australia became an additional source of 'replica' styles. It also meant that fortified wine was the main wine style consumed for decades. Up until the late 1960s, over 70 per cent of Australia's production was fortified. Fortified wine production is far more limited today, but the legacy of this long tradition survives and there are several key producers, particularly in Rutherglen (see page 224–226) who continue to craft magnificent examples. Many classic styles continue to be made but naming conventions have had to shift over time.

Fortified tawny and fortified vintage are the modern names for what used to be called Port in Australia. Tawny styles are common. Most are of very high quality, and some are truly world class, such as those made in the Barossa Valley by Seppeltsfield (see page 114).

Apera is the modern name for what used to be called Sherry. The full array of styles exist but of the fortified wines being produced in Australia today, Apera is the most limited. Seppeltsfield has decided not to make any Apera styles in the future. I certainly appreciate the economic realities, but it does seem a shame.

Rutherglen Muscat is a magnificent, uniquely Australian fortified Muscat style. The best examples are discussed in the regional section on Rutherglen on page 221.

Rutherglen Topaque is the modern term for what used to be called Rutherglen Tokay. The name was changed because of the similarity to that of the famous Hungarian wine region, which the original style was modelled on. There seems to be a collective shift in the region however with producers using the name Muscadelle, which makes sense seeing as that is the grape being used. Topaque did seem like an odd name.

Fortified producers to look for

While I cannot think of a producer in Australia that is solely focused on fortified wine production, many wineries, especially the older, more established ones, still produce small amounts and are really worth seeking out.

- **Seppeltsfield** (www.seppeltsfield.com.au). One of the greatest fortified wine producers in Australia (see p. 114 for full details). They have a stunning array of fortified tawnies under the Para label. They still have a brilliant selection of Apera too so try them before it is too late. Look out for Para Grand Tawny, Para Rare Tawny and any of the vintage dated Para Tawnies. The DP117 Dry Flor Apero and DP38 Rich Rara Apero are a couple of the best Sherry-style wines you will try outside Jerez.

- **Penfolds** (www.penfolds.com). Penfolds produces an excellent range of fortifieds. Try the Fortified Vintage, Father Grand Tawny and one of my favourites, Great Grandfather Tawny.

- **Yalumba** (www.yalumba.com). Several excellent fortified wines can be found at Yalumba. The Antique Tawny and Antique Muscat are great places to start. They also have a 21-year-old, 30-year-old and an absolutely stunning 50-year-old tawny.

- **John Kosovich Wines** (www.johnkosovichwines.com.au). Established in 1922, this historic Swan Valley producer has always made excellent fortifieds. Look for the Rare Muscat and Vintage Fortified Shiraz.

- **Rockford Wines** (www.rockfordwines.com.au). Try the PS Marion Tawny and the Fortified Vintage Shiraz.

- **d'Arenberg Wines** (www.darenberg.com.au). Among the bevy of wines produced at this classic McLaren Vale property are three excellent fortified wines: Nostalgia Rare Tawny, Fortified Vintage Shiraz and the very rare, limited production Daddy Longlegs Tawny.

- **Kaesler Wines** (www.kaesler.com.au). Kaesler in the Barossa has a very cool fortified wine called Cottage Block Fortified White NV. It is made from old-vine Palomino planted in 1961.

- **Kay Brother Wines** (www.kaybrothers.com.au). Kay Brothers make a fantastic, well priced Pounders Old Tawny and Grand Liqueur Muscat and a brilliant Rare Muscat.

- **Simão & Co Wines**. This is a project by Simon Killeen of Stanton and Killeen in Rutherglen. He is passionate about Portuguese varieties and makes a killer fortified vintage.

Rutherglen Muscat and Topaque (Muscadelle) producers are recommended in the regional chapter on Rutherglen.

THE EVOLUTION OF AUSTRALIAN WINE STYLES

Brian Croser AO was a very important figure in helping mould the modern Australian wine style. His first winemaker role was with Thomas Hardy and Sons in 1969. He then founded a winemaking consultancy and developed the wine science course at Charles Sturt University in New South Wales. As a consultant and an educator, Brian had a huge influence on Australian winemakers in the 1970s and 1980s, mentoring and shaping the community. He and his colleague Dr Tony Jordan essentially taught a generation of winemakers how to make good wine. Jordan and Croser were advocates of anaerobic, also known as reductive, winemaking. By excluding oxygen from the winemaking process, and using stainless steel and refrigeration, they taught winemakers to produce clean, fruit-forward and delicious wines, even in warm climates.

A generation of boutique winemakers followed. Louisa Rose from Yalumba, Jeffrey Grosset from the Clare Valley, Rick Kinzbrunner from Giaconda in Beechworth and Tim Kirk from Clonakilla in the Canberra District played important early roles in shifting perceptions of what was possible for premium, regionally expressive wines. Many more have followed.

These wine styles were the catalysts for the strong export successes from the 1980s through to the mid-2000s. Vibrant, varietally expressive and affordable wines combined with premium boutique wines captured the imagination of a wine-drinking world that was mostly used to European wine styles. By around 2007 or 2008, enthusiasm had waned and the image of Australian wine diminished. The mass-market brands had lost their sheen. The boutique producers who were seduced into making overripe, over-oaked wines as a result of high scores by certain American critics, watched sales slide as boredom and exhaustion crept in. The problem was compounded by an unrealistically strong Australian dollar making exporting even more of a challenge. Australian wine exports languished through a period of torpor based largely on perceptions of what Australian wine was rather than what really existed. The mid-2000s was actually the start of a rapid evolution that bordered on revolution. Australian wine was changing – dramatically.

Several factors have shaped the look and feel of wines being made in the last 10–15 years, as noted in the individual regional chapters, but the following gives a tidy snapshot of some of these changes. The approach to farming vineyards has been rationalized, with the adoption of biodynamics, organics and sustainable farming practices becoming far more common than in the past. Many producers want to work more naturally, picking earlier to preserve acidity and minimizing additives. There is more use of alternative forms of fermentation and maturation vessels such as concrete, larger format oak barrels, ceramic eggs and clay amphorae, and a move away from heavy reliance on new oak. The exploration of alternative varieties has been an exciting development, with varieties such as Fiano, Vermentino, Nero d'Avola and Montepulciano offering up new flavours and textures. A better understanding of some traditional varieties, such as Grenache, is adding another dimension of character and quality. The changes over the last 15 years are astonishing. Styles have shifted, new varieties and blends are available and the presentation of classic wines and varieties has evolved. There is always something new and exciting to explore in Australia right now. If you can get access to the full range of Australian wines being made today, it is impossible to be bored.

FIRST NATIONS PEOPLES
(Aboriginal and Torres Strait Islander peoples)

I grew up and went through school in Australia. We were taught very little of what really happened to the original inhabitants of Australia. This book is not a forum for discussion of this, nor do I have the experience or knowledge for a detailed explanation of the tragedies that we now know occurred. It is a complicated and sensitive subject. Recognition and reparations are an ongoing process. Language as we move forward is important and some background on this should be helpful.

There is growing recognition in Australia of the importance of protecting and advancing the rights of First Nations peoples. Protecting First Nations heritage and enabling First Nations to access and to speak for Country and to carry out traditional practices is very important for the well-being of this group. There still needs to be more inclusion and empowerment of Indigenous people in heritage decision-making and management, and legislative reform to ensure that these obligations are met.

In late 2023, Australians will vote in a referendum that has the ability to amend the nation's constitution. The subject of the referendum is recognition of Aboriginal and Torres Strait Islander peoples, who have been largely disenfranchised throughout Australian history. If successful, First Nations groups will get permanent representation in the government. This referendum comes after the Australian government announced earlier in the year that it would give A$424 million in funding to 'improve the lives of Australia's original inhabitants'.

Some background to and explanation of Welcome to Country and Acknowledgement of Country

The meaning of traditional 'Country' goes some way beyond the dictionary definition of the word. For First Nations Australians, it might mean homeland, or tribal or clan area and might mean more than just a place on the map. Country is a word for all the values, places, resources, stories and cultural obligations associated with that area and its features. It describes the entirety of the ancestral domains. While they may no longer necessarily all be the title-holders to land, Aboriginal and Torres Strait Islander Australians are still connected to the Country of their ancestors and most consider themselves the custodians or caretakers of their land and waters.

A Welcome to Country is a ceremony to welcome people on to the land of the custodians. A local traditional custodian performs a Welcome to Country. The welcome can take many forms. It might offer safe passage to visitors or outline any responsibilities while on Country. An Acknowledgement of Country is something anyone can do. It is a way a person of any descent can pay respect to the local community and nation(s). It acknowledges the custodians of the land on which a meeting is being held. And it recognizes the local community's ongoing connection to, and care for, Country. Both are simple but important ways of paying respect. They redress the erasure of Aboriginal and Torres Strait Islander peoples on their own lands.

In the regional chapters in the book, I have tried to use the First Nations country name in conjunction with the wine region name as we know it today. I used the AIATSIS Map of Indigenous Australia as a source for the original names. Some of the current wine regions overlap several different First Nations/Countries. Where possible, I have tried to recognize that fact. I accept that there may be mistakes and apologize in advance. I would rather live with a few inaccuracies or omissions than not address the subject at all. There are alternative spellings which can cause confusion. I stuck to the map as it is presented today.[4] I have also

---

4   Indigenous Australia map: https://aiatsis.gov.au/explore/map-indigenous-australia.

provided a link to the alternative spelling of the First Nations Country names.[5]

To date, there is very little First Nations involvement in viticulture and winemaking. There are some encouraging initiatives. While not wine related per se, I visited Coranderrk in the Yarra Valley in 2022. This is a very special place and should provide a guiding light on future collaboration to better understand land and culture, as demonstrated in the letter below, which was shared with me during my visit:

> *Despite a dark history, Coranderrk has always been a place of hope and inspiring firsts. It was the first self-governed Aboriginal mission station, established in 1863, with homes, kilns, schools, a dairy and farm, until it closed in 1924. Later in 1998, 220 acres of the original 4750-acre property were brought back with funding from the Indigenous Land Corporation, with Wandoon Estate established to manage it. Communities Australia-wide have always looked to Coranderrk as an example of possibility. It's often cited as among the first Indigenous-led campaigns for land rights and self-determination, paving the way for successful land rights claims. It's our plan to continue to set an example, to lead the way in reconciliation through meaningful partnerships that benefit the land and connect people.*
>
> *This property represents so much more than just the remnants of Coranderrk mission statement and something that happened in history. We are not history. We do not belong in museums. We are still here, we are alive, we are active. This place has been asleep for 75 years and we are waking it up again, but we are not just waking it up again for ourselves, we're waking it up for the rest of the people who want to know.*
>
> Wurundjeri Elder Dave Wandin, 2021
> Coranderrk: Wandoon Estate Aboriginal Corporation

In May 2021 a group of winemakers, winery owners and journalist Max Allen, convened at Coranderrk to meet the Wandins and connect with Country. This marked the start of subsequent visits by winemakers and viticulturalists.

The connection between the concept of terroir and Aboriginal notions of belonging to country motivated Yarra Valley winemaker Mac

---

5   A list of alternative spellings is given here: https://aiatsis.gov.au/sites/default/files/2020-08/aamapalternatespellings.pdf

Forbes to connect with the people at Coranderrk. Mac has always been interested in the different terroirs within Yarra Valley and of how introduced species, in this case grape vines, adapt and express character, 'I feel rejuvenated when I go to Coranderrk,' he says. 'I come away with more questions than answers, but I feel more open to what's possible. And I feel we can all contribute to that conversation.' This type of meaningful engagement is important for the development of wine culture in Australia. A deeper understanding of land is at the heart of quality wine production and there is so much more to learn about Australian terroir.

In Margaret River, Vanya Cullen has also been working towards seeking better acknowledgement of and connection to Country and to Wadandi indigenous culture in the region. She says:

All of our staff have been through cultural training with the Undulap association. Since 2017 we have acknowledged the Wadandi (Saltwater) peoples on our wine labels with respect for elders past, present and emerging, and have removed naming of white folks involved in Wadandi cruelty and killings from our text at Cullens. We have also been to sessions about cultural burning[6] after harvest rather than during the heat of the growing season, as is usual. This reduces the carbon load and also doesn't kill plants and animals as it is cool. The country is then protected from future burns.

Vanya is also involved in an initiative titled Yorgas Yarning. This programme has two major components, cultural connections of students to Country and overall improved mental health and well-being for Waalitj Kaatitjin Yorgas (girls and women).

Working with First Nations/Indigenous Australian communities is and will continue to be part of an evolution of Australian wine culture. The work that people like Mac and Vanya have initiated and the interactions at Coranderrk should serve as a call to action for our industry to make the effort to engage and learn. There are other examples but we can and should do more. Below are a couple of wine projects that are really exciting.

---

6 Cultural burning is fire deliberately put into the landscape, authorized and led by the Traditional Owners of that Country for a variety of purposes, including but not limited to, ceremony, protection of cultural and natural assets, fuel reduction, regeneration and management of food, fibre and medicines, flora regeneration, fauna habitat protection and healing Country's spirit.

Mt Yengo Wines

www.mtyengowines.com.au

A venture started by Gary Green and Ben Hansberry, Mt Yengo was created to fuse the culture and values of the First Nations People of Australia with the more recent culture surrounding wine. The aim is not just to create a wine brand. It is about community. A community that values bridging the cultural divide, instilling cultural understanding, and embracing reconciliation and diversity. Gary Green is a Gamilaraay and Githabul man from New South Wales. He founded a premium Australian Wagyu wholesaler called Mr Wagyu Beef, as well as Gondwana Wines, in 2016. This was rebranded as Mt Yengo Wines in 2019.

They source from many sites across Australia, especially Adelaide Hills. In 2020, they joined forces with Bisous Estate in New South Wales' Hunter Valley to establish a more permanent home for Mt Yengo. A portion of the proceeds of each bottle sold goes to the National Indigenous Culinary Institute. This is an industry inspired and initiated programme designed to create highly skilled Indigenous chefs. NICI offers elite training and experience for aspiring Indigenous chefs, who will be trained and mentored by top Australian chefs at host restaurants such as Rockpool Bar and Grill, Bistro Guillaume, Catalina, Aria, The European, Movida, The Dolphin Hotel, Icebergs Dining Room and Bar, and more in Sydney and Melbourne.

Munda Wines

www.mundawines.com.au

This is a collaboration between Paul Vandenbergh and Damien Smith. Vandenbergh is a Wirangu and Kokotha man from the west coast of South Australia. Munda means *land* in his language. Smith is non-Indigenous and has a long career in the wine business. Vandenbergh says, 'In winemaking, the importance of the ground, of land, is really critical. But Munda is broader than that. It's also about recognizing and acknowledging Country.'

Smith is quick to point out that this is not a marketing or a money-making exercise. It is a long-term project. Munda will work in conjunction with the Tjindu Foundation to create pathways in an industry that traditionally hasn't attracted young Indigenous people. This is designed to guide young Indigenous kids to learn viticulture, winemaking and hospitality.

Smith says, 'Five years down the line, we'd love Munda to have an Indigenous winemaker. That's our goal.' Munda is focusing solely on premium wine production. Chalk Hill Wines' award-winning wine-maker Renae Hirsch made the 2021 Syrah. Marco Cirillo from the Barossa made the 2022 Ngadjuri and Peramangk Country Grenache. Both are A$45.00 per bottle. Vandenbergh designs the labels.

2

LANDSCAPE AND CLIMATE

The areas most suited to fine wine production in Australia are in the south-east and south-west of the country. The primary factors influencing the suitability of a region for vine growing in Australia are:

- Latitude – higher latitudes (further from the equator) are cooler, therefore southern Australia is much cooler than the north. However, the citing of broad elements and how they impact potential growing regions can be misleading. Hobart is Australia's southernmost city and has the same southern hemisphere latitude as the northern hemisphere latitude of Perpignan in southern France. The two could not be more different.
- Altitude – the varied hills and ranges in the south-west and south-east areas, combined with higher latitudes, create ideal conditions for viticulture.
- Soil types – as detailed below, Australia is a very old continent. The underlying geology in many wine regions is several hundred million years old. The soil types are varied, complex and for the most part, quite fragile. Detailed work in identifying the connections between soil types, grape varieties and wine character is still new.
- Weather patterns – prevailing breezes from the cold Southern Ocean moderate the warm northerly influence of the hot inland. It is important to remember that there is nothing but cold ocean between southern Australia and Antarctica. The Southern Ocean is effectively the refrigeration unit that tempers the climate in the southern part of Australia.

GEOGRAPHY AND TOPOGRAPHY

Australia's land mass is considerably larger than that of Europe and almost equal to that of the contiguous states of the US – Australia is just 4 per cent smaller. Australia sits between the latitudes of 12°S and 44°S. This clearly indicates that most of the Australian continent is not suited to grape growing. Large parts of the north are tropical, and the centre is too hot and dry. Except for some regions in Queensland and far northern New South Wales, all the quality growing regions are in the southern part of the country between 30°S and 44°S. These are the necessarily cooler latitudes, but latitude alone is not enough to make an area suited to viticulture. Other factors are important. Australia is a relatively flat continent overall. Its highest peak is only 2,228 metres. France has 75 peaks higher than this. That doesn't mean elevation is not important when discussing regional climate and viticulture in Australia. The standard calculation is that for every 100 metres of elevation, the average temperature drops by 0.6°C. So, a region sitting at just 300 metres above sea level is almost a full two degrees cooler overall. Australia has many regions that sit at between 250 and 500 metres above sea level, with several that are between 800 and 1,100 metres elevation, providing a valuable cooling effect in more northerly regions.

There are three main mountain ranges that impact the viticultural areas in Australia. Darling Scarp in Western Australia is situated at the edge of the Yilgarn Craton and rises to 400 metres. Many fantastic regions in Western Australia are on or affected by this escarpment, from Perth Hills down to Pemberton. The Mount Lofty Ranges in South Australia rise to 936 metres and make viticulture possible in Adelaide Hills, Clare, Barossa Valley, Eden Valley and McLaren Vale. The Great Dividing Range in Eastern Australia is a major landform consisting of mountains and uplands. Mount Kosciuszko is the highest peak in the Great Dividing Range, at 2,228 metres. This range is important to most of the Geographical Indications (GIs) in Queensland, New South Wales and Victoria. Its height brings reduced temperatures and it acts as a barrier to the tropical rain systems that come down the east coast, as it effectively creates a rain shadow. The only major wine region on the 'wrong' side of the range is the Hunter Valley, which typically experiences mid-summer and harvest rain.

GEOLOGY AND SOILS

Australia has been an individual land mass for over 100 million years and is the oldest and therefore most eroded continent. Some of the oldest geological structures and minerals on the planet are found in Australia. For example, it is home to the largest concentration of zircon of any country in the world. In geological settings, the development of various types of zircon occurs after hundreds of millions of years. Hadean zircon grains found in the Jack Hills in Western Australia were determined to be 4.4 billion years old – only 200 million years younger than the planet. A further example of Australia's great geological age comes in the form of the craton. Cratons are outcrops formed predominantly of granite and are the oldest formations of land on the planet. Australia has three cratons: two in Western Australia, the Yilgarn and Pilbara Cratons, and one in South Australia, the Gawler Craton. Scientists have determined that the Pilbara region in Western Australia has vast formations of iron-rich rock, formed prior to the existence of oxygen and life, is the best-preserved example of the world's most ancient crust. While other global iron deposits are thought to have formed at a similar time, the surface of the Pilbara remains unburied and undisturbed by geologically cataclysmic events.

Wine is produced on the edge of the Yilgarn Craton in Western Australia. While there are ancient geologies and soils there are also younger soils made up of sand and limestone and many areas of volcanic origin. The net result is that tremendous soil variation exists, not only from region to region in Australia but also within the regions themselves. So why is this relevant and what does it mean when it comes to discussing grape growing and winemaking in Australia? The complexities make generalization about regional soils challenging in many instances. This is true of other grape growing areas in the world but the difference is that Australia is, viticulturally speaking, a relatively young country, compared to the classic regions of Europe. Not as much work has been done to identify and illuminate the diversity of geology and soil type on a sub-regional, individual site and indeed within individual sites as it has within the world's older wine regions. Coonawarra is a notable regional exception, having included, albeit with vigorous debate and compromise, its prized terra rossa soils as part of the Geographic Indication. Work has been done in other areas of note. McLaren Vale conducted exhaustive studies on its complex geology. More than 40 different geologies were identified, and they vary in age from 15,000 years to over 550 million years. The geology of the McLaren Vale wine region map was first published in 2010. A wide variety of soil types were identified in the region too; red-brown sandy loams; grey-brown loamy sands; yellow clay subsoils interspersed with lime, distinctly sandy soils, and patches of red and black friable loam. This remains an ongoing study and provides a lens into the links between geology, grape variety and wine style. Has this detailed work paid off? Slowly but surely, certain sub-regions are developing reputations for superior fruit quality based on the soils and geology which is incrementally displaying economic benefit. Grenache grown in the Blewitt Springs area, with its distinctly sandy soils has commanded the highest price paid per tonne for grapes in McLaren Vale over the last couple of vintages. Until recently, most Australian vine growing was less concerned with the links between soil type, vine variety and quality. Climate, temperature and variety were the primary considerations in shaping the general styles. Terroir has become more of a focus as Australian wine evolves. While in its infancy compared to, say, France, developing a deeper understanding of climate and soils at the regional, sub-regional (macro), site (meso) and individual sections within site (micro) levels will be an important factor in the future of Australian fine wine production. Australia's appellation system (GIs) does not dictate what can and can't be grown so there is freedom to experiment with varieties.

CLIMATE AND CLIMATE CHANGE

As well as understanding the soil of a region, an appreciation of the general climate is also important. It sets the stage for deeper investigation into varietal possibilities and wine style. Australia is a hot, dry and drought-prone country overall. As detailed in the regional chapters, factors such as cooling ocean influence and altitude are important in mitigating what would otherwise be a hostile environment for quality grape growing and winemaking. There are cyclical patterns that affect the weather conditions across the country and impact annual region climate. Each year is different and follows the two cycles of La Niña, which results in a wet vintage, and El Niño, which results in a dry vintage. These are linked to and indeed dictated by the Indian Ocean Dipole influence. The Indian Ocean Dipole is defined by the difference in sea surface temperature between two areas or poles – a western pole in the Arabian Sea (western Indian Ocean) and an eastern pole in the eastern Indian Ocean south of Indonesia. The Indian Ocean Dipole affects the climate of Australia and is a significant contributor to rainfall variability in this region. The weather patterns are quite predictable based on these cycles.

This outlines the overall climate patterns in Australia. However, the more I learn, teach and write about Australian wine the more frustrated I get with sweeping statements about regional climate and soil. It is every bit as complex a subject in Australia as it is in Europe and requires just as much work. The problem is that many of our Geographic Indications are quite large and, as mentioned earlier, the work on identifying sub-regional and individual site soils and climate is in its infancy. The concept of macroclimate, mesoclimate and microclimate is important, but that level of detail is neither possible nor necessary in this book. Broad statements about climate and soils exist at the beginning of each regional chapter, so I am guilty of the very thing that annoys me, but where possible, I have indicated the curiosities. Most major wine regions in Australia have anomalies – exceptions that prove the rule – and it boils down to differences in macro-, meso- and in some instances, micro-climate. For example, the overall climate in Barossa is warm, but there are sites in Eden Valley that produce world-class Riesling. Domaine A is a top shelf Cabernet Sauvignon made in Tasmania but that does not mean that Tasmania overall is an ideal place to grow Cabernet Sauvignon. My aim, therefore, has been to give the reader a general idea of the overall climate and how that impacts varieties grown and wine styles produced. It clearly does not address the intricacies and variables of every site, nor can it assess in any detail the future impact of climate change.

A climate change initiative

Adapting to a changing climate is something that viticultural areas globally have to manage. A discussion with Dr Liz Waters, General Manager of Research and Innovation at Wine Australia provided a succinct snapshot on how climate change is affecting the wine industry in general and in Australia specifically.

What are the main challenges?

Liz Waters: As with all industries and countries, the wine sector is likely to face challenges as climate change continues. Our sector has been investing in climate change research for at least two decades. Currently, we're seeing changes to the vine's physiology, particularly that wine grapes are ripening earlier than they used to, leading to vintage compression. While this can seem like a vineyard challenge only, it also puts pressure on small- to medium-sized wineries when fruit comes in quickly as many do not have the processing capacity in terms of fermentation vessels and the additional tank space compressed vintages demand. Other challenges may arise in the form of diseases and pests, and as the environment warms and dries further, water needs will be a consideration. These are the challenges that research and development investments are already looking into.

What changes are projected for the future in Australia?

Liz Waters: Generally, it is going to be warmer and drier everywhere. Rainfall patterns will also change – for example there is likely to be less rain in winter and more in summer than we record now. Climate variability, particularly season-to-season, will increase, as will the frequency of weather extremes that increase the risk of events like severe bushfires. However, Australian viticulture is equipped to manage the effects of climate change for a couple of reasons. Firstly, Australia already has a naturally variable climate, so grape growers and winemakers are adept at responding to the ups and downs of climate year-to-year. And secondly, we have invested in extensive research for two decades that has resulted in a suite of adaptive strategies. Vineyard management in many Australian wine regions will need to adapt as rainfall patterns change and temperatures and extreme events such as heatwaves increase under climate change. These challenges are already occurring in many regions of the world. However, there is widespread awareness of adaptation options that help reduce the impact of weather risks under current conditions, and this knowledge will help winegrowers adapt.

What is the industry in Australia doing about climate change?

Liz Waters: A complex problem such as climate change requires multiple solutions, so we are looking at new solutions and technologies as well as strengthening practice changes in the vineyard to address the impacts of a changing climate and allow informed decisions to be made on future management and investment.

For example, currently, we are investing in research and development projects on smoke taint, vintage compression, dry winters, improved forecasting of extreme climate events and rootstock and variety breeding for improved stress tolerance. We have practice change and adoption programmes in irrigation best practice, cover crops and functional biodiversity, all of which are designed to help producers build climate resilience and manage their land in a sustainable fashion.

Our investments are also helping the sector reduce its carbon footprint by developing a roadmap to help grape growers and wineries reduce their carbon emissions to zero. Collectively our sector has set a goal through Vision 2050 [a project developed by Australian Grape & Wine, in collaboration with Wine Australia[7]] to have net zero carbon emissions by 2050. We believe that we can get there sooner. The roadmap will set achievable targets, guide the sector collectively towards those targets and provide practical information for producers to manage their emissions. We're also going to establish a baseline of greenhouse gas emissions so that we can track progress and identify opportunities for reduction.

7   Additional information can be found at https://www.agw.org.au/about-australian-grape-and-wine/the-grape-and-wine-sector/vision-2050/

Wine Australia, in conjunction with the University of Tasmania, has developed the Climate Atlas. This was a three-year project that brought together an extensive, multidisciplinary research team to consider the impact of seasonal climate variability and longer-term climate trends on the wine sector in Australia. It has generated the finest available climate projections for Australia's wine regions and provided detailed information about how the climate may change in the near, mid and long-term time horizons. This is a free online resource of climate information for all Australian GIs. The atlas aims to help answer questions on what specific regional climates will look like in the future. This is essential knowledge for making good management decisions, based on decadal changes, and supporting strategic decisions over the longer term, both within and between regions. Tailored climate indices were calculated for every Australian GI and include detailed information on:

- Temperature – growing season temperature (GST); growing degree days (GDD).
- Rainfall and evaporative demand – annual, monthly and seasonal rainfall; growing season rainfall; number of rainy days during harvest;

annual, monthly and seasonal aridity; number of dry spells before harvest.

- Heat Extremes – extreme heat factor (EHF) during a heatwave; heatwave duration and intensity; number of days per year exceeding temperature thresholds; frequency of days with high human heat stress.
- Cold Extremes – number of days at risk of frost during the growing season; daily minimum temperature; annual chilling degree days; number of days per year temperature falls below temperature thresholds.

This is a valuable resource for the industry and for those wishing to dig deeper into climate. More information can be found here: https://www.wineaustralia.com/growing-making/environment-and-climate/climate-atlas

Sustainability in Australia

Launched in July 2019, Sustainable Winegrowing Australia (SWA) is a relatively young programme that draws on the strengths of its predecessor programmes, including Entwine Australia and Sustainable Australia Winegrowing (SAW). It is dedicated to promoting and progressing the sustainable production of Australian grapes and wine among the grape growers and winemakers that make up its membership. Sustainability is a nebulous term and can be misleading. The programme covers many aspects. Sustainable Winegrowing Australia provides a broad definition and the goal of the programme:

Growing and making wine sustainably is a holistic approach to production that evolves the environmental aspect of the craft. It looks at how we can better use energy and water to create efficiency, support regions and communities, and establish a business that is resilient and thriving. Where organic and biodynamic practices look specifically at environmental management, sustainable winegrowing takes a broader view to improve social and economic performance. Many growers and makers in Australia are practising sustainability already; it's just getting into the habit of documenting everything to make it official. As part of the Sustainable Winegrowing Australia programme, information collected allows a greater understanding of what's happening in the vineyard or winery. It allows our community to know where they are and have a view to where they want their practice to be. So, they can be proactive, rather than reactive.

The programme focuses on six key areas:

- Land and soil: members aim to protect and enhance the soil, providing vital nutrients and enhancing fertility for long-term productivity.

- Water: reducing environmental impact by increased efficiency in water use in both the vineyard and the winery.

- Biodiversity: active land management to conserve, develop and enhance the ecosystem.

- Energy: aims to lower greenhouse gas emissions, including efficient energy use and investment in green sources of power, reducing the impact of the wine business on climate change.

- Waste: reduction and elimination of waste to help the Australian wine community achieve its zero-waste target by 2050.

- People and businesses: by building relationships within the supply chain and with the local community both the business and the land can benefit.

It is a solid programme with many high-profile members. More information can be found at www.sustainablewinegrowing.com.au.

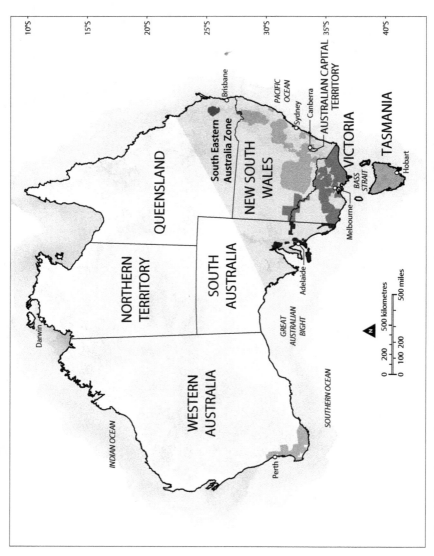

Map 1: The wine-producing regions of Australia. As noted on page 17, the areas suited to wine production are concentrated in the south of the country. Individual GIs are shown on the detailed state maps.

3

LABELLING LAWS IN AUSTRALIA

THE LABEL INTEGRITY PROGRAM

In the late 1980s, legislative changes – instigated and funded by winemakers – set up what was known as the Label Integrity Program (LIP). The LIP essentially controls truth in labelling. Many gaps existed however, not the least of which was a lack of regulation determining regional boundaries. In 1994 the Australian Wine and Brandy Corporation Act helped to rectify that by establishing a sort of system of appellation. There now exists a hierarchy of regional descriptions. A wine region is internationally protected and defined as a single tract of land that usually produces at least 500 tonnes of wine grapes in a year, and comprises at least five independently owned vineyards of at least 5 hectares each. The area of land must be discrete and homogeneous in its grape-growing attributes. An 85 per cent rule applies in Australia, which means at least 85 per cent of the wine must be from the named region in order for it to appear on the label.

Rules apply to all variety claims, stipulating the minimum amount of a single grape that a wine must contain for that wine to be labelled as a single variety. In Australia, it is down to the 85 per cent rule again, that is, at least 85 per cent of the wine must be from the grape variety in question.

GEOGRAPHIC INDICATIONS (GI)

The largest region as it relates to the labelling of wines in Australia is South Eastern Australia. Then there are the individual states of Victoria,

New South Wales, South Australia, Tasmania, etc. Within each state there are **zones** such as Adelaide Super Zone, Murray Darling Zone, etc. Each zone can be divided into **regions**, such as Barossa Valley, Clare Valley, etc. Each region can be divided into **sub-regions**,[8] for example, Lenswood and Piccadilly are sub-zones within Adelaide Hills.

Zones, regions and sub-regions are all known as Geographic Indications (GIs). There are currently over 65 Geographic Indications in Australia.

The criteria for determining Geographical Indications is quite detailed but below are a few key elements that outline the basic requirements that must be met and the process for awarding of a GI.

Applications for new geographical indications (GIs) are made to the Geographical Indications Committee (GIC). Applications may be made by a declared organization representing winemakers and/or grape growers, an individual winemaker or a wine grape grower.

To be eligible for determination as a GI, a grape-growing area must:

- usually produce at least 500 tonnes of grapes per year;
- include at least five wine-grape vineyards of at least 5 hectares each (that do not have common ownership);
- be a single tract of land.

There is an application fee of $27,500. An application cannot be considered until trademark owners (or those with applications pending) or other persons have been invited to object, through the Registrar of Trade Marks. Oppositions can be made to the Registrar of Trade Marks on the grounds that determination of the proposed GI is likely to cause confusion with an existing trademark, or that the proposed GI is used in Australia as the common name of a type or style of wine or as a name of a variety of grapes.

Applications for the review of a final determination may be made to the Administrative Appeals Tribunal (AAT) within 28 days. Appeals against an AAT decision can be lodged with the Federal Court. If no appeals are lodged, or if appeals are not successful, the GI is entered on to the Register of Protected Geographical Indications and Other Terms.

Once a GI is entered on to the Register of Protected Geographical Indications and Other Terms, the blending rules apply to it. This means

8   The legislation is a bit vague and the difference between a region and a sub-region is very subtle.

that if the single GI is used, at least 85 per cent of the fruit used to make the wine must have been sourced from within the boundary of the GI. Use of registered GIs is regulated by Wine Australia through its Label Integrity Program.

4

GRAPE VARIETIES IN AUSTRALIA

There are over 150 different grape varieties grown in Australia today. Some are widely planted, and others are either relatively new or have limited geographical distribution. The industry in Australia informally categorizes them into major varieties and alternative varieties. I have loosely followed this with my own interpretations. This is not a comprehensive list of all the grape varieties grown in Australia. It is a brief overview of the varieties that have shaped the wine styles of Australia to date and some that will be important for the future. Major, or classic varieties are those that have history, broad regional distribution and have formed the backbone of a wide cross-section of regionally expressive wines. Determining which varieties qualify as alternative is a bit untidy. Journalist and author Max Allen is writing a book on alternative varieties, titled *Alternative Reality* (due in 2023), and we both agree that while alternative is not ideal it is the term that the Australian industry is comfortable with and follows the lead of the Alternative Varieties Wine Show. This show started in 2001 and for over 20 years it has looked at all the newer varieties and the different styles of wines they can produce.

More important than nomenclature is the changing landscape of varieties being grown and how they are shaping the look, feel and taste of Australian wine. Many varieties of southern Mediterranean origin have been planted over the past 20 years. The initial motivation was to look to the future and our changing environment. The varieties that are being introduced are better suited to warmer climates, can hold their natural acidity and make wines that are not only delicious but require less manipulation. Australian GI regulations do not stipulate what can and can't be grown, which means that Australia has been on the front foot in experimenting with new varieties. It is also important to note that some varieties that have been in Australia for decades are now re-emerging as stars. Grenache is the most obvious example.

Recent commentary from award-winning winemaker Steve Pannell adds another angle on the extremes that are presented by climate change and which newer varieties are best suited to cope:

> For me, and considering the 2023 vintage, it's a sweeping generalization to say that the climate changing is only resulting in warming. I agree with the science on warming, however I'd say the effect for us is an increase in extremes and as such we are planting varieties that deal with the extremes in our regions better than those traditionally planted. The 2023 harvest was the latest and coolest in my memory. The third year of a muti year La Niña has resulted in rain and early onset cold that made ripening difficult and delivered acidity in some varieties unlike any I have seen in 43 vintages. Fortunately, it is the Southern Italian, Iberian and Grenache wines that have delivered the best results, retaining flavour at lower Baumes and a focus on the tannins, which is what I am most eager to continue exploring.

MAJOR WHITE VARIETIES

Chardonnay

Chardonnay has been in Australia since the early 1900s but it didn't become popular until the 1970s. Tyrrell's bottled the first varietally labelled Chardonnay in 1971, Craigmoor in the Mudgee in 1972. Also in 1972, David Wynn from Mountadam Vineyards planted Chardonnay at the highest point in South Australia's Eden Valley. This was Australia's first noteworthy cool-climate Chardonnay. Chardonnay is planted in virtually every region in Australia and makes a wide variety of styles from light-bodied, crisp and unoaked through to full-bodied, complex barrel matured versions. The beauty of Chardonnay as a variety is its adaptability. It is relatively easy to grow, and you can fashion interesting wines from fruit grown in varied climates. It is a vigorous variety that requires proper canopy management to control yields. It is also a variety that responds well to various winemaking techniques; indeed, you could argue that it needs the intervention of the winemaker.

It was, in fact, a Chardonnay that put modern Australian wine on the map. In 1981 Rosemount Show Reserve Chardonnay 1980 won a rare double gold medal at the International Wine and Spirits Competition in London. The wine press and merchants took note. What followed were many years of rich, ripe heavily oaked styles. Subtlety and structural complexity were not a consideration in those days. Ripeness ruled, and we all loved them! But exhaustion inevitably set in.

Premium Australian Chardonnay has evolved dramatically and there are several factors that have shaped this change. First, growers have gained access to and developed experience with new Chardonnay clones. Dijon (Barnard) clones became available in the mid-1990s. At the time, these were considered to be the premium clones and it was important to see what was possible in Australia with newer plant material. Ripeness in many areas in Australia is not the issue. So the second factor involved growers taming ripeness by planting in cooler regions and cooler sites within those regions as well as being more thoughtful about picking dates to ensure natural acid balance is maintained.

However, a different approach to winemaking might be the biggest influence on how the best wines look today. Oak use has shifted. Today's winemakers use better quality oak, larger format barrels, a lower percentage of new oak and give their wines less time in oak. This, combined with a more thoughtful approach to lees management and malolactic conversion has led to a more restrained and balanced style. There was a period during the early shift in style where many wines were tight, restrained, overly acidic and lacked the textural charm and subtle richness that top Chardonnay exhibits. Mercifully, this is all but in the past and there has never been a better time to drink Chardonnay from Australia's best regions. There are many regions growing Chardonnay of various styles and quality levels. The very best, premium, examples are covered individually in the regional chapters. The top performing regions for Chardonnay in Australia at present are Margaret River, Adelaide Hills, Yarra Valley, Beechworth, Mornington Peninsula, Macedon Ranges, Tasmania, Tumbarumba and Orange.

Riesling

Australia has a long history of Riesling production, with the first recorded plantings being in 1838 near Penrith, New South Wales. Riesling was the most planted quality white grape variety in Australia until the late 1980s. Australia is second only to Germany in terms of total plantings of this variety and, while plantings have declined since the 1980s, it is still grown in many regions across the country. Generally, the better wines are from cooler sites within cooler regions. The classic style of regional Riesling is dry and full flavoured with typical youthful citrus characteristics. The top wines from Clare Valley and Eden Valley have defined how people view Riesling in Australia and for good reason. The best are vibrant and lively with electrifying acidity and the capacity to age for decades, developing toasty characters and, at times, the distinctive and controversial petrol or kerosene-like aroma (see box, below). Other regional expressions and styles have emerged. Off-dry and sweeter styles are more common, as are wines with additional complexity and texture because of a little skin contact and fermentation in different vessels, such as amphorae or concrete eggs. While Clare Valley and Eden Valley have a long history and deserved reputations for producing some of Australia's most noted examples there are pockets of fantastic Riesling vineyards spread across the country and specific producers are highlighted throughout the book in their respective, sometimes lesser-known regions. Regions where you will find thrilling examples are Clare Valley, Eden Valley, Great Southern (especially Frankland River), Tasmania, Henty, Canberra District and Grampians.

That pesky petrol/kerosene character of aged Riesling

Riesling lovers are familiar with a very specific character that aged wines from the variety often display. Producing aromas variously referred to as petrol or kerosene-like, the compound responsible is 1,1,6-trimethyl-1,2-dihydronaphthalene, usually referred to as TDN. It is found in other white varieties, but Riesling appears to contain more of it. At low levels it can be viewed as additional complexity, but most people are not charmed by it. A deeper technical breakdown is offered by Dr Jamie Goode:

TDN belongs to a group of compounds called C13-norisoprenoids. It is formed from precursors in the grapes that develop higher levels with sunlight exposure and also water stress. Riesling wines typically have both free TDN in them and also the bound precursors, with far more of the latter, and some of the bound reserve becomes free during fermentation and then ageing. But some of the free is lost, too, so there is a sort of flux with more being

> *released as some is lost. It is thought that after a few years most wines reach*
> *a stable peak, before the levels fall once the bound reserves are used up.*
>
> Many producers of Riesling in Australia generally aim to mitigate overt kero-
> sene characters. A whiff can be charming. Too much can dominate the flavour
> profile and detract from the pure, vibrant fruit charm of Riesling. Keeping the
> fruit zone shaded, with careful canopy management, leading to dappled light
> rather than direct sunlight on the fruit, is common.

Semillon

Semillon arrived in Australia in 1832 as part of James Busby's collection. It is a vigorous variety that is relatively easy to grow. It is quite
disease resistant and can maintain high yields, so it became quite popular. It initially found a comfortable home in the Hunter Valley and subsequently the Barossa Valley but can now be found in several regions.
The Hunter Valley remains its spiritual home in Australia. Early Hunter
Semillons were often labelled as Hunter River Riesling, Rhine Riesling,
Shepherd's Riesling, Hock, White Burgundy or even Chablis such were
the lack of tight labelling laws. Those were common naming conventions in Australia at the time but did nothing to promote the inherent
qualities of Semillon as a standalone variety. Today, the Hunter Valley
has old Semillon vines dating back to the early 1900s. While this variety has a long history in Australia it still flies under the radar in terms
of broad popularity. Wines are made in a range of styles but the classic
unoaked Hunter Valley expression is unique and one of Australia's most
singular white wine styles. Picked early to preserve natural acidity, wines
are typically fermented in stainless steel and bottled immediately. When
young, they are crisp, dry and lemony and could quite easily be passed
off as simple and straightforward as I have witnessed in blind tastings.
But with 6–8 years of bottle age the texture changes and complex flavours emerge. Fig, honey and toasty notes develop that often lead in-
experienced tasters to swear that the wines were aged in oak. Exactly
where the toasty notes come from is still unclear (see box, opposite).
Hunter Semillon is capable of ageing gracefully for well over 20 years.

Semillon also has a long history in the Barossa Valley where there
are several old vine vineyard sites. The Barossa version tends to be more
full-bodied, with peach and citrus flavours and is sometimes fermented
and/or aged in oak. It is an important variety in Margaret River, where

it typically partners with Sauvignon Blanc in varying proportions. The Hunter Valley, Barossa Valley and Margaret River are the three most noted regions for Semillon in Australia.

The aged character of Hunter Semillon

Peter Godden at the Australian Wine Research Institute (AWRI) explains some of the theories around the appearance of toasty notes in aged Semillon:

In short, we don't really know for sure which compound or compounds are responsible for the toasty character in aged Semillon. Wine lactone (3S,3aS, 7aR)-3a,4,5,7a-tetrahydro-3,6-dimethyl benzofuran-2(3H)-one) probably contributes. It has aromas of coconut and lime and can increase in concentration over time. Phenylacetaldehyde is probably also contributing, with an aroma often described as honey-like. However, the key compound might be TPB (E-1-(2,3,6-Trimethylphenyl)buta-1,3-diene), and more work needs to be done on this. Ultimately it appears to be a combination of these three compounds. TDN (the petrol-like character more associated with aged Riesling) might also be a factor, but is usually obvious if it is present, and not necessarily part of classic 'toasty' aged Semillon character.

The Muscat Family

The various clones of Muscat – Muscat of Alexandria (Muscat Gordo Blanco), Muscat à Petits Grains Rouges and Muscat Blanc à Petits Grains – have a long and colourful history in Australia. While it is used for many different styles today, the legacy of Muscat in Australia rests with the classic sweet, fortified wines from the Rutherglen area in north-eastern Victoria. The Muscat à Petits Grains Rouges, often called Brown Muscat in Australia, is the variety of Muscat mostly used here. The grapes are picked very ripe, and the wine is fortified quite early in fermentation to preserve the natural sweetness. Older wines are blended with younger wines and the result is a wine of extraordinary richness and complexity, unlike any other fortified wine in the world. (See page 223 for additional details on this style.) The global enthusiasm for Moscato d'Asti and similar successful styles produced in the US and elsewhere, created a large market for the style in Australia. Australian versions are similarly light-bodied, 5–8% abv, frothy and relatively sweet and can be made from any of the three major types of Muscat listed above. Muscat is also used in Pet Nat production and there are many fantastic, skin-contact dry versions emerging from the low-intervention sector.

Sauvignon Blanc

Records indicate that Sauvignon Blanc was first grown in Australia in the 1800s, but planting of the variety was intermittent until the 1990s. The popularity of Marlborough Sauvignon Blanc from New Zealand inspired rapid growth in the Australian market. It is a vigorous variety that thrives in cool but sunny climates and has now become firmly established in several regions in Australia. Elevated, cooler sites in Adelaide Hills have proven to be ideal and it has become a signature variety for the region. The style of Adelaide Hills Sauvignon Blanc tends towards ripe, tropical flavours of passionfruit and guava, with a little herbal life rather than an overt herbaceous character. Margaret River does produce varietal Sauvignon Blanc, but it is more common in this region to find it in the classic blend of Semillon and Sauvignon Blanc. This style ranges from light, crisp, lemony and herbal through to fuller flavoured and more tropical with some barrel fermentation and/or ageing. Adelaide Hills and Margaret River are the two most notable regions for Sauvignon Blanc in Australia but there are also delicious examples from Yarra Valley, Tasmania and Orange.

Pinot Gris/Pinot Grigio

Pinot Gris was another variety that reputedly came to Australia in the 1832 Busby collection. It seemed to languish in obscurity until 1994, when Kathleen Quealy and Kevin McCarthy brought it into focus, planting Pinot Gris vines for their new T'Gallant winery project in the Mornington Peninsula. This was the beginning of the popularity surge for the variety in Australia. Whether to label it Pinot Gris or Pinot Grigio still causes confusion. In theory, a style modelled on the light, crisp northern Italian iteration would be labelled Pinot Grigio, whereas a richer, more textural style would be labelled Pinot Gris. The reality is that many styles overlap. A light, fresh, zesty style could be labelled Pinot Gris. A rich, lees-matured, textural style could be sold as a Pinot Grigio. One half of a tank (or barrel) of the very same wine could be bottled under a Pinot Grigio label, the other half under Pinot Gris. Ultimately it is a marketing-driven decision by the producer. The vast majority is made into a fresh, vibrant juicy style intended for early consumption. A large proportion of plantings are in the Murray Darling region, destined to produce affordable, entry-level wines. It is also made with varying levels of skin contact. Ramato style Pinot Gris is popular in Australia. It is modelled on the historical Italian version from Friuli in which the wine is left on skins, so it develops a coppery tone and a little more grip and texture. The term comes from the Italian word for copper – *rame*. More extended skin contact versions end up as orange wines, and there are styles that fit in between. There is not one specific region in Australia where you can comfortably say that Pinot Gris is the focus, benchmark variety. Premium Pinot Gris/Pinot Grigio is being made in several regions. Mornington Peninsula, Adelaide Hills and the distinctly Italian influenced region of King Valley produce some very interesting, complex versions. I often come across random, interesting versions from unlikely places. It is a good time to explore this variety in Australia.

Viognier

The first serious plantings of this variety in Australia were in Heathcote in 1978 but Yalumba also planted vines in the Eden Valley in 1979. Yalumba's enthusiasm is largely responsible for the success and visibility of the variety in Australia. To begin with, there was lots of trial and error, according to Louisa Rose, Yalumba's head winemaker. Learning how to manage the variety in the vineyard was the first step. Picking according to acid and sugar numbers was not the answer. Viognier needs to be very ripe to capture the classic floral and apricot characters. Rose also says that native yeasts and oxidative handling have been the key to success. Yalumba winery is also responsible for much of the early work on clonal selection, at their vineyard nursery. Today there are now hundreds of wineries producing a version of this variety. Most Viognier is made into a varietal wine or forms part of a white blend. The practice of co-fermenting it with Shiraz is quite common although the rampant enthusiasm for this has slowed, leaving a smaller but better collection of wines attempting the style. You can find classic, premium, straight varietal Viognier in the Barossa, with especially good examples from Yalumba's Eden Valley sites. Yalumba makes five different versions of the variety from entry level through to their ultra-premium Virgilius. It does well in Heathcote and there are some interesting skin contact and low intervention wines (see Kalleske, in the Barossa Valley, p. 108).

Marsanne

Australia is home to the oldest Marsanne vines in the world. Tahbilk's 1927 Vines vineyard, on the banks of the Goulburn River in Nagambie

Lakes, represents the current oldest plantings of the variety. Records show that it was first introduced to the region in the 1860s from the Yarra Valley. Tahbilk has been the flagbearer of Marsanne as a varietal wine and is home to the largest single vineyard plantings of this variety in the world. A lot of Australia's Marsanne is blended with Roussanne and/or Viognier. Due to the Tahbilk legacy, Nagambie Lakes is, by default, the region in Australia best known for this variety but there really isn't a region that solely specializes in the variety. There are several really lovely examples, either blended or varietal. Tahbilk has its flagship 1927 Vines version, along with its Museum Release, aged Marsanne and a fresh, lively regular bottling. Ben Haines and Alkimi in the Yarra Valley, and Mitchelton in Goulburn make excellent varietal examples. Mount Mary and Yeringberg in the Yarra Valley both use Marsanne in a blend.

Verdelho

There is not a lot of Verdelho in Australia, but it has a long history in Australia and makes some very interesting wines, which is why I am including it. Verdelho first made its way from Madeira to Australia in the 1820s and has always done well in the hot, drier areas. The Hunter Valley in New South Wales and the Swan District in Western Australia are known for a vibrant juicy style, typically made for early consumption

A FEW ALTERNATIVE WHITE VARIETIES

Vermentino

This native southern Italian variety is doing well in many areas. Most versions to date are made with a relatively straightforward and/or low intervention approach and while they are not the same as southern Italian versions (nor should they be) the lemony, textural element of the variety exists in the better versions. Excellent examples can be found in McLaren Vale, Heathcote and the Riverland.

Fiano

Fiano is another beauty from southern Italy that is thriving in the warmer regions of Australia. This is a variety that has continued to charm me over the last 10 years. It maintains its vibrant, natural acidity when fully ripe and has the added bonus of doing well in drier years as it does not require as much water to grow successfully. It typically shows a vibrant lemony character and the better examples have weight, texture and a faint saline element. Excellent examples come from McLaren Vale, Riverland and Heathcote. Keep an eye on this one as it is showing up in many regions. In 2022 I tried a delicious tank sample at Tyrrell's in the Hunter Valley.

Roussanne, Grenache Blanc, Grenache Gris, Picpoul, Clairette and Bourboulenc

I am adding this collection of southern French varieties because there is a lot of chatter, especially in the Barossa and McLaren Vale about their suitability. I have tried enough examples of varietal wines and blends of the above to predict comfortably that the future of white wine in both Barossa and McLaren Vale will include a hefty proportion of these varieties. Coriole in McLaren Vale has made a delicious Picpoul for many years. Pete Fraser is crafting brilliant wines using these varieties at Yangarra. Yangarra Roux Beauté Roussanne is a textural, savoury masterpiece. Yangarra's delicious Ovitelli Blanc is a Grenache Blanc dominant white blend that typically sees the inclusion of Roussanne, Clairette, Picpoul and Bourboulenc. Pete Schell at Spinifex in Barossa had this to say:

> Grenache Gris delivers wines with texture, weight and freshness. It's early to harvest, acid retentive and robust in the vineyard. I'm still building a perspective with Grenache Gris but from the very small parcels I've handled – the first one in 2005 – I think it's going to be super useful. The better wines I've seen were firm, fresh, mid-weight numbers, with ripe citrus, dried herb and wild honey characters. Clairette gives wines with delicate aromatics and discrete flavours – white flowers, soft, sweet, herbal, pale pear-like fruit – and has a fullness without a lot of weight, which is appealing and useful in the Barossa, where it's easy for things to become a little heavy-handed. Like the Grenache Gris it has good acid retention and copes very well with heat and aridity.

Max Allen is also a fan of these newer varieties, saying:

> I am very excited about the Grenache Blanc and Grenache Gris I have tried – perfect white grapes for warmer climates such as McLaren Vale. I think Aglianico is very special as is Sagarantino, though the

latter's fierce tannins and deeply meaty/earthy qualities scare people off. Assyrtiko, currently only grown by Jim Barry has enormous potential and I would love to see more of it grown here. Nerello Mascalese (not yet planted) is going to be an adventure. Some Greek and Cypriot varieties are in the process of being imported and evaluated.

The excitement these varieties are generating is obvious in the discussions I have had with growers and winemakers, especially in warmer areas. Judging by what they are delivering in the glass I too share the excitement and will be watching this space closely.

MAJOR RED VARIETIES

Shiraz/Syrah

Shiraz was one of the original varieties brought to Australia and is certainly one of the most successful. This is Australia's heritage variety. There are still many vineyards scattered throughout the country with vines that are over 100 years old. It is grown in virtually every region in Australia and produces varying styles, from cooler climate, medium-bodied and spicy styles through to more full-bodied, richly flavoured and textured warmer climate versions. There are many fantastic regions for Shiraz but the most historic area, with a large repository of old vines, is the Barossa Valley. Other well-established regions for Shiraz in South Australia include McLaren Vale, Clare Valley and Eden Valley. The cooler climate areas of Victoria such as Grampians, Heathcote, Yarra Valley and Nagambie Lakes produce varying styles but tend towards the savoury and medium-bodied. In New South Wales the cooler climate of Canberra District produces a restrained and aromatic style, and the Hunter Valley is known for distinctive medium-bodied, savoury and age-worthy wines. Shiraz partners well with several other varieties. The classic blend of Grenache, Shiraz and Mourvedre in varying proportions has a long tradition as does the Shiraz–Cabernet blend. More recently co-fermenting a small proportion of Viognier with Shiraz has led to the trendy Shiraz–Viognier style. There are so many brilliant wines from different regions that listing good regional examples is difficult. Benchmark examples can be found in Barossa Valley, Eden Valley, McLaren Vale, Clare Valley, Langhorne Creek, Heathcote, Nagambie Lakes, Grampians, Yarra Valley, Hunter Valley and Canberra District.

However, with deference to the storied history and glowing praise heaped on this variety in Australia, its great success may be creating issues selling wines to more discerning customers. Particularly in export markets there seems to be a growing weariness with Shiraz, with the variety appearing in too many mundane, nondescript wines. Producers will have to work hard to convince customers that Shiraz is a variety that can produce interesting and nuanced wines. For more on this see the box below.

The Shiraz Conundrum

Shiraz is not as popular as it once was, in either Australia or in several export markets. Recent retail data for the UK produced by IRI still has Shiraz as the top selling Australian variety but purchases are heavily skewed towards cheaper price points. China was once a big market but given the import levies imposed it is not part of the current discussion (though this market may be on the radar again soon). In the United States, the general sentiment among the trade is one of lukewarm interest. Ask any of the top importers, and they will all agree that selling Shiraz right now is a challenging proposition.

Australia is home to the oldest plantings of this variety in the world. Shiraz is the grape behind some of the most iconic wines ever made in the country. There is no place on earth that can show the full range of what this variety can achieve better than Australia. So, what is the problem? I spent a decent amount of time over the last 12 months asking Australian growers, winemakers, and journalists this very question. Responses varied but most agreed on one thing: there are too many middle of the road, one-dimensional, boring examples. The early popularity of the variety also meant that it was planted widely and perhaps in certain areas, other varieties may fare better and make more interesting wine. One could argue that the cheap and cheerful style of supermarket Shiraz is debasing the value and character of the variety.

I am not convinced that this is where the image problem lies. Mass market wine is traded on price and these wines are not necessarily the ones that people use to judge the quality and character of Shiraz. I feel more blame rests with the expansive range of Shiraz that sits at moderate price points, around A$20–A$30. There are exceptions, but the sea of sameness in this segment is numbing. Most are simplistic wines with nothing more than ripe fruit and a few lashings of oak. It doesn't take long to get worn down by the disappointments. I have lived, eaten and breathed Australian wines for close to 20 years and rarely reach for this type of Shiraz. To be fair, I have recently tasted several examples of newer, fresher styles of Shiraz at this price point, some of which are juicy, fresh and delicious, which is encouraging. However, I would still argue that other varieties often deliver more character and interest at the same price point. For example, the Spinifex Papillon, priced at A$28, a Grenache Cinsault blend from the valley floor in Barossa Valley, is absolutely delicious: red-fruited, savoury and spicy. It has freshness but it also screams where it is from, with Barossa warmth and comfort. Similarly, the Coriole Nero from McLaren Vale is priced at A$30. Fragrant, fresh and juicy, it has lively black fruit overlayed with a charming herbal element. So why buy a moderately priced Shiraz when wines like this are on offer?

Pete Fraser is rationalizing his plantings at Yangarra. He is pulling out some Shiraz vines in sections of the estate and planting another 4 hectares of Grenache Gris and Grenache Blanc, as these two white varieties have performed particularly well. He is also planting three more hectares of Picpoul for the same reason. In addition he plans to add eight more hectares of Grenache. If we wish to continue to praise Shiraz and hail it as our heritage grape, we need to ensure that we keep it interesting. Old vine and other special sites where world-class wines are being made should be highlighted. More thought needs to go into site suitability for future plantings. It is so easy to demonstrate the diversity, character, and quality of this variety in Australia. Nobody else can do what Australia can do with this variety but if we populate store shelves with one-dimensional, simplistic examples it will be a long hard road to get the image of Shiraz back to where it belongs.

Cabernet Sauvignon

Considered around the world to be one of the noble red grape varieties Cabernet Sauvignon has a long history in Australia, dating back to the mid-1800s. It is a variety that does not do well with heat stress and drought and consequently took a while to find a comfortable home. It became very fashionable in 1970s and 1980s and plantings increased dramatically. It is now grown in more than 30 different regions across the country. Cabernet Sauvignon is often blended with other varieties; Merlot, Malbec and Petit Verdot are common partners. The classic Cabernet–Shiraz blend has a long history in Australia (see p. 101) and is made in many regions, most notably Langhorne Creek, Coonawarra and Barossa. The terra rossa soils and moderate climate of Coonawarra have proven to be well suited to the production of classically structured, age-worthy wines. The maritime climate and gravelly soils of Margaret River have also proven to be fantastic for this variety. These two areas have developed the best reputation for Cabernet Sauvignon in Australia. There are many other regions producing great wines. Yarra Valley, Pyrenees, Langhorne Creek, McLaren Vale, Clare Valley and Barossa are all note-worthy Cabernet-producing regions in South Australia.

Pinot Noir

Pinot Noir was one of the varieties that first came to Australia with the Busby collection in 1832. MV6 is a noted clone of Pinot Noir and is supposed to have been collected by Busby when he visited Clos de Vougeot on his travels. It was a variety that was not talked about very much in the early years, when warmer climate varieties like Shiraz and Grenache seemed to fare better. The challenges of growing Pinot Noir are well documented. It is a notoriously fickle variety, which likes temperate climates: understanding this made successful plantings possible. In Australia it does best in regions with cooling influences from either the ocean or altitude. The evolution of Pinot Noir is not dissimilar to that of Chardonnay. Access to Dijon clones in the mid-1990s gave winemakers a broader palate of raw material,and a better understanding of how and where to grow the variety followed. A deeper understanding and appreciation of the MV6 clone was also helpful. Given that the original cuttings arrived in 1832, MV6 is a clone that has 190 years of adaptation to the Australian environment.

Abel Clone Pinot Noir at Tolpuddle, Tasmania.

Experience making Pinot Noir was also necessary to the success of these wines. I have been in the wine business long enough to watch the evolution of this variety in several New World areas, especially California, Oregon and New Zealand, and all seem to have experienced a similar steep learning curve to Australia. In the 1990s I would carefully recommend certain Pinot Noirs by name. Today, you can comfortably experiment with Australian Pinot Noir at your leisure. There are so many fantastic wines being made in many regions. Yarra Valley, Mornington Peninsula, Geelong, Gippsland and Macedon Ranges, Orange and Tumbarumba all produce very high-quality examples. Being surrounded by the cooling effect of the Southern Ocean, Tasmania does particularly well with this variety. The complex and varied region of Adelaide Hills is also home to very fine examples. Pinot Noir figures prominently in the production of traditional method sparkling wines in Australia, with fruit from Tasmania, Yarra Valley and Adelaide Hills in high demand for its balance of delicate flavours and high acidity.

Grenache

Grenache has a long history in Australia, with the first vines also arriving with the Busby collection in 1832. It is an early budding, late ripening variety and thrived in the warmth of the Australian climate. As a result, there are many vineyard sites, especially in McLaren Vale and Barossa Valley, that have vines dating back to the late 1800s. Cirillo's 1848 vineyard is the oldest Grenache vineyard in the world. It was used for fortified wine production in the early years and formed the backbone of many red blended wines but seemed to be viewed, rather strangely, as a secondary citizen. I remember it being referred to as 'a rather coarse variety' by a well-respected Master of Wine. In recent years the status of Grenache has been elevated, as growers and winemakers realize its inherent charm and beauty. It has been referred to as warm climate Pinot Noir, a statement I embraced initially, given the soft red fruit and ethereal qualities that can be coaxed from varietal Grenache, but that statement inherently positions it as inferior to Pinot. Steve Pannell sums it up beautifully:

> *I often wonder whether the perception of Grenache as warm climate Pinot Noir is misleading. McLaren Vale Grenache is nothing of the sort. It is definitively medium bodied, with appealing red spectrum*

fruits (if handled without obvious oak), and balanced by dark spice and a unique iodine/umami finish. The freshness is derived from the balance of acidity to fine tannin that gives length and creates the classic fan shape on the back palate. It is the textural interest. Grenache seemingly manages to deliver in all conditions if the picking window is carefully monitored. We aim to pick at a Baumé of 13.5 and sometimes the difference between meeting or missing that window is 48 hours. McLaren Vale Grenache is unique and worthy of its own place in the world of fine wine, without comparison.

This is the red variety in Australia that has captured my imagination for the past 15 years (see Ochota Barrels Fugazi Grenache, p. 313). Varietal Grenache, especially from McLaren Vale, is setting a new standard of quality for this variety globally. McLaren Vale should be your first port of call if you want to understand this evolution, but there are also brilliant wines from the Barossa Valley. It still forms the backbone of the classic red blends, partnering beautifully with Shiraz and Mourvedre among other varieties. Grenache is also used in the production of rosé and is still the go-to variety for fortified wine production. Outside McLaren Vale and Barossa Valley, top-notch Grenache-based wines can be found in Clare Valley, Riverland, Heathcote and Swan Valley in Western Australia.

Pruning Grenache vines at Cirillo – the vines were planted in 1848.

Merlot

Merlot was first planted in Australia in 1965. It is not a variety that has a long history and until recently it had a negative reputation. Most argue that the issue in Australia was the original clonal material not being ideal (although some say the problem was viticulture). The D3V14 clone was introduced from UC Davis in 1965. New clones arrived in 2006. Mike Miller from Mertite Wines in Wrattonbully conducted extensive trials in his vineyards to determine which Merlot clones were best suited to Australia's growing conditions. (For his findings, see the box below.)

Production of varietal Merlot has increased in Australia but, in the past, it typically served as a blending partner to other varieties, most notably Cabernet Sauvignon. The best examples to date are from Margaret River, Coonawarra and Wrattonbully. There are smatterings of really good Merlot from other regions but it often appears to be individual producers excelling rather than any sort of regional focus. Chris Carpenter's The Revivalist Merlot from Hickinbotham Clarendon Vineyard in McLaren Vale comes to mind.

Regardless of any issues there may previously have been with the variety, there are now all manner of interesting Merlots to look for. I think it is a variety to keep an eye on.

Merlot clones in Australia

In 2006 the new Merlot clones Q45, 8R, 181 and 343 were introduced to provide alternative vine stock to the D3V14 clone from UC Davis, which had been grown in Australia since the 1960s. One of the best Merlot producers in Australia, Mike Miller from Mertite Wines in Wrattonbully, performed extensive trials with newer clones and the results showed that the newer clones performed better in his vineyard in general than the old UC Davis clone. He found the following, with a caveat for a cool climate site with high UV.

D3V14 Clone. This is planted on own roots only, requires an extra pass in the vineyard for vigorous canopy and trunk shoots, and has smaller leaves to higher crop load ratio so is unbalanced in a cool climate. It is more vulnerable to poor fruit set and hen and chicks/millerandage. Berries are bigger, leading to a larger bunch weight, averaging 120 grams. Later seed development and ripening, holding on to green flavours for typically 10–14 days longer. Regularly has more seeds in the grape – often 2–3 seeds. Seeds remain tactile and with a green film until around 14.5 Baumé. Mulberry and riper flavour profiles in the wine.

8R Clone. This is planted on low vigour rootstocks and own roots. It has bigger leaves than D3V14 to a smaller crop load. Berries are smaller, providing better colour and flavour concentration in the wine. Flowering and set are more reliable. Seeds become ripe two weeks earlier so it may be harvested when acidity is higher, giving flavours of a less-ripe profile, when seeds taste like toasted pine nuts and pop-crunch in your teeth. Blue and black fruits, high quality tannins, and typically lower alcohol wine.

Q45 Clone. This is planted on low vigour rootstocks and own roots. Bigger leaves than D3V14 to a smaller crop load. Berries are smaller, providing better colour and flavour concentration in the wine. Flowering and set are more reliable. Seeds become riper two weeks earlier so it may be harvested when acidity is higher, flavours less ripe, when seeds taste like toasted pine nuts and pop. Red fruit flavours, prominent tannins, and typically lower alcohol wine.

343 Clone. This is planted on low vigour rootstocks and own roots. Bigger leaves than D3V14 to a smaller crop load. Smaller berries than D3V14, providing better colour and flavour concentration in the wine. More reliable flowering and set. Seeds become riper two weeks earlier so it may be harvested earlier. Red fruits and aromatics in the wine, and typically lower alcohol wine.

181 Clone. This is planted on low vigour rootstocks and own roots. Bigger leaves than D3V14 to a smaller crop load. Smaller berries than D3V14, providing better colour and flavour concentration in the wine. More reliable flowering and set. Seeds become riper two weeks earlier so it may be harvested earlier. Red fruits and aromatics in the wine, and typically lower alcohol wines.

In summary, Miller says of the new clones, 'If you can imagine the load in the harvest bin going to the winery, it will have a higher concentration of colour and flavour, with higher quality seeds providing fine tannins, and berries at a more even ripening stage in the load, so hardly any greenness, and at a higher natural acidity at harvest time. In short: A-grade Merlot!'

Mourvèdre/Mataro

Mourvèdre originates from Spain, where it is known as Monastrell. It is sometimes labelled Mataro in Australia, a name derived from that of a town on the Mediterranean coast between Barcelona and Valencia. Being a late ripening variety, it does well in the warmer climate regions of Australia and has a long history in the Barossa Valley in particular.

Along with Shiraz and Grenache it was one of the original varieties that thrived and although not as widely planted, there are still 100-year-old Mourvèdre vineyard sites. There are many superb varietal wines. Hewitson's Old Garden Mourvèdre is from the Koch Vineyard, which was planted in 1853, the oldest Mourvèdre vineyard in the world. It is still an important element in the various Shiraz, Grenache and Mourvèdre blends, labelled either GSM, MGS or SGM depending on the make-up of the final wine. There are many regions growing Mourvèdre but Barossa Valley is the best known region for this variety.

Koch Vineyard old-vine Mourvèdre, planted in 1853.

Malbec

Malbec used to be a popular variety in Australia but it fell out of favour in the early part of this century. It is now making a minor comeback, especially in Margaret River, where it has become increasingly important as a blending partner in Cabernet Sauvignon dominant blends. Bleasdale in Langhorne Creek has always produced a varietal wine from Malbec and it is an important variety at Wendouree in Clare Valley. (Those in the know, know.) The Cabernet–Malbec might be the best wine, which is saying something given how good everything is at Wendouree. The Shiraz–Malbec is also legendary. Malbec is an important variety in Clare Valley, Langhorne Creek and Margaret River

A FEW ALTERNATIVE RED VARIETIES

Sangiovese

The UC Davis Sangiovese clone H6V9 was first brought to Australia in the 1960s but was not planted in Australia until the early 1970s. Penfolds trialled it in their Kalimna vineyard in the Barossa Valley using the UC Davis clones, and Carlo Corino at Montrose in Mudgee also established some trial plantings. It was Mark Lloyd at Coriole in McLaren Vale who drew attention to this variety in a more serious and commercial way. Lloyd particularly wanted to use something non-French when he planted it in 1984, making it one of the original alternative varieties in Australia. By 1999, several producers were working with the variety, to the extent that Jenni and Bruce Chalmers, Dr Rod Bonfiglioli from the Chalmers Nursery, and Stefano de Pieri of Mildura were able to plan a 'Long Italian Lunch', which included the inaugural Australian Sangiovese Awards. Twenty-eight Australian Sangiovese or Sangiovese blends were entered in the first Sangiovese Awards. This inspired the creation of the Australian Alternative Variety Awards Show in 2001. Exciting Sangiovese is being produced in many regions now, including McLaren Vale, Barossa Valley, King Valley, Heathcote, Beechworth, Yarra Valley, Riverland and the Riverina

Tempranillo

The interest in alternate varieties in Australia has resulted in increased plantings of Tempranillo. From a small base of about 50 hectares in 2001 plantings had grown to 739 hectares by 2015 (individual variety statistics have not been reported since 2015). The 2021 National Vintage Survey indicated that 5,874 tonnes of Tempranillo were crushed that year, which is less than 0.5% of the total annual crush.

The Riverland represents about 20 per cent of the total crush, the Murray Darling (Victoria and New South Wales combined) is 22 per cent, Riverina 9 per cent and the Barossa Valley 7 per cent. The balance is made up across several other regions. I have had delicious examples from Adelaide Hills, Heathcote, McLaren Vale, Beechworth and King Valley. Minuscule statistics aside, it is a variety that is presently quite popular on the domestic market. You don't see a lot of varietal Tempranillo from Australia in export markets. The sentiment shared by several producers was that Tempranillo would be a challenge in export markets given the competition and price points of Tempranillo from Spain. A sound theory, I think. There are many exciting varietal examples as well as various blends. SC Pannell's Tempranillo Touriga is wonderful and ages gracefully. Excellent varietal examples can be found at SC Pannell, Gemtree and Paxton (McLaren Vale), Fighting Gully Road (Beechworth) and La Linea (Adelaide Hills).

Petit Verdot

Petit Verdot is a late ripening variety and grows particularly well in several regions in Australia. Australia's largest plantings of Petit Verdot can be found in the Riverland region. It is also grown with success in the Barossa, McLaren Vale, Langhorne Creek, Margaret River, Padthaway, Coonawarra and Riverina. Its ability to retain acidity in warmer climates is key. It typically makes full-bodied wines with a flavour profile similar to that of Shiraz, with red berry fruit, black pepper spice and floral notes. It is still more likely to be found in a Cabernet based blend but is clearly a variety that is well suited to Australia.

Touriga Nacional

A classic variety from the Douro region in Portugal, Touriga Nacional has small presence but long history in Australia, where it has mainly been blended with Shiraz and Durif to make Port-style wines. Touriga is a very low-yielding vine that produces small, thick-skinned berries with a high skin-to-juice ratio. Firm tannins are a feature of the variety. In the 1990s, Dr Baily Carrodus from Yarra Yering in the Yarra Valley planted it alongside four other Portuguese varieties. Originally used to make a vintage fortified wine, it is now blended with the other Portuguese varieties to make Dry Red No. 3. Many of the oldest plantings are in Rutherglen, but the variety grows well in McLaren Vale, Barossa, Langhorne Creek and the Riverland.

Nebbiolo

Australia's first plantings of Nebbiolo date back to the mid-1980s. Carlo Corino experimented with Nebbiolo at Montrose in Mudgee, where conditions proved too warm for this fickle variety. It is now grown in several cooler climate areas with notable wines now being made in King Valley, Yarra Valley, Beechworth, Adelaide Hills, Canberra District, Orange and Tasmania. Fred Pizzini notes that, 'it's a frustrating variety with as many clonal variations as Pinot Noir. Nebbiolo is a difficult grape to grow and equally challenging to make.' Despite this, the Pizzinis have been growing and making Nebbiolo since 1990 – with great results (see p. 232).

Nero d'Avola

This is one of the more recent Italian red varieties imported into Australia, but it seems to be drawing a lot of attention. In the early 2000s a partnership with Italian nursery Vivai Cooperativi Rauscedo, with the assistance of Dr Alberto Antonini, saw several Italian varieties brought into Australia, Nero d'Avola among them. Chalmers first planted Nero in the Murray Darling region at their original nursery in Euston in 2002, and subsequently in their Heathcote vineyard. The first commercial wine was made from fruit from Euston in 2009, so we are still in the early stages of understanding what this variety is capable of. McLaren Vale is a hotbed of interesting examples at present but there are several other areas where this native Sicilian variety is shining. Great examples can be found in the Riverland, Heathcote, Murray Darling, Barossa Valley and Granite Belt. Today, there are more than 50 vineyards planted with Nero. Ashley Ratcliff of Ricca Terra Farms in the Riverland planted Nero originally with the sole motivation of coping with the long-running drought his region was experiencing in the early part of the century. Results exceeded expectations: 'We now use about half the water of more traditional varieties,' says Ashley. Nero is a variety that needs warmth, and it is clearly adapting to the Australian environment.

Montepulciano

Here is yet another southern Italian variety excelling in Australia. Not much was planted until the early part of this century but you can find dozens of juicy, fresh and vibrant versions from many different regions, including Riverland, McLaren Vale, Barossa Valley, Heathcote, Riverina, Adelaide Hills and Granite Belt.

5

AUSTRALIA'S OLD VINES

Grape vines are not native to Australia. Early European settlers brought the original cuttings on the First Fleet in 1788. The cuttings were collected in Rio de Janeiro and the Cape of Good Hope. There are limited records of viticulture and winemaking in these early years. In *Riesling in Australia*, Ken Helm and Trish Burgess note that in a dispatch dated 16 October 1791 the then Governor stated that 'he had 3 acres of vineyard in the Government House grounds at Parramatta and that Phillip Schaffer, a German from Hessen had planted one acre of vines on his property on the North Bank of Parramatta River thus entitling him to be recorded as the first vigneron of Australia'.

Some historians have suggested that the vines were also brought in to make wine for practical reasons. Early settlers did not know what to expect so vines were likely planted to make wine for the eventual journey back to Britain. Water on long ship journeys needed to be stabilized and wine served that purpose. One bottle of wine mixed with six bottles of water achieved the necessary stability. There was no understanding of the complexities of chemistry in those days but the vinous addition would have lowered the pH, making the water safe to drink.

Vines were haphazardly brought to Australia throughout the next 40 years but the most significant year for vine importation was 1832. Botanist James Busby travelled to Europe in 1831 and collected vine cuttings from southern Spain and France. From what he had witnessed so far, he was convinced that vine growing and winemaking would be very successful in the new colony.

The following excerpt from his journal, dated 6 January 1832, highlights his systematic and impressive work.

I had the good fortune to find in the Botanic Garden at Montpellier a collection of most of the vine varieties cultivated in France, and in other parts of Europe, to the number of 437, and, on application to the professor of Botany, he, (with the greatest liberality) permitted me to take cuttings from the whole. I afterwards, added to this collection 133 from the Royal Nursery of the Luxembourg at Paris, making in this whole 570 varieties of vines, of all of which, with two or three exceptions, I obtained two cuttings.

It is my wish to place this collection at the disposal of His Majesty's Government, for the purpose, should it be deemed expedient, of forming an experimental garden at Sydney, to prove their different qualities, and propagate, for general distribution, those which may appear suitable to the climate.

Busby's request was granted, and his collection was shipped to Sydney. In total, 363 vines survived the journey and were planted in the Botanical Gardens in Sydney. A duplicate collection was planted at his property in the Hunter Valley and subsequent cuttings made their way to various parts of New South Wales, Victoria and South Australia, as well as to New Zealand, where Busby later moved. This distribution marked the start of a more systematic and detailed approach to vine growing in Australia. As a result, many of Australia's old vines can be traced back to the original Busby collection. The timing of his trip was additionally fortuitous as it preceded the outbreak of phylloxera in Europe by 30 years.

Phylloxera has a history in Australia with outbreaks in the early 1900s in parts of Victoria – notably Geelong and Rutherglen. Current issues exist in the Yarra Valley but many regions in Australia remain unaffected. Phylloxera has never been detected in the state of South Australia. This, combined with distribution of vines from Busby's collection, means that Australia is home to the largest repository of ungrafted, pre-phylloxera vines anywhere on the planet.

DEFINING OLD VINES

What constitutes old vines is vague as there is no universal definition. As such, the term is used liberally in many countries and regions. The Barossa is home to the largest acreage of old vine sites in the world and is the only region in Australia that has codified the use of the term old vines. The Old Vine Charter was originally conceived at Yalumba winery but quickly snapped up by the region as a way of classifying and honouring these old vine sites. The Old Vine Charter has four classifications, all based on minimum age.

- Old Vines: 35 years or older
- Survivor Vines: 70 years or older
- Centenarian Vines: 100 years or older
- Ancestor Vines: 125 years or older

While this is a Barossa only classification it serves as a useful benchmark for other regions across the country. Perhaps we may see an Australian Old Vine Charter in the future? There is nothing in the works at present, but it would be helpful as there are many old vine sites spread across the country.

AUSTRALIA'S OLD VINE REGIONS

Thirty-five years old is a useful minimum standard for defining old vines but virtually all of Australia's wine producing regions would qualify on some level! The following is a snapshot of regions that have either extensive old vine plantings or historically significant old vine sites.

The Barossa, which encompasses both the Barossa and Eden Valleys, is one of the most historic wine-producing regions in Australia and has vineyard sites that date back to 1843. Barossa is the queen bee when it comes to old vine vineyard sites. A separate chapter could be written on the subject, hence the disproportionate space dedicated to them here. There are sixth- and seventh-generation grape-growing families who have served as custodians to these beautiful old-vine vineyard sites. Within a 5-kilometre radius you can visit the oldest vineyards of Shiraz, Grenache and Mourvèdre anywhere on the planet: Langmeil Freedom Shiraz vineyard, Cirillo 1848 Grenache vineyard and a Mourvèdre vineyard planted in 1853 by Friedrich Koch, the fruit of which is used to produce Hewitson's Old Garden Mourvèdre. The Cabernet Sauvignon vines at Penfolds Kalimna Block 42 were planted in 1885, making it one of the oldest Cabernet vineyards in the world.

Shiraz, Mourvedre, Grenache, Cabernet Sauvignon, Riesling and Semillon make up the bulk of varieties that qualify. Below is the full list, taken from Barossa Grape and Wine, of old vine plantings still in production today. Even if you take out the Old Vine level (minimum age

35 years) you are still left with 410 hectares (1,013 acres) of vineyard sites that are at least 70 years old.

Old-Vine Shiraz

- Barossa Ancestor Vine: 12.54 hectares/30.99 acres
- Barossa Centenarian Vine: 100.62 hectares/248.64 acres
- Barossa Survivor Vine: 88.48 hectares/218.64acres
- Barossa Old Vine: 589.06 hectares/1,455.60 acres

Old-Vine Mourvèdre

- Barossa Ancestor Vine: 2.63 hectares/6.5 acres
- Barossa Centenarian Vine: 5.39 hectares/13.32 acres
- Barossa Survivor Vine: 12.2 hectares/30.14 acres
- Barossa Old Vine: 45.5 hectares/112.43 acres

Old-Vine Grenache

- Barossa Ancestor Vine: 7.55 hectares/18.66 acres
- Barossa Centenarian Vine: 23.49 hectares/58.05 acres
- Barossa Survivor Vine: 93.51 hectares/231.07 acres
- Barossa Old Vine: 302.98 hectares/748.67 acres

Old-Vine Cabernet Sauvignon

- Barossa Ancestor Vine: 4.44 hectares/10.97 acres
- Barossa Centenarian Vine: 4.65 hectares/11.49 acres
- Barossa Old Vine: 121.1 hectares/299.24 acres

Old-Vine Riesling

- Barossa Centenarian Vine: 6 hectares/14.83 acres
- Barossa Survivor Vine: 16.24 hectares/40.13 acres
- Barossa Old Vine: 321.47 hectares/794.37 acres

Old-Vine Semillon

- Barossa Ancestor Vine: 3.75 hectares/9.27 acres
- Barossa Centenarian Vine: 1.98 hectares/4.89 acres
- Barossa Survivor Vine: 26.4 hectares/65.24 acres
- Barossa Old Vine: 84.65 hectares/209.17 acres

In McLaren Vale, Shiraz and Grenache are the main old vines. The region has set up an old vine register. Whereas the Barossa Old Vine

Charter extends to what terms can be used on labels, this merely serves as a list of varieties that qualify as old vines, categorized in brackets of 35 or more years old, 50 or more years old, 75 or more years old and 100 or more years old. The extent of plantings is not quite the same as Barossa but impressive, nonetheless.

As of December 2021, there were 37 hectares of vines aged 100 years or more, mostly Shiraz and Grenache and 53 hectares of vines of 75 years old or more. These are also mostly Shiraz and Grenache but there are a few surprises such as Chenin Blanc, Sangiovese and Sagarantino.[9]

The Hunter Valley is Australia's oldest producing wine region, with vineyards dating back to the 1860s, and home to some of the oldest vine stock. While it doesn't have as broad a collection of old vine vineyards as Barossa, there are some historically significant vineyards.

Old Malbec vines at Wendouree in the Clare Valley.

9 The full list can be accessed at www.mclarenvalewine.au/wine/old-vine-register

There is a notable amount of ungrafted, old-vine Shiraz in the region. Tyrrell's 4 Acre was planted in 1879 and the Stevens Shiraz was planted in 1867. Mount Pleasant Old Hill was planted in 1880. Semillon was part of the Busby collection and found a comfortable home in the Hunter. There are several old vine sites of significance, including Tyrrell's Johnno's Vineyard and Tyrrell's HVD Vineyard, both 1908. There are not a lot of old vine Chardonnay sites in Australia, however Tyrrell's owns the oldest. Chardonnay was planted in the HVD vineyard in 1908 making it one of the oldest Chardonnay vineyards in the world.

Grape growing and winemaking in the Clare Valley dates back to 1852, when Austrian Jesuits established the Sevenhill winery. There are many old-vine sites scattered across the valley but the most significant is the iconoclastic Wendouree. I am not a fan of the term 'unicorn' wine but in the true sense of rare and hard to find, Wendouree qualifies. The dry-grown Shiraz vines were planted in 1893 and there is an old block of Malbec planted in 1898.

Langhorne Creek is also home to sixth-generation grape-growing families and several significant sites. Brothers in Arms winery is custodian of the world's oldest family-owned Cabernet Sauvignon vines, planted in 1891 in the Matala Vineyard.

Nagambie Lakes is a Geographical Indication (GI) that sits within the Goulburn Valley region and the old-vine story here is all about Tahbilk. This is one of the oldest wineries in Australia and has the oldest Shiraz vineyard in Victoria – planted in 1860. Tahbilk is also the custodian of Australia's oldest plantings of Marsanne. The original vines were planted in 1927 and the site has expanded to be the largest single vineyard of Marsanne in the world, at just under 41 hectares (100 acres).

Great Western is a subsection within the Grampians GI. There are a few old vine sites scattered across the region but the story at Best's is remarkable. In 1866, Henry Best planted what would become some of the oldest vines in Australia. He planted whatever he could get at the time and this original site, now known as the nursery block, is believed to have the greatest variety of pre-phylloxera plantings in Australia – and possibly the world. Recent work has shown that there are 32 different grape varieties in the block. The Pinot vineyards were first planted in 1868, comprising about 85 per cent Pinot Meunier and 15 per cent Pinot Noir. The original Shiraz vines were planted in 1868 and there's a block of Dolcetto reputedly planted in 1889.

DO OLD VINES MAKE BETTER WINES?

There is something special about tasting a wine made from vines planted over 100 years ago. Apart from contemplating a vine that has continuously produced for that length of time we just don't regularly consume agricultural products with lengthy history. While I believe strongly that preserving and honouring these special sites is important, the obvious question is: so what? Do old vines matter? Do they make better wine?

A common refrain in the Barossa is that 'old vines don't make great wines, great wines make old vines', the implication being that those old vines produced good wines right from the start. If they didn't, they were pulled out. There is truth to this. Vines planted in good sites typically make better wines but I can't help thinking that this is a bit simplistic and undermines the story of old vines. The discussion around the character and quality of wines made from old vines has, until recently, been mostly anecdotal save for a few practical and physiological realities.

Sarah Ahmed wrote an excellent article on this subject after an old vine tasting and panel discussion in London in 2016.[10] On the subject of old vine versus young vine physiology the panel noted that research has shown that older plants are more efficient than younger ones. As for whether better efficiency translates into better wines? This could be extrapolated to suggest that given the same amount of energy, older vines can go further through their biochemical pathways, producing the flavours and riper tannins that we associate with quality.

With trunk girths and root systems that are both larger, old vines have more carbohydrate reserves, giving the vine a jump start to the season. And it has been observed that vines can draw upon these reserves during times of stress later in the growing season too. The more developed root system of an older vine allows for better access to potential water and nutrients that exist in the different subsoil stratas. In Dean Hewitson's Old Garden Mourvèdre site, vine roots go down 10 metres, which he believes helps them to deal with extremes of weather, whether it's cool and wet or hot. He sees an evenness in ripening year on year.

---

10 The full article can be found here: https://thewinedetective.co.uk/blog/do-old-vines-make-better-wines-australia-under-the-microscope

Naturally balanced canopies could be an explanation for better fruit quality in older vines. Panellist Jamie Goode, who has a PhD in plant biology, speculated that during a vine's first year or two of fruiting, the ratio between vegetative growth and fruit growth is in balance – but only briefly. For a period after this it appears that, in his words, 'adolescent vines push towards growing more shooting tips rather than fruit, canopies grow larger so fruit to canopy growth is out of whack'. His comparison to an energetic, awkward, gangly, growing teen seemed appropriate. Old vine canopies come back into a natural balance of fruit and vegetative growth. The balance of the very young vines Goode mentions does explain the anomaly of some historically famous wines that were produced from young vines. Quinta do Noval Nacional Vintage Port 1931, Stags Leap S.L.V. Cabernet 1973 and many 1961 Bordeaux (arguably one of the greatest vintages ever) were all produced from three to four year-old vines.

Epigenetics

When Australian Dylan Grigg wrote his PhD on old vines, a key element of his investigation focused on epigenetic modification.[11] What is epigenetics? It is the study of stable phenotypic changes (known as *marks*) that do not involve alterations in the DNA sequence. Epigenetics most often involves changes that affect the regulation of gene expression. The term can also be used to describe any heritable phenotypic change. Such effects on cellular and physiological phenotypic traits may result from external or environmental factors or be part of normal development.

Grigg aimed to assess scientifically the influence of vine age on grape and wine production to find out if the quality of fruit and wine produced went beyond the perception of the wine industry and media. He found that old vines (with a minimum age of around 50–60 years) use epigenetic modification to learn from stress, essentially bookmarking weather events. Over time there's an accumulation of markers, preconditioning the vine to adjust quickly in the event of similar conditions arising. These characteristics are also heritable, meaning that they can be passed on, but this is where it gets tricky. Experiments taking cuttings from old vines and replanting them showed that the new vines did not in fact retain the traits. The heritable characteristics were, however, evident in vines that were established by layering from the parent vine, leaving it connected for five to six years before separating – basically giving the

11 His thesis can be found here: https://digital.library.adelaide.edu.au/dspace/handle/2440/113314

new vine an umbilical cord until it was established. Grigg was quick to point out that this is an area where more research is needed, and as detailed as his work was, it is just the tip of the iceberg. The study also noted that large differences in vine age did not produce differences in basic grape composition, however, the older vines consistently produced grapes with lower pH at similar Brix levels to grapes from younger vines.

So we now have something beyond anecdotal evidence that old vines do matter. With this information we can say with a modicum of confidence that they produce more consistent and potentially better quality fruit than younger vines. Does this mean they make better wine? Theoretically the fruit sourced from the older vines should produce better wines, but much lies in the skill of the winemaker.

PART 2
THE REGIONS

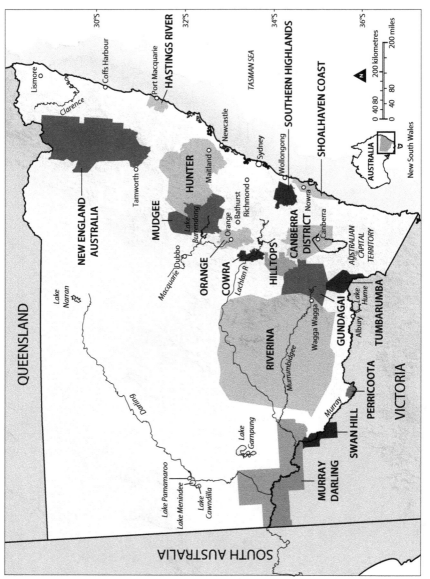

Map 2: The Geographic Indications of New South Wales

6

NEW SOUTH WALES

The area around Sydney has the longest history of grape growing in Australia. Vines came with the First Fleet and initial plantings were at Sydney Cove, in the Governor's gardens, in 1788. This was followed by the Macarthur plantings near Camden, and Blaxland's vineyards around the Parramatta River in the early 1800s. By early 1820, vine plantings extended to Camden, Bathurst and the Hunter Valley. James Busby's collection of 362 vines in 1832, originally planted where the Botanical Gardens now sit, was the most significant development in Australia's early viticultural history. Cuttings of these vines made their way to other parts of New South Wales, Victoria and South Australia. Expansion of vineyard plantings continued in various parts of the state for the next several decades but slowed in the early 1900s. James Halliday astutely notes in his 2014 edition of the *Wine Atlas of Australia*, that 'between 1815 and 1912 the viticultural map of the state had been drawn, encompassing the Sydney metropolitan area, Hunter Valley, Mudgee and the Riverina. That map was to remain largely unchanged until 1973 when the first vines were planted in Cowra. So it is that 11 of the 15 New South Wales wine regions have come into existence since 1973.' Given the long tradition of wine growing, New South Wales has in fact been a slow developer in the broader scheme of regional expansion.

The GIs of New South Wales

Hunter Valley Zone

This zone encompasses the region of Hunter and its subregions – Broke Fordwich, Pokolbin and Upper Hunter.

Central Ranges Zone

This zone encompasses the regions of Cowra, Mudgee and Orange.

Southern New South Wales Zone

This zone encompasses the regions of Canberra District, Hilltops, Gundagai and Tumbarumba.

South Coast Zone

This zone includes the regions of Shoalhaven Coast and Southern Highlands.

Big Rivers Zone

This large zone encompasses the regions of Riverina, Perricoota and portions of Murray Darling and Swan Hill. The latter two are covered in the chapter on Victoria.

Northern Slopes Zone

Contains one region, New England Australia.

Northern Rivers Zones

Contains one zone, Hastings River.

Western Plains Zone

There are no individual regions in the Western Plains Zone.

HUNTER VALLEY

(Wonnarua Country)

By 1823, 8 hectares of vineyards had already been planted on the northern banks of the Hunter River. The early pioneers of the Hunter Valley's long winemaking history were George Wyndham of Dalwood, William Kelman of Kirkton and James King of Irrawang. It was a replica set of cuttings from Busby's 1832 collection, planted at Kirkton, that established the Hunter Valley's claims to viticultural fame. By 1840 there were 200 hectares of vineyards planted in the region. In the latter part of the nineteenth century, four families established vineyards in the area: the Tyrrells, Tullochs, Wilkinsons and Draytons, alongside the well-known Dr Henry Lindeman.

Area under vine

2,605 hectares[12]

Climate

Hunter Valley's climate is distinctly warm and humid. Rain falls during harvest in some years, which can create challenges, especially for the red varieties. Rain, humidity, cloud cover and gentle sea breezes mitigate the warmth. The Upper Hunter has lower rainfall.

Soils

Soils across the region are quite varied. Shiraz does best on friable red duplex and loam soils, while Semillon does best on the sandy alluvial flats. Soils in the Upper Hunter Valley consist mostly of black, silty loams over clay loam.

Varieties

Semillon, Chardonnay, Shiraz and Verdelho.

12 Source: National Vineyard Scan 2020 and ABS

Before the Geographical Indications (GIs) were laid out, the industry simply referred to the region as the Hunter Valley and unofficially divided it into the Upper Hunter and Lower Hunter, and many still talk about the region using those terms. In what seems to be another quirk in the GI listings, the Hunter Valley is a zone that includes the region of Hunter and the subregions of Upper Hunter Valley, Broke Fordwich and Pokolbin. It is north-west of the city of Newcastle and about a two and a half hour drive from Sydney. It is the closest region to Australia's largest metropolitan area and has reaped the benefits of this proximity.

For simplicity, the Hunter regional statistics are listed above rather than being separated into region and subregions. As noted, the Hunter climate is warm and humid but it is unique in that the wine styles present more like cooler climate wines in the glass. Climate classification systems don't always capture the nuances of regional climate and Hunter is a prime example. Daytime temperatures are warm and consistent but don't usually see the spikes that might occur in other warm or hot regions in Australia. Rain at harvest is a threat and this leads to a slightly shorter, more condensed season, and that shapes the wines dramatically.

Main wine styles

While Semillon is grown in other parts of Australia and across the globe, there is nothing that compares to the styles produced in the Hunter. This is a unique expression. Picked early, vinified in stainless steel and bottled fairly quickly, Hunter Semillon is not about fancy winemaking techniques. Most sit between 10.5% and 11.5% abv and can be drunk young. The crisp acidity and light, lemony freshness has considerable appeal as an aperitif and works well with many dishes. But for classic Hunter Semillon, the magic happens after around 8–10 years in bottle. The acidity softens and flavours develop from citrus to honey, toast and nuts. They can be aged gracefully for decades especially given the use of screwcap (Stelvin) by most producers.

Shiraz is generally more medium bodied with red and black fruit flavours and a distinctly savoury, earthy element.

Verdelho has been in the region for a long time and produces easy-drinking, fresh floral and fruity wines. Although it is a pleasure to drink, winemakers in the region often treat it like the cousin nobody wants to speak of. I love it and always have a glass of it when there.

Tyrrell's Vat 47 Chardonnay 1971 (labelled Pinot Chardonnay) was the first varietally labelled Chardonnay in Australia so there is a long history of this variety in the region. In fact, it was a Hunter Valley Chardonnay that put Australia on the modern wine producing map back in 1981. Rosemount Roxburgh Chardonnay won a competition in London and the wine press started paying attention to what was happening in Australia. There is some very good Chardonnay still produced in the region and worth seeking out.

Producers

Tyrrell's

www.tyrrells.com.au

An iconic Australian producer. This generational family-run business has been steered by the inimitable Bruce Tyrrell for the last few decades. He is slowly handing the reins over to his son Chris but will always be on hand to taste and chat. His analogies always make me laugh, such as: 'smells a bit like the southern end of a north bound sheep', while tasting a less than stellar natural wine. Vat 1 Semillon is the best, most age-worthy Semillon produced in the region. Any of his Sacred Sites wines are worth seeking out, especially the 4 Acre Shiraz. Made from grapes planted in 1879 this should be on the list of must try Shiraz for any red wine lover.

Vat 47 Chardonnay is fantastic and if you can find a bottle of the HVD Chardonnay it is made from grapes planted in 1908, the oldest Chardonnay vineyard in Australia, maybe anywhere.

They have been toying with Fiano and a tank sample tried in 2022 looked very interesting.

Brokenwood

www.brokenwood.com.au

Brokenwood produces an excellent range of Semillon, especially the ILR. The regional Shiraz is delicious, and if you can cellar it for at least 10 years the Graveyard Shiraz will repay that patience handsomely.

Margan Family

www.margan.com.au

Andrew Margan and his wife Lisa run their 100-hectare property out in the Broke Fordwich subregion, with a great range of wines. The aged release Semillons are fantastic, and they have tinkered with Barbera and Albariño for some time. There is also a fantastic restaurant on site.

Charteris Wine

www.charteriswines.com

PJ Charteris worked for many years at Brokenwood before returning to his native New Zealand to make wine. He is back in the Hunter and his regular Shiraz bottling is a classic example of the regional expression. His Semillon is a forward and delicious version that I would be happy to drink on release with a plate of fresh oysters.

De Iuliis Wines

www.dewine.com.au

All the classics are made here: Chardonnay, Shiraz and Semillon. All are fantastic and worth trying. Owner and winemaker Mike De Iuliis is also playing around with alternative varieties, including a zippy, fresh Pecorino and a juicy Montepulciano.

Keith Tulloch Wines

www.keithtullochwine.com.au

Tulloch is a legendary name in wine in the Hunter. Keith is making some of the most compelling Semillons in the region, some sourced from his own vineyards and others from growers. There is plenty of great wine in the range but my picks would be The Field of Mars Semillon and the Museum Release Semillon.

Mount Pleasant Wines

www.mountpleasantwines.com.au

McWilliams is one of Australia's storied wineries and have interests in several other regions – see Riverina and Tumbarumba. The Mount Pleasant range is the very best of their Hunter Valley wines. The Lovedale and Elizabeth Semillons are fantastic and age gracefully for decades. They have several old-vine Shiraz sites which are bottled separately – Old Hill (planted in 1880), Rosehill (planted in 1946 and 1965) and Old Paddock (1921). The Maurice O'Shea bottling is expensive but worth the investment.

Agnew Wines

www.agnewwines.com.au

The Agnew family purchased the famous Audrey Wilkinson vineyard in 2004 and acquired Cockfighter's Ghost and Poole's Rock brands in 2011. It is a large and impressive stable of wines now all made at the same winery facility but with all three brands maintaining their own identities. Xanthe Hatcher took over the reins as head winemaker in 2019 and seems to have brought an additional elegant touch to the best wines.

The best examples from the three brands include the Wilkinson Winemakers Selection from **Audrey Wilkinson** (www.audreywilkinson. com.au). A great range that includes the top notch Marsh Vineyard Semillon and really lovely Tempranillo. **Cockfighter's Ghost** (www. cockfightersghost.com.au) makes The Single Vineyard range, which is solid top to bottom, particularly the Barbera, Semillon and Pinot Gris. At **Poole's Rock** (www.poolesrock.com.au) it is all about single site wines and the Centenary Block is a beauty: classic raspberry scented, spicy, leathery Hunter Shiraz. The Soldier Settler Semillon is from a site planted in 1918 and is one of the best in the region.

Pepper Tree

www.peppertreewines.com.au

This venture was started by John Davis in 1991. He also has vineyards in Orange, Coonawarra and Wrattonbully. Look for the Alluvius Single Vineyard Semillon and the Conquun Platinum Shiraz. The very talented Gwynn Olsen made the wines at Peppertree for some years but recently moved to Barossa to take on the head winemaker role at Henschke. Ex-winemaker Jim Chatto (see Chatto Wines in the chapter on Tasmania) is back as consultant winemaker.

Vinden Wines

www.vindenwines.com.au

Alex Vinden is a young rising star in the region. He is making fun, easy drinking wines. I particularly like the Charmless Man, an unconventional blend of Alicante Bouschet, Cabernet, Tempranillo and Shiraz, which is juicy, lively and fresh and sits at 11.5% abv. The Pokolbin Blanc changes yearly but is a blend of different varieties and typically fun to drink too.

Usher Tinkler

www.ushertinklerwines.com

Usher Tinkler is one of the cool cats of the Hunter, producing classic and contemporary wines. Death by Semillon is a skin contact version; a textural, savoury and fun departure from the typical Hunter style.

Château Pâto

www.chateaupato.com.au

Pato is a really solid estate that was established in 1979. The OPV (Old Pokolbin Vineyard) Shiraz was planted in 1968 and is a perennial beauty. The DPJ Shiraz is from a site that they planted in 1981. Look too for the Oakey Creek Semillon, a regional classic made from old vine Semillon.

Lake's Folly

www.lakesfolly.wine

Established in 1963 by Doctor Max Lake, in early 2000 Lake's Folly was purchased by Peter and Lee Fogarty and family who, along with Hunter born and bred winemaker Rodney Kempe, have continued to maintain the integrity and direction of this significant vineyard. There are two flagship wines. Lake's Folly Chardonnay shows the richness of the regional style but manages to be elegant and restrained at the same time. The Cabernets is a Cabernet Sauvignon-dominant wine with Petit Verdot, Merlot and Shiraz in varying proportions. It is a structured, tightly woven wine that can age gracefully. It has been well regarded for decades.

Thomas Wines

www.thomaswines.com.au

This relatively small producer is worth seeking out for its top notch range of Semillons, with the Braemore Semillon being of particular note.

Harkham Wines

www.harkhamwine.com.au

This is a small family-run business that made its first vintage in 2005. It operates sustainably and is thoughtful about vineyard practices and winemaking techniques. Minimal intervention is the mantra. There are lots of fun wines to play with here. The Aziza's Shiraz was the first wine I tried from Harkham and remains a favourite. Fruit for this wine is handpicked and fermented using natural yeasts. No sulphur is added and the wine is unfined and unfiltered to give pure, unadulterated Hunter Shiraz flavors. The Aziza's Semillon is made the same way and is a very interesting departure from classically styled Hunter Semillon, being more savoury and textural.

Len Evans – a true Australian legend

Discussion of Len Evans rightfully belongs in a chapter on the Hunter Valley even though his love for Australian wine extended way beyond the region's boundaries. Len was one of the first people to champion the quality of fine Australian wine and recognize that the future lay in table wines, not the fortified wines that were widely consumed when he was growing up. His parents were Welsh, but he was born in Felixstowe, England. He migrated to New Zealand in 1953, then to Australia in 1955. He became the first regular wine columnist in Australia in 1962 and was the founding director of the Australian Wine Bureau in 1965. He wrote the first major encyclopedia of Australian wine in 1973. Evans was chairman of Rothbury Wines from 1969 until 1996, and

Petaluma from 1978 until 1992. He was chairman of Evans Wine Company, Evans Family Wines and Tower Estate. Len Evans made blind tasting a competition sport with his Options Game and there is not a single person in the Australian wine business today that does not know how to play. His list of achievements and awards in the wine and culinary world is long, and he was appointed an Officer of the Order of the British Empire in 1982 and an Officer of the Order of Australia in 1999. Len Evans was a true legend in the Australian wine world. Jancis Robinson MW, a friend of Evans for more than 30 years, articulates Len's character succinctly: 'Autocratic, didactic, caustic – all these words applied to Len. But he was also unfailingly enthusiastic, uproariously entertaining and an unstoppable force for good in wine. Unlike many famous wine people, he really understood what wine was for: drinking. In fact, he had run out of many of the great Australian wine classics in his own cellar – so rapacious was his thirst and so generously and enthusiastically did he entertain. He transformed the all-important Australian wine shows into disciplined arenas truly designed to "improve the breed" and perhaps his most lasting legacy will prove to be the annual Len Evans Tutorials at which he exposed hand-picked young Australian tasters to some of the finest wines of the world, and not a little ridicule if they failed to recognize their greatness. No one could fail to recognize his.'

Len Evans passed away in 2006.

CENTRAL RANGES ZONE

Central Ranges lies on the western slopes of the Great Dividing Range, west of the Blue Mountains. There are three regions within this zone, Mudgee, Orange and Cowra. Vineyards that don't sit within these three regions use the zonal GI.

MUDGEE
(Wiradjuri Country)

The original vineyards of Mudgee were planted in 1858, and the discovery of gold in 1872 brought prosperity to the region. Situated on the western slopes of the Great Dividing Range, Mudgee has relatively high vineyard sites ranging from 450–1180 metres above sea level. It is essentially a red wine producing area with Cabernet Sauvignon and Shiraz being the most planted varieties. There is also a history of quality Chardonnay in the region.

Area under vine

1,900 hectares[13]

Climate

Frosts and cold nights delay budburst but sunshine hours are long. Rainfall and humidity are low so irrigation is essential on many sites. The harvest here is four weeks behind the Hunter because of the higher altitude.

Soils

The soils are brown loam or sandy loam over neutral clay subsoils. Topsoil and subsoil are quite well drained. Some of the most favoured sites have shale, quartz and seabed sandstone.

Varieties

Cabernet Sauvignon, Shiraz and Chardonnay are the main varieties but some Italian varieties also have history in the region, most notably Sangiovese, Barbera and Nebbiolo.

13 Source: National Vineyard Scan 2020 and ABS

Main wine styles

Cabernet Sauvignon is historically one of the strongest varieties in the region; richly fruited with velvety tannins. Shiraz is generally medium to fuller bodied depending on site and features rich black and red fruit flavours. Chardonnay has a long history in Mudgee. Craigmoor made a varietally bottled Chardonnay in 1972.

Producers

Mudgee wines are not widely exported so are hard to find. Some producers have cellar doors located in Mudgee and also showcase wines from Orange. Look for wines from the producers below.

Gilbert Family Wines

www.gilbertfamilywines.com.au

The Gilberts have vineyards in Mudgee and Orange and often blend fruit sourced from both regions. Gilbert Shiraz is a ripe, peppery example of the Mudgee style. The Preservative Free Shiraz is fresh, juicy and designed to be drunk young.

Craigmoor

www.craigmoor.com.au

The oldest winery in Mudgee, this is now owned by the Robert Oatley group. They also own another historical Mudgee winery, Montrose. This now sits as a separate brand under Craigmoor. Look for the Craigmoor Artist Series Chardonnay and Montrose Black Shiraz.

Logan

www.loganwines.com.au

Logan has vineyards in both Orange and Mudgee. They have a strong range of approachable wines under the Weemala label with all the fruit coming from their Mudgee vineyard of the same name. Look for the intense, spicy Tempranillo and the very easy drinking Pinot Gris under this label. Wines are well priced, too.

ORANGE
(Wiradjuri Country)

This altitude-influenced, cool-climate region has long been famous for apples. It is located on the western side of the Great Dividing Range and many of the top vineyards are situated at between 600 and 1,000 metres above sea level.

Area under vine

1,075 hectares[14]

Climate

The climate is strongly influenced by elevation. Overall, mild to warm midsummers mean temperatures seldom rise above 32°C (90°F); days are offset by cool to very cool nights during the growing season. The rainfall predominates in winter and spring and wind is common. Although this helps to reduce the major threat of spring frosts it can interfere with fruit set. The undulating hills make site selection critical.

14 Source: National Vineyard Scan 2020 and ABS

Soils

The soils vary widely but fall into four main groups:

- Well drained, friable, deep red-brown clays derived from basalt found near Mount Canobolas.
- Deep red-brown, yellow-brown clay loams.
- Red-brown podzolic clay loam over a clay and shale base.
- Patches of terra rossa associated with visible limestone at the lower elevations.

Varieties

Sauvignon Blanc, Chardonnay, Pinot Noir and Shiraz.

Main wine styles

Sauvignon Blanc is one of the key varieties that excels, with typical ripe, herbal notes combined with tropical flavours. Chardonnays are medium bodied with citrus and stone-fruit flavours. The Shiraz is elegant, fragrant and expressive – textbook cool-climate style Shiraz. Cabernet Sauvignon needs to be in the right site but can be very good, showing the more medium-weight characters of the variety. It can be green and herbal in cooler vintages and/or sites. Not a lot of Pinot Noir is grown but there are some lovely fragrant examples.

Orange Producers

Orange wines are exported a little more widely than the wines from Mudgee but you still do need to search hard to find many wines from this region overseas, which is a pity as there are many vibrant, delicious wines. The following wines from these top producers should be on your list.

Printhie Wines

www.printhiewines.com.au

This producer makes excellent traditional method sparkling wines, especially the Vintage Swift Blanc de Blancs. Also recommended are the Millwood Single Vineyard Pinot Noir and Swift Family Heritage Shiraz.

Canobolas-Smith Wines

www.canobolassmithwines.com.au

This is one of the older, more significant Orange producers. They have always made good Chardonnay, Cabernet Franc and Pinot Noir and have recently been taken over by Jonathan Mattick who used to be the winemaker for Handpicked Wines. His new wines were still in barrel in early 2023, but word from an insider source is that this is a space to watch.

Philip Shaw

www.philipshaw.com.au

Philip Shaw has a long history in Australian wine, having worked at Rosemount for many years. His sons are now running the property. I've rarely tried anything I didn't like from this extremely reliable producer. Look for the No 8 Pinot Noir and No19 Sauvignon Blanc.

Bloodwood Wines

www.bloodwood.biz

Rhonda and Stephen Doyle planted Merlot on free-draining gravelly soils on their property in 1983. They did extensive research leading up to the choice of Orange as a region and were equally exhaustive searching for a site and deciding what to plant. Bloodwood Cabernet Sauvignon is a beautifully fragrant, medium-weight example of the variety. The Cabernet Franc is also delicious, as are the two Chardonnays. Bloodwood Maurice is a blended selection of the best barrels in a given vintage and, as such, changes from vintage to vintage. Sometimes you get 100 per cent varietal wine, sometimes a blend. Hands on. Attention to detail. Lovely wines. A pioneer producer in the region.

ChaLou Estate Wines

www.chalouwines.com.au

This venture was started in 2020 by Steve Mobbs and Nadja Wallington, both of whom have extensive experience in the industry. Their first crush at ChaLou was in 2021. They make delicious Riesling and a beautifully balanced, fragrant, fine-boned Pinot Noir. A new producer to keep an eye on.

Ross Hill Wines

www.rosshillwines.com.au

Established in 1994, Ross Hill is another excellent producer in the region, with many really good wines. Look for the Pinnacle Series Sauvignon Blanc and Merlot and the Founder's Reserve Merlot.

Cumulus Vineyards

www.cumulusvineyards.com.au

This is one of the larger producers in the region. The vineyard site is just over 500 hectares. There is a full range of good wines under various bottlings: Chasing Clouds, Rolling, Climbing, Inkberry Luna Rosa, Block 50 and ALTE. The picks of the bunch are ALTE Chardonnay and ALTE Shiraz.

Hoosegg

www.hoosegg.com

This is Philip Shaw's new venture. Hoosegg is the dream that Philip Shaw says he has been working towards for nearly 60 years. In 2015, he made the decision to transfer the management of Philip Shaw Wines to his sons, Damian and Daniel. 'I wanted time to fulfil my dream,' he says, 'to make small parcels of wine that can stand among the finest wines from anywhere. This reflects my philosophy on winemaking: select an exceptional site and the right varieties. Marry the vineyard and the winemaking. I want to make wines that are elegant, vibrant, varietal, intense and complex.' I don't typically recommend wines I haven't tried but it's Philip Shaw whose experience and pedigree suggest that this is a safe bet. Go ahead and experiment!

COWRA
(Wiradjuri Country)

The first grape planting in the region was in 1973. Vineyards are mostly situated on gentle slopes in the foothills of the western side of the Great Dividing Range. Cowra is the furthest south of the three Central Ranges regions but is the warmest due to the lower altitude.

Main wine styles

Chardonnay is the most successful variety in the region. The wines are rich in style with texture and length.

Area under vine

950 hectares[15]

Climate

The climate is classic continental; warm and dry. Spring frosts mean that careful site selection is required.

Soils

Brown, loamy sand to clay loam – red clay subsoils.

Varieties

Chardonnay, Cabernet Sauvignon and Shiraz are the main varieties. Other varieties grown include Petit Verdot, Sangiovese, Grenache and Mourvèdre.

15 Source: Wine Australia

Cowra Producers

Not many wines are exported widely. However, I came across an interesting natural wine producer, **Benson and the Mooch** (www. bensonandthemooch.com). Partners Benson and Joel make wines from various sites in the Central Ranges. The Central Ranges Rosé is fun and fruity. Golden Girl is a blend of Zibibbo, Chardonnay and Fiano and is fun, fruity and friendly. Sauci is a light, crunchy, red blend of Mourvedre and Shiraz.

SOUTHERN NEW SOUTH WALES

This zone includes the regions of Canberra District, Hilltops, Gundagai and Tumbarumba.

Being influenced by the proximity of the Great Dividing Range, altitude is a key element in shaping the varieties grown and wine styles produced.

CANBERRA DISTRICT
(Ngunawal Country)

Grapes have been grown and wine made in the Canberra District since the 1840s. Like many smaller, cool climate regions in Australia, interest waned, and production had declined significantly by the early 1900s. Plantings increased in the 1970s and 1980s and although this is a small region in terms of vineyard plantings, its reputation is large. Some very high quality wines are produced in Canberra District. The topography of the region is quite varied with undulating hills and distant views of the Snowy Mountains forming a picturesque backdrop to many of the vineyards. Slope and aspect are all important.

Area under vine

450 hectares[16]

Climate

The climate is strongly continental, with very warm, dry days but cold nights during summer. Autumn temperatures are cool, with rain at harvest a potential threat. Spring frost is a yearly threat.

Soils

Soils are typically brownish, shallow clay loams, often overlying shale or clay.

Varieties

Shiraz and Riesling have a long history. Newer varieties include Tempranillo, Sangiovese, Pinot Noir and Chardonnay. Some producers source fruit from nearby regions, especially Tumbarumba.

16 Source: Canberra Wine District Regional Website

Main wine styles

Shiraz had its reputation sealed by the character, quality and success of Clonakilla (see opposite). Shiraz from this region typically displays classic cooler climate characteristics of raspberry and blackberry fruit with spicy, peppery, savoury notes. Helm (below) did for Riesling what Clonakilla did for Shiraz in this region. Rieslings are vibrant, focused and expressive.

Producers

Helm

www.helmwines.com.au

Helm was established by Ken Helm in 1973 and, although small, has an outsized reputation. This is partly because of the character that Ken Helm is, and his passionate pursuit to craft quality Riesling. The Premium Riesling is vibrant, tightly focused and bristling with energy and lime zest flavours. A must try wine from this region.

Clonakilla

www.clonakilla.com.au

Established in 1971, Clonakilla is not only one of the region's stars, it is one of the very best producers in Australia. Tim Kirk took over from his father in the 1990s and a visit to Côte-Rôtie shaped his approach to the Shiraz they were producing. He came back and experimented with a Shiraz Viognier co-fermentation. The results were astonishingly good. The first time I tried it I was stopped mid-sentence. Clonakilla Shiraz–Viognier is exceptional. It has power and intensity while maintaining fragrance, elegance and delicacy, a very tricky tightrope to walk. This is one of Australia's great wines and one that you simply must try. The O'Riada Shiraz is also fantastic. Ceoltoiri is a blend of Grenache, Mourvèdre, Shiraz, Counoise, Cinsault and Roussanne and is unfortunately only sold at the winery but is delicious.

Shiraz–Viognier ferment at Clonakilla.

Ravensworth Wines

www.ravensworthwines.com.au

Founder Bryan Martin honed his skills at Clonakilla, where he was the winemaker for 16 years. He currently makes 25 wines under four labels from around 30 different varieties. The estate wines are in a more classic mould and as you might imagine, the Shiraz Viognier is brilliant. With a vibrant core of fruit, it is lifted and aromatic with beautifully structured, silky tannins. The Hilltops Nebbiolo is a lovely, gentle iteration of the variety with soft strawberry fruit and a lingering savoury finish. The Riesling is minerally and savoury and his Project C Tumbarumba Chardonnays, experimental in nature, show a cool insight into various handling techniques. There are three versions using the variety, all made very differently. The first is in a fully oxidative style, aged in 600-litre barrels for 10 months, and neither topped up nor looked at. The next is treated more reductively in a large foudre and the third is fermented in a ceramic amphora and left on skins for 8 months. This is a super cool producer where you can try classic and contemporary Canberra District wines all in the same place.

Mount Majura

www.mountmajura.com.au

This excellent producer makes a range of wines, with a particular focus on Tempranillo. The regular estate bottling is lovely but there are three single-block Tempranillo wines worth seeking out – Little Dam, Dry Spur and Rock Block.

Eden Road Wines

www.edenroadwines.com.au

This Canberra-based producer also sources fruit from nearby regions such as Gundagai and Tumbarumba. The Cullerin Block 71 Syrah shows all the classic cooler climate hallmarks of Canberra District Shiraz/Syrah. The Organic Syrah is also worth seeking out as is the delicious Riesling. (Look for an additional Eden Road recommendation in Gundagai and Tumbarumba, see page 84.)

Lark Hill Winery

www.larkhill.wine

Excellent, biodynamic producer and one of the first in Australia to produce Grüner Veltliner in 2009. The regular Lark Hill Vineyard Riesling is delicious and the Ley-Line Riesling bottling, from the original 1978 plantings is an intense, lime zest laden mouthful of excellence. Positively bristling with energy.

Lerida Estate

www.leridaestate.com.au

Top shelf Shiraz producer. Look for the regular Lerida Estate Shiraz and the Lerida Cullerin Syrah.

Nick O'Leary Wines

www.nickolearywines.com.au

Nick O'Leary is a noted Riesling and Shiraz specialist so that is the best place to start here, but it is also worth taking a peek at some of the other varieties he is playing with like the Tempranillo and the Sangiovese.

HILLTOPS
(Wiradjuri Country)

Europeans first settled in the area in 1820. The Gold Rush encouraged further growth and development. Croatian immigrant Nicole Jasprizza planted the first vines in the 1860s and grape growing continued up until the Second World War, when labour shortages all but ended viticultural endeavours. Barwang vineyard was established in 1969 and vineyard planting resumed a slow growth.

Area under vine

590 hectares[17]

Climate

Elevation plays a strong role in shaping the climate. Overall, it is a classic continental climate with warm days and cool nights. Spring frosts are common, which makes site selection an important consideration. The summers are typically quite dry and it is not unusual to see some snow in the winter months.

Soils

Overall, soils are quite rich and deep, consisting of dark red granite clays with basalt.

17 Source: National Vineyard Scan 2020 and ABS

> ## Varieties
> Shiraz, Cabernet Sauvignon, Riesling and Chardonnay are the most planted varieties. Many alternative varieties have been planted, with Tempranillo and Nebbiolo showing real promise.

Producers

Clonakilla is among a host of wineries who source fruit from Hilltops. Clonakilla's Hilltops Shiraz is a beauty and a slightly more affordable entry into their excellent range of wines. **Chalkers Crossing** (www.chalkerscrossing.com.au) is a solid producer making the full range of Hilltops varieties. Their Hilltops Shiraz and CC2 Hilltops Shiraz are both excellent. They also source fruit from Tumbarumba. **Grove Estate** (www.groveestate.com.au) produces primarily Shiraz and Cabernet Sauvignon but also has a lot of alternative varieties. They planted Zinfandel in 1996 so that is worth a try and their Nebbiolo is really good.

TUMBARUMBA
(Ngarigo Jaitmatang Country)

This remote region sits in the foothills of the Australian Alps. The first vines were planted in Tumbarumba in 1982 so it is a relatively young viticultural region. Elevation plays a key role in shaping the character of the wines from this region. The majority of vineyards sit at between 500 and 830 metres above sea level. These elevated sites have helped the region develop a reputation as a source for top quality, cool climate fruit, especially for use in sparkling wine production. Most vineyards are small and family owned, and a large proportion of fruit is sold to bigger wineries in other regions. Penfolds has sourced Chardonnay from this region for use in their top white wine, Yattarna, and until recently produced a 100 per cent Tumbarumba Chardonnay – Bin 311. McWilliams has also produced a range of Tumbarumba wines for some time.

Producers

As noted, many producers from outside the region source fruit from Tumbarumba growers. Penfolds Bin 311 Chardonnay is still predominantly Tumbarumba fruit and a great wine to get a feel for the lean, taut, tightly focused nature of Chardonnay from this region.

Estate grown and produced wines from Tumbarumba are hard to find outside the region but the following are worth tracking down. **Courabyra Wines** (www.courabyrawines.com) make really good sparkling wines and lovely Pinot Noir and Pinot Meunier. **Coppabella** of Tumbarumba (www.coppabella.com.au) have very good Chardonnay and Pinot Noir and an excellent NV sparkling wine. **Eden Road Wines** (www.edenroadwines.com.au) are based in Canberra District but make a lovely, fine-boned Pinot Noir and elegant Chardonnay from Tumbarumba. Keep an eye out for **Nick Spencer**'s (www.nickspencerwines.com.au) delicious Chardonnay using fruit sourced in this region.

Area under vine

300 hectares[18]

Climate

The climate is cool overall, but the effects of air drainage and inversion make sweeping generalization difficult. Summer days are sunny but nights are quite cool. Frost is a hazard, so site selection is important.

Soils

The soils are predominantly granite based, with many vineyards on fertile, well-drained granitic sandy loams. A number of vineyards are planted on patches of fertile red basalt soil while others are located on slightly more shaley soils.

Varieties

Chardonnay and Pinot Noir are the main varieties. Also grown are Sauvignon Blanc, Riesling, Pinot Meunier, Pinot Gris, Gamay, Shiraz, Merlot, Tempranillo and Sangiovese.

18 Source: Tumbarumba Wine

GUNDAGAI
(Wiradjuri Country)

The first vines were planted in the area in the late 1840s. The most significant nineteenth-century development was that of John James McWilliam, who established Mark View near Junee in 1877 before moving to the Riverina in 1912. These early successes were followed by a dormant period from the 1920s to the mid-1990s. Interest in the area started again in 1995, which in effect makes it a new region. A broad range of varieties and styles of wine can be made here given the difference in climate within the region.

Area under vine

595 hectares[19]

Climate

Quite a range of climates depending on location. The north-east section of the region is warm to hot whereas the south-eastern corner of this region is quite cool and indeed cold in certain parts.

Soils

Predominantly red loam with some variability along the major rivers and creeks.

Varieties

Cabernet Sauvignon, Shiraz and Chardonnay are the primary varieties.

19 Source: Wine Australia

Gundagai producers

As is the case in Tumbarumba, a decent proportion of fruit grown here is purchased by wineries from other regions. Locally grown and produced wines are hard to find outside the region.

Tumblong Hills

www.tumblonghills.com

Established by the talented Simon Robertson, this producer makes excellent Shiraz and a delicious Chenin Blanc. Simon also more than dabbles with newer varieties; Barbera, Sangiovese and Fiano are all worth seeking out.

Eden Road Wines

www.edenroadwines.com.au

This Canberra District based estate has sourced Gundagai Shiraz for its successful Long Road Syrah. They also have an interesting Sangiovese made from fruit grown at Tumblong.

Nick Spencer

www.nickspencerwines.com.au

Nick is definitely a producer to keep an eye on. He is making wines from Tumbarumba, Gundagai and Hilltops fruit. His Tumbarumba Chardonnay is pure and vibrant with textural peachy fruit and tight, lemony acidity. Also look for his light and lively LDR (Light Dry Red) a blend of Pinot Noir, Sangiovese and Shiraz with crunchy, juicy red fruit flavours.

SOUTH COAST ZONE

The South Coast Zone covers an area that stretches from Newcastle in the north to the Victorian border in the south. The two GIs within this long, slender zone are Shoalhaven Coast and Southern Highlands.

SHOALHAVEN COAST
(Tharawal and Yuin Country)

The Shoalhaven Coast wine growing region stretches from Kiama in the north to Milton in the south, and west to Kangaroo Valley on the south coast of New South Wales. Output consists largely of small production wines sold mostly to an eager tourist trade.

Area under vine

45 hectares[20]

Climate

Growing season temperatures are quite warm, though extremely high summer temperatures are uncommon due to the moderating influence of the Pacific Ocean. High humidity and heavy summer rainfall is common, which significantly increases the risk of downy and powdery mildew and botrytis. Site selection is important – exposed, north-facing slopes are best.

Soils

Predominantly red and brown loam.

20 Source: Wine Australia

> ### Varieties
> Chambourcin has a history in the region due to its resistance to rot and mildew. Chardonnay, Semillon, Cabernet Sauvignon and Shiraz are also grown.

Shoalhaven Coast Producers

Most wine is sold to visiting tourists and hard to find outside the region. The following producers are worth noting. **Coolangatta Estate** (www.coolangattaestate.com.au) have a Verdelho and a Chambourcin worth looking out for. **Cambewarra Estate** (www.cambewarraestate. com.au) produces a simple, juicy Chambourcin. **Lyrebird Ridge** (www. lyrebirdridgewinery.com.au) has organically farmed vineyards; the Chambourcin is solid.

SOUTHERN HIGHLANDS
(Tharawal Country)

The Southern Highlands form part of the Great Dividing Range. Most vineyards sit at between 500 and 700 metres above sea level. There are records of table grape production dating back to 1886, but there wasn't really any serious viticulture during the early twentieth century. Modern wine history of the region dates back to the 1980s, when the Joadja Vineyards and Winery were established.

> ### Area under vine
> 140 hectares[21]
>
> ### Climate
> The region has a moderately continental climate with mild summers and cool winters. Rain falls throughout the year, increasing the incidence of fungal diseases, including downy and powdery mildews. Botrytis can also present problems in very warm vintages.
>
> ### Soil
> The principal soils are derived from basalt – red and brown ferrosols with a high clay content. There are also some shale- and sandstone-derived yellow earths.
>
> 21 Source: National Vineyard Scan 2020 and ABS

> ### Varieties
> Chardonnay, Sauvignon Blanc and Pinot Gris are the primary varieties. Pinot Noir, Shiraz, Cabernet Sauvignon and Merlot are also grown.

Producers

As with Shoalhaven Coast, most wines are sold locally. Notable producers include **Tertini Wines** (www.tertiniwines.com.au), who make an excellent Pinot Noir. **Joadja Estate** (www.joadjawinery.com.au) is the oldest vineyard and winery in the Southern Highlands. Look for their Cabernet Merlot.

BIG RIVERS ZONE

The Big Rivers Zone occupies the entire south-western corner of New South Wales. It contains the significant GIs of Riverina, Murray Darling and Swan Hill,[22] and diminutive Perricoota.

RIVERINA
(Wiradjuri Country)

The first plantings in the region were around Wagga Wagga in the 1840s. The subsequent decade saw a lot of expansion in nearby areas, especially around Albury, which is technically not within the GI boundaries today. It is significant because, according to the Australian Town and Country Journal of 25 July 1874, by the 1870s Albury wine production was the highest of any area in the colony. As land became available for sale as a result of the Murrumbidgee Irrigation Area J.J. McWilliam established vineyards around Griffith in 1917. The McWilliam family remains in the region six generations later. Italian immigrants were also attracted to the region after the First and Second World Wars. The De Bortoli, Calbaria and Bruno families are still all part of a strong Italian cultural influence in the Riverina today.

Riverina is a flat tract of land on the state's south-west plains and is centred on the city of Griffith. The GI is 77,974 square kilometres in size. It is the largest wine producing region in New South Wales and the

---

22 The GIs of Murray Darling and Swan Hill straddle the Murray River and sections of both sit in the state of Victoria and are covered in the section on that state.

second largest in Australia. This is a region that defined and perfected broad-acre grape farming in Australia. Mechanization is a critical factor in achieving the necessary price points to remain competitive. This extends to most vineyard practices from planting, pruning and canopy management to harvesting and fruit processing. Irrigation is a critical piece of the equation so water access is important. This is not an issue at present (2023) but Australia is a drought-prone country, which means water will forever be a topic of importance if not concern in areas that depend on it for survival. I find a certain charm to the region, mostly due to the Italian cultural influence that established the area rather than scenic vistas. This is a wine land of function over form and remains important for that reason.

Area under vine

22,000 hectares[23]

Climate

This is a vast, flat region with ample sunshine during most of the summer. Relative humidity is generally low until the latter part of the growing season. This late-season humidity can provide good conditions for the development of botrytis or noble rot, which is not common in many areas in Australia. Because of this, one of Australia's most famous dessert wines is produced here (see entry under DeBortoli, opposite). Irrigation is essential in this region.

Soils

Relatively homogeneous soils. The main type is red-brown loam over reddish-brown lime containing clay. Some sands and gravels embedded in clays. Many of the soils contain limestone rubble.

Varieties and styles

Durif is an important variety, as are Shiraz and Chardonnay. Botrytis affected Semillon is notable. Montepulciano and Pinot Grigio plantings have increased.

23 Source: www.riverinawinemakers.com

Producers

DeBortoli

www.debortoli.com.au

DeBortoli is famous in this region for the glorious Noble One botrytis affected Semillon, one of Australia's best dessert wines. They also produce large volumes of easy drinking, affordable varietal wines. The Durif is delicious.

Casella Family Brands

www.casellafamilybrands.com

The export success of [yellow tail] sealed the reputation of this family forever. It is a remarkable story but is often dismissed in elitist wine circles. I often hear that the image problem Australia has in certain export markets, especially the United States, sits on the shoulders of [yellow tail]. This is a glib assessment of a complex subject. The image problem stemmed from copycat brands flooding the market and trying desperately to capture a slice of the [yellow tail] success. The quality of the wines has always been rock solid and the Casella team is smart, hardworking and innovative. Their easy-drinking, affordable wines are still around … and the copycats have dwindled.

McWilliams Family Wines

www.mcwilliams.com.au

McWilliams is a long-established producer in the region. The McWilliams Hanwood range of wines are all well made, affordable and eminently drinkable.

Calabria Family Wines

www.calabriawines.com.au

The family has a history in the region dating back to 1945. They now have property in Barossa but the Richland series of wines pays homage to their roots in the Riverina. It's a full range of well made, affordable varietal wines.

Lillypilly Estate Wines

www.lillypillywines.com.au

The Fiumara family came to Australia in the 1950s, and started out growing and selling fresh fruit and vegetables. They ventured into viticulture in the 1980s and now make a fun range of traditional and alternative varietal wines. Try the Tramillon, a blend of Gewurztraminer and Semillon. They won a trophy for the first vintage of it in 1983. There is also a delicious Vermentino.

Nugan Estate

www.nuganestate.com.au

The winery is Riverina based but they also make wines from fruit sourced in King Valley, McLaren Vale, Coonawarra and Langhorne Creek. The Manuka Grove Durif is good as is the Scruffy's Shiraz. Both are single vineyard wines from the Riverland.

PERRICOOTA
(Waveroo Country)

Perricoota is a small GI that sits on the Murray River, right on the border of Victoria. The region, which takes its name from a grazing property established in 1840, achieved Geographical Indication status in 1999.

Area under vine

410 hectares[24]

Climate

Days throughout the growing season are typically warm and sunny but the region is slightly cooler overall than Riverina.

Soils

Red and brown clay loams predominate.

Varieties

A broad range of varieties is grown but the region is mostly known for Chardonnay, Cabernet Sauvignon and Shiraz.

24 Source: Wine Australia

Producers

Morrisons Riverview Winery (www.morrisons.net.au) is the only well known property in the region and is mostly noted for the restaurant on site rather than the wines.

NORTHERN RIVERS ZONE
(Worimi, Biripi, Dainggatti, Gumbainggir and Bunjalung Country)

This zone stretches along the coast from just north of Newcastle to the Queensland border. A catch-all zonal GI for any producers that fall outside the boundaries of the only regional GI, Hastings River.

HASTINGS RIVER
(Biripi Country)

Hastings River has a history of viticulture and winemaking that dates back to 1837. As in many other Australian wine regions, disease and competitive pressures in the early 1900s led to a halt in production of wine. In 1980, the Cassegrain family began planting vines. This inspired additional development along the northern New South Wales coast.

Area under vine
15 hectares[25]

Climate
This is a warm region with high summer humidity and high rainfall. It also receives the tail end of tropical cyclones that come south from Queensland. Its proximity to warm waters of the Pacific Ocean also creates challenges for viticulture. The best vintages are the driest; those in which the late summer rains are below average. These factors explain the necessity and success of the French-bred hybrid Chambourcin, which is resistant to mildews.

Soils
The gently rolling hills afford a selection of different aspects. The soils vary from rich free-draining alluvial to red volcanic soils.

Varieties
Chambourcin, Verdelho, Chardonnay and Semillon.

25 Source: National Vineyard Scan 2020 and ABS

Producers

Cassegrain Wines (www.cassegrainwines.com.au) is the most established producer in the region and the one you are most likely to encounter. They own vineyards and source fruit from other New South Wales regions and are now more of a multi-regional winery. Try the NV sparkling Chambourcin.

NORTHERN SLOPES ZONE
(Nganyaywana and Kamilaroi Country)

This zone covers a large area of the inland slopes of the Great Dividing Range. It stretches from just north of Dubbo up to the Queensland border. New England is the sole regional GI within the Northern Slopes Zone. The correct name for the GI is New England Australia even though this area, prior to the formation of a GI was always known as New England. Perhaps the fear of litigation from other places in the world is the reason?

NEW ENGLAND AUSTRALIA
(Nganyaywana and Kamilaroi Country)

Wine growing in New England began early in the nineteenth century and by the 1880s, the district was winning international prizes for its wines. In 1882 it was described as 'one of the foremost wine producing regions in the colonies' in the *Sydney Daily Mail*. As was the case for so many during the first half of the 1900s, wineries slowly ceased production. The First World War, tough economic times and a distinct swing towards fortified wine consumption all but ended production in this region. Vine planting started again in 1968 and a slow viticultural expansion began.

New England is diverse due to its topography. There are cool-climate vineyards along the spine of the Great Dividing Range, while the lower altitude vineyards on the western edges of the New England tablelands are warmer. There are several vineyards planted above 1,000 metres. Being this far north in Australia, elevation is key in creating suitable growing conditions. While classic varieties are well established, there are many producers experimenting with different varieties and alternative techniques, making this region a place to pay attention to. There is a lot to be excited about in this area. The crying shame is that it is not easy to find wines from this region outside Australia.

Area under vine

100 hectares[26]

Climate

Summers are warm but with consistently cool nights. Rainfall is common in late summer and early autumn. Late frosts and even snow are possible until November.

Soils

Soils are varied and complex depending on location. There are rich, alluvial soils in the south near the town of Tamworth. Granite soils predominate along the steeply rising slopes and are the prized sites in the region. Around Inverell, in the western section, the soils are black loam. Along the spine of the hilltops, basalt predominates. In the far north, around Tenterfield, granite shows up again with some sandy loams. The region is also the only place in Australia where terra rossa soils exist at high altitude.

Varieties

Cabernet Sauvignon, Shiraz and Chardonnay are mainstay varieties but there's real excitement with some of the other varieties being produced in a wide range of styles. These include Gewurztraminer, Pinotage, Tempranillo, Barbera, Nebbiolo, Petit Manseng, and many others.

26 Source: Wine Australia

Producers

Topper's Mountain

www.toppers.com.au

The first wine I tried from this region was Topper's Mountain Gewurztraminer. It is a zippy, lively beauty with all the lovely, floral and lychee characteristics we love about the variety but without being overbearing. There is excellent Nebbiolo and a really delicious Petit Manseng. You basically cannot go wrong with this producer.

Jilly Wine Co

www.jillywines.com.au

This small batch, low intervention producer has some really exciting wines. The Nebbiolo is tense, taut and grippy. There is delicious rosé too. They make a bunch of wines from fruit sourced in other regions. The Banana Girl is a Sauvignon Blanc–Chardonnay blend with skin contact. It is actually made from fruit sourced in Orange and Central Ranges, but if you can find a bottle, get it, it's delicious. It is an irides-cent yellow colour that makes you want to pour it into a tumbler and gulp it down. I have only had a couple of their wines but will be looking for more in the future. A cool producer.

Merilba Estate

www.merilbaestatewines.com.au

The estate makes very good Chardonnay and sparkling wines.

WESTERN PLAINS ZONE

(Wiradjuri and Wongaibon Country)

This is a large zone in the far north-west of New South Wales. The north-western edge of this zone is where the states of South Australia, Queensland and New South Wales meet. It is a desert out there so it is unclear why the boundary of the GI stretches out to this extreme, but there must be some logic behind it. The area of interest is in the south-eastern section of the zone, around the town of Dubbo where grapes were being grown in the 1870s and 1880s. Wineries today are mostly located in this area. The most notable producer in the region is **Canonbah Bridge** (canonbah.com.au), which makes easy-drinking wines from classic varieties. Always affordable, they are exported to many countries.

7

SOUTH AUSTRALIA

South Australia was founded as a free colony in 1836, a year after Colonel William Light came from England to survey a site for a new colony. He selected a site on what is now the Torrens River and named it Adelaide after Queen Adelaide.

South Australia is the largest wine producing state, consistently responsible for almost 50 per cent of Australia's annual production. It is also home to some of the most famous regions, historic estates and oldest vines in the country. It is the driest state in Australia but is diagonally bisected by the Murray River which supplies critical water for irrigation in many regions. There is a multitude of different soil types and local mitigating influences such as altitude and cooling ocean breezes that allow for a wide range of wine styles.

The GIs of South Australia

There are 8 zonal GIs that encompass 19 regional and 3 subregional GIs.

Adelaide Super Zone

A large catchall zone that includes the zonal GIs of Barossa, Mount Lofty Ranges and Fleurieu.

Barossa Zone

This small zone captures the regional GIs of Barossa Valley and Eden Valley and the Eden Valley subregional GI of High Eden.

Mount Lofty Ranges Zone

Encompasses the regional GIs of Adelaide Plains, Clare Valley, Adelaide Hills and the Adelaide Hills subregional GIs of Piccadilly and Lenswood.

Fleurieu Zone

Encompasses the regional GIs of McLaren Vale, Langhorne Creek, Currency Creek, Kangaroo, Island and Southern Fleurieu.

Limestone Coast

A broad, sweeping zone that captures the regional GIs of Coonawarra, Padthaway, Wrattonbully, Robe, Mount Benson and Mount Gambier.

Lower Murray Zone

Includes the large regional GI of Riverland.

Far North Zone

Captures the regional GI of Southern Flinders Ranges.

Peninsulas Zone

Captures the Southern Eyre Peninsula region.

ADELAIDE SUPER ZONE

This is a somewhat strange zone in that it encompasses three other zonal GIs – Mount Lofty, Fleurieu and Barossa. It essentially exists to allow for multi-regional blends labelled under the name Adelaide and to capture a few vineyard sites that do not fall within the boundaries of the other zones. There are a few notable wineries that use the GI labelling of Adelaide (Hewitson, Patritti and Penfolds Magill Estate). Technically the Mount Lofty Ranges zone could also be used as they fall into that zone too. So, while it may be a tad confusing it does provide options. From a South Australian wine producers' perspective, the word Adelaide on a label resonates better than Mount Lofty Ranges. The awarding of zonal GIs in Australia is, for the most part, quite logical. It facilitates the ability to blend wines from multiple regions and have a suitable appellation to use on the label. There are a few that do seem to add a layer of confusion.

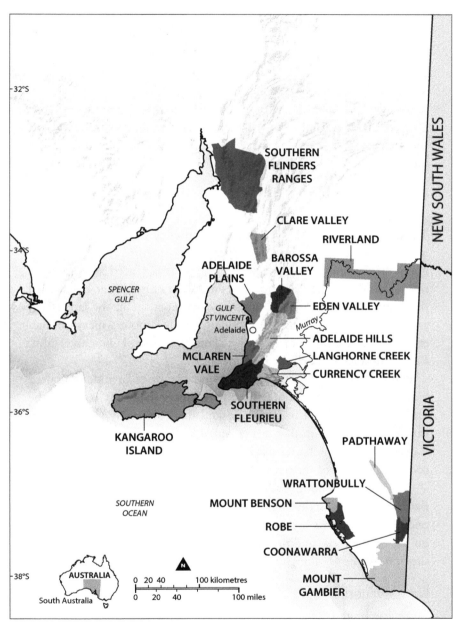

Map 3: The Geographic Indications of South Australia

BAROSSA ZONE
(Peramagnk Country)

The Barossa Zone includes the Barossa Valley and Eden Valley GIs. There are just over 14,000 hectares under vine (11,800 hectares in Barossa Valley; 2,380 hectares in Eden Valley) which represents about 10 per cent of Australia's planted area. This is a tight, smart zonal GI that frequently ends up on labels. A label that just uses the word Barossa indicates that it is a blend of fruit from Barossa Valley and Eden Valley.

BAROSSA VALLEY
(Peramagnk Country)

There are more than 175 years of grape growing and winemaking history in this region. Although established by the British, Lutheran emigrants fleeing religious persecution from Prussia played an important role in cementing the unique wine and food culture that has shaped this region. German was the most spoken language in the late 1800s and early 1900s in this region and many of the famous winery producer names are a legacy of this emigration: Henschke, Lehmann, Hahn, Burge, Lindner and Schultz to name a few.

Barossa is home to Australia's largest plantings of old, ungrafted vines. Langmeil's Freedom vineyard (planted in 1843) is likely the oldest Shiraz vineyard in the world and there are many vineyard sites throughout the region that were planted between 1850 and 1900. The Barossa Old Vine Charter was established as a way of celebrating and codifying the use of the term Old Vines (see p. 54)

There is also a long tradition of fortified wine production in the Barossa. Fortified styles may not hold the economic importance they once did but there's a strong sense of stewardship, with many intent on preserving these traditional styles. For this we should be thankful as they can be breathtakingly complex and long lived.

Newer varieties to watch

There has been a lot of attention given to new varieties recently. It is largely a direct result of a search for solutions to combat a changing environment – heat and drought tolerance, better retention of natural acidity, later ripening, reduced water requirement, etc. It is also about growing varieties that can be shaped into wines that deliver freshness and vibrance. When I asked Pete Schell from Spinifex Wines (see p. 110) to pick the new varieties that are doing well he chose Cinsault, Grenache Gris and Clairette saying, 'From a Barossan point of view, these three varieties have an innate durability and resilience in the vineyard – they work well with our warmth and aridity, the fruit holds condition and freshness, and this shows in the wines.' He sums up each variety below:

- Cinsault gives medium to lightweight wines with good aromatic depth of savoury brown woody spices and sour-edged red and dark fruits. It can be a little structurally incomplete but this weakness can be a real strength as for us its real value is as a blender to temper wines that have a natural tendency to aromatic and palate fruit sweetness – Grenache in particular. In the vineyard it grows well, yields well with minimal to no water and copes with heat and aridity. It's a no-nonsense peasant variety.
- Grenache Gris delivers wines with texture and weight – with freshness. It is early to harvest, acid retentive and robust in the vineyard. I'm still building a perspective with Gris but from the very small parcels I've handled – the first one in 2005 – I think it's going to be super useful. The better wines I've seen were firm, fresh, mid-weight numbers, with ripe citrus, dried herb and wild honey characters.
- Clairette gives wines with delicate aromatics and discrete flavours – white flowers, soft, sweet herbals, pale pear-like fruit. It has a fullness without a lot of weight, which is appealing and useful in the Barossa where it's easy for things to become a little heavy handed. It has good acid retention and copes very well with heat and aridity.

Area under vine
11,800 hectares[27]

Climate
The climate is warm and dry with low humidity and rainfall during the growing season. Nights are cool to very cool and summer days are hot.

Soils
There are complex and varied soils due to a multitude of hills and sub-valleys. In general they range from clay loam through to sandy with relatively low fertility.

27 Source: Barossa Grape and Wine

> ## Varieties
>
> Shiraz, Cabernet Sauvignon, Grenache and Semillon are the most recogniz-able varieties in Barossa Valley. There are several others that are either new arrivals or have some history but will be key in shaping the future. Cinsault, Carignan, Touriga Nacional, Counoise, Grenache Gris, Grenache Blanc, Clairette and Vermentino are all showing real promise (see p. 98).

Main wine styles

Shiraz occupies 60 per cent of the vineyard plantings and is by any measure *the* variety in this region. Barossa Shiraz did develop a reputation for being overly ripe and heavy with lots of oak and alcohol. That is probably an unfair and simplistic assessment but the fact remains that there were a *lot* of wines made in this mould and many were exported with a curious sense of pride. Barossa Valley Shiraz has evolved. The warm climate means it is not difficult to craft rich, full-flavoured wines with power and concentration. Tempering and managing these attributes requires work in the vineyard, sensitivity around harvest times, creativity and a gentle hand in the winery. Barossa Valley Shiraz should have power and intensity, but this should not come at the expense of balance, complexity and freshness. The best examples today show power, richness and Barossa Valley's trademark plush, velvety tannins. The difference is clarity and purity of fruit. There are still some heavy, intensely ripe, rich and raisin-scented styles (and there is a market for them); however, freshness is at the core of postmodern Barossa Shiraz.

While Grenache doesn't occupy the vineyard acreage it used to, it has a long history in this region. Historically blended with both Shiraz and Mourvedre to produce a classic complex and textured red it also formed the backbone of most fortified wine styles, which seemed to relegate it to secondary status compared to Shiraz. The evolution of single varietal Grenache has been nothing short of a revelation. Earlier picking, whole bunch inclusion, longer post-fermentation maceration and maturation in seasoned oak has revealed a much broader spectrum of weight, aromatics, flavours and textures. Grenache may be an original classic of the Barossa Valley, but it will also be key to shaping the future styles.

Cabernet Sauvignon tends to do best in the cooler sites and in cooler vintages. The style is generally richer with riper fruit character and softer tannins than Coonawarra and Margaret River. Shiraz–Cabernet is one of the regions' famous and historic blends (see below).

Semillon has a long history in the region and there are many old vines and different clones. There are various styles, ranging from light, fresh and crunchy from earlier picked fruit through to full flavoured, textured wines that see skin contact and/or oak maturation.

Although made in much smaller quantities than in the past there is a strong history and legacy of fortified wine production in Barossa. Tawny styles are the most common but a full range, including sherry styles exist. Seppeltsfield produces world class examples. The 100-year-old Para Liqueur is in a league of its own and one of the greatest fortified wines you will ever have the pleasure of tasting.

The Cabernet–Shiraz blend

The blending of Cabernet Sauvignon with Shiraz dates back a long way in the history of Australian red wine production but it is hard to nail down precisely when and where it started. The first vintages of Penfolds Grange had small amounts of Cabernet in the blend and Yalumba has been making its classic Signature Cabernet–Shiraz since 1962. Deeper investigation is complicated prior to varietal labelling. Many red wines in Australia were labelled Claret or Burgundy and there is a good chance that many of those labelled Claret were likely Cabernet–Shiraz blends. When Louisa Rose was showing me through the Yalumba vintage cellar she paused to show me a red wine from 1910 that she said was likely a Cabernet–Shiraz. Wherever it started, Cabernet–Shiraz is one of Australia's most classic and important combinations. The blend has always made sense. Cabernet Sauvignon provides structure and framework with its firmer tannins and higher acidity and Shiraz fills out the mid-palate with plush fruit and complex earth and spice characters. The sourcing of fruit is varied but a classic approach is to blend Coonawarra Cabernet Sauvignon with Barossa Shiraz. One of Penfolds most legendary wines, 1962 Bin 60A, was made from this combination.

Tyson Stelzer and Matthew Jukes host a competition called the Great Australian Red where they judge this blend only (www.thegreataustralian-red.com). Now in its seventeenth year, it provides a contemporary list of the best examples. Perennial picks of this Australian classic for me are: Yalumba Signature, Yalumba The Caley, Penfolds Bin 389, Wynn's V&A Lane Cabernet–Shiraz, Elderton Ode to Lorraine, Tapanappa Whalebone Vineyards Cabernet–Shiraz, St Hugo Cabernet–Shiraz, Majella The Mallea, Hickinbotham Clarendon The Peake Cabernet–Shiraz.

EDEN VALLEY
(Peramagnk Country)

Joseph Gilbert planted the first vineyard in this region in 1847 at Pewsey Vale. Eden Valley is technically part of the greater Barossa region, but the vineyards sit at higher altitudes (380–550 metres) so ripening is generally a week or two later. Harvest is also later and takes place in cooler conditions. Protection from the strong breezes in the rocky, exposed region is important, so site selection and aspect are critical. The northern section is a little lower in altitude and more suitable for reds. Henschke's famous red wine sites are located here. The southern section is at higher altitudes and is where the subregion of High Eden is located. Riesling does particularly well in this part of the region.

Area under vine

2,380 hectares[28]

Climate

Climate is varied, but overall it is cooler than Barossa. Harvest takes place up to two weeks later and in cooler conditions. Elevation leads to varied climates within the region. Certain sites are excellent for white varieties, but it is a struggle to ripen red varieties. Wind is common and protection from it is a consideration when choosing vineyard sites.

Soils

These are varied, due to altitude and topography. Sandy loam and clay loam are both common. Ironstone gravels and quartz gravels are present in some areas.

Varieties

Riesling, Chardonnay, Viognier, Shiraz and Cabernet Sauvignon.

28 Source: Barossa Grape and Wine

Main wine styles

Riesling is the most important white variety of the region. It yields classic lime flavours and aromas but with a distinct mineral tinged edge and can age gracefully for 10 years or more. Eden Valley Riesling is one of Australia's classic expressions of the variety.

The style for Shiraz differs from that of the Barossa Valley. Black pepper, blackberry/blackcurrant and sage aromas and flavours are common. Wines are generally medium- to full-bodied with supple tannins and balanced acidity. Henschke Hill of Grace and Mount Edelstone vineyards are located in Eden Valley.

The first serious planting of Chardonnay was at Mount Adam in 1973. The style is medium-bodied with melon and fig flavours augmented in the best cases with careful oak maturation.

Site selection is critical for Cabernet Sauvignon in this region, and it only represents about 10 per cent of production. Overall quality is very high, with classic cassis, cedar and herbal notes in the best versions. There are several really good Cabernets from Eden Valley.

The strength of Viognier here is based on the work Yalumba started when they first planted it in 1980. It took some time to find its feet and most of that rested on learning how to capture the perfume and distinct apricot character while maintaining balance and purity. Yalumba has nailed it (see p. 105).

Barossa Valley and Eden Valley producers
Henschke
www.henschke.com.au

If there were such a thing as royalty in Australia wine, Stephen and Prue Henschke would be King and Queen. This is a sixth generation, family-run estate. Henschke grows many different varieties and makes a dazzling array of wines but there are two jewels in the crown that shine just a little brighter than the others. Henschke are the custodians of two of Australia's greatest single-vineyard Shiraz sites, Hill of Grace and Mount Edelstone. Tasting Hill of Grace in situ with Stephen and Prue has brought many experienced wine professionals to tears. It is a wine of incredible depth, complexity, texture and length. It is rare and expensive, as it should be. Mount Edelstone is a slightly more affordable lens through which to view Eden Valley Shiraz and the brilliance of Henschke. It is unique, and the most singular expression of Shiraz anywhere on the planet, never mind Australia, with supple, velvety tannins and the classic blackberry, black pepper Shiraz flavour. And there is a herbal note. Not green and stemmy, more sage and bay leaf. There is also a distinct blackcurrant note, not a typical Shiraz character but it exists in this wine.

Cyril Henschke is their top Cabernet Sauvignon and stands among the better expressions of this variety in Australia. Eden Valley is not

Under-vine straw mulching for weed control and moisture retention –
Hill of Grace vineyard.

ideally suited to Cabernet Sauvignon but this is the exception that proves the rule. Julius Riesling is a laser-sharp, lime and mineral-scented example and shows why this variety excels in Eden Valley.

Standish Wine Company

www.standishwineco.com

Dan Standish has been making brilliant wines for a couple of decades now. He is all about small batch production Shiraz, and his fastidious attention to detail is obvious. The wines are rich, concentrated, textural and complex. Dan's strategy is to 'sell more wine than he makes', in other words for demand to outstrip supply (he usually has a waiting list), so declassification is a critical piece of the puzzle. Only 30 per cent of what he has access to makes it into a Standish Wine Co. wine. Everything he makes is a pleasure to drink and all are worth seeking out. The Relic is from the Hongell Family vineyard in Krondorf and is co-fermented with 1 per cent Viognier. The Standish is from the Laycock Vineyard in Greenock, The Schubert Theorem is from six different small parcels of fruit (all handled separately) from the Schubert Vineyard in Marananga. These three wines are all top-notch, small production Barossa Valley Shiraz. The Lamella is the wine that really stands out, which is saying something in a line-up like this. From a vineyard in Hutton Vale planted in 1961 using cuttings from Henschke's Mount Edelstone Vineyard, it is a wine of incredible perfume, depth and complexity. This is one of the very best boutique Barossa producers.

Sami Odi

www.sami-odi.com

Fraser McKinley started Sami Odi in 2006 after stints with Rockford, Standish and Torbreck. He has typically sourced all the fruit for his wines from the Hoffman vineyard in Ebenezer. He continues to do so but also planted his own site, behind his house, in 2017. The first crop and bottling of Our Hill was 2020 and the joy and pride of finally having his own vineyard site is obvious. Fraser has a relaxed, easy-going style but his attention to detail is evident. He is, along with Dan Standish, making some of the best, small production wines in the Barossa. He moves to the beat of his own drum and that is reflected in the way he makes and labels his wines. Little Wine is made every year and is typically a blend of seven back vintage wines in descending order. Little Wine #11 is the 2021 release. You can't go wrong with any of his wines. Production is tiny (1,000 cases) and the wines are difficult to find but it is well worth the effort.

Yalumba

www.yalumba.com

Established in 1847, Yalumba is the oldest family-run wine company in Australia. Louisa Rose has been the head winemaker for many years and their best wines just keep getting better. You really can't go wrong with anything from Yalumba but the following varieties and wines are the shining stars for me.

Pewsey Vale Rieslings: this vineyard located in Eden Valley was initially planted in 1847 but fell into disuse and was purchased by the Hill Smith family in 1960. All Riesling, all delicious and among the finest in the country. Regular releases include the late, aged-release Contours and an even later release Museum bottling. There is also a 1961 Block Riesling. Try them all!

Viognier has been a pet project here since 1980 and Yalumba has nailed it. They make several cuvées but the Eden Valley and Virgilius bottlings are some of best expressions you can find of this variety outside the northern Rhône.

Grenache: the Samuels Collection Bush Vine Grenache is a delicious example of modern, fresh and juicy Barossa Grenache. The Tricentenary is from a Grenache vineyard planted in 1889 and is on the more serious, age-worthy side. Its a spicy, fragrant and lovely expression of the variety.

The Signature is a Cabernet–Shiraz blend that they have been making since the 1960s and I think it is their best red wine. The blend is always in the neighbourhood of a 50:50 split between the varieties and rarely disappoints. It is a perfect melding of the richness of Shiraz with the structure of Cabernet Sauvignon and it can age gracefully for 20 years or more.

John Duval Wines

www.johnduvalwines.com

It is always a pleasure to be in the company of John Duval, a gentle-natured, thoughtful and passionate man who has constantly tinkered with his approach. He has more than 50 vintages under his belt, but he is not old school. He spent 29 years at Penfolds and for 14 of those he was the man responsible for Grange. RWT was his baby, and that wine continues to be made today. He struck out on his own in 2003 and now has a stable of impressive wines. His son, Tim, is gradually taking the reins under John's watchful eye. Entity Shiraz is my barometer for assessing the current vintage of Barossa Shiraz. Plexus Red and Plexus White are both consistently delicious. The Annexus Grenache and Annexus Mataro are beautifully crafted old vine versions of those varieties. An excellent, impressively consistent producer.

Rockford

www.rockfordwines.com.au

If a visit to Rockford doesn't restore your faith in old-school, family-run estates then it might be that you are dead and just haven't realized it yet. It is impossible not to be charmed by the traditional, fastidiously restored old equipment and buildings. Once you try the wines, the deal is sealed. Rockford was started by Robert O'Callaghan in 1984 and he ran it solo for the first few years. It did not take long for his wines to garner praise. His small batch winemaking approach also captured the attention of the younger generation. The list of winemakers who have history at Rockford is a veritable who's who of superstars. (Aussie wine journalist Nick Ryan wrote a brilliant piece on this in *Gourmet Traveller Wine* entitled 'The School of Rockford'. See Appendix III.) The Rockford Academy, as O'Callaghan calls it, has been important in shaping the attitude and approach of so many brilliant winemakers in the Barossa, attention to detail being a primary attribute. It is almost like Rockford was the first small batch winery in Barossa. It is not that attention to detail was lacking in Barossa prior to Rockford but small batch production as a business model was rare. The Basket Press Shiraz is the pride and joy and a must-try wine. The Sparkling Black Shiraz is one of the best examples of this style in the country. Rod and Spur is the Cabernet–Shiraz blend and I secretly love the White Frontignac with its juicy, peachy floral flavours, low alcohol and absolute gulpable charm.

Eperosa

www.eperosa.com.au

Brett Groeke is a sixth-generation Barossan. His family started growing grapes in the Krondorf area of the region in the 1840s and has owned and farmed vineyards ever since. The wines he now makes are not from the original family sites but from vineyards he purchased in 2013. Brett also spent time at Rockford. He is a softly spoken, thoughtful guy who is passionate about the Barossa. His wines captured my attention the first time I met him which was around 2013, just as he was striking out on his own. His farming practices follow organic and regenerative principles, and the winemaking is small batch and hands on, with great attention to detail. One of the sites he owns is called Magnolia and is in the Vine Vale sub-district of Barossa, the other is in Krondorf. Both sites are now a mix of the very oldest vines and some newer planting made since 2013. Magnolia 1941 is a textured, delightful Semillon and the Magnolia 1896 Shiraz is a concentrated, richly textured beauty that comes exclusively from the oldest vines in the vineyard. His Stonegarden Grenache was the first of his wines I ever tried and remains a favourite. It is from fruit sourced at the famous Stonegarden vineyard in Eden Valley which was planted in 1858, making it one of the oldest vineyards in Barossa. Here you will find the epitome of quality small production Barossa.

Langmeil

www.langmeilwinery.com.au

The first vineyards were planted at Langmeil in the 1840s. This is a historic property located in Tanunda. In 1996 the Lindner family purchased the property, which was somewhat run down, and refurbished the winery. They also acquired a 2-hectare plot of Shiraz that was planted in 1843. This is the oldest Shiraz vineyard on the planet and is bottled as the Langmeil Freedom Shiraz. It is a rich, seductive, gloriously textured wine that is best with 8 years bottle age at the minimum. A very Shiraz-dominant winery, all of which are delicious and classic. The Three Gardens Grenache Shiraz Mourvedre and the Fifth Wave Grenache are both fantastic, and one of my favourite Barossa Cabernets is their Jackaman's Cabernet Sauvignon.

Kalleske Wines

www.kalleske.com

The Kalleske family has been growing grapes on their Greenock property since 1853, and up until 2002 sold the fruit to various wineries. In 2002, Troy and Tony Kalleske decided it was time for the family to produce their own wines from the estate. This makes Kalleske a sort of old, new winery. There are so many things to like about what they do. The vineyards have been organic and biodynamically farmed since 1998 and rather than the younger generation encouraging the switch to better farming, it was Troy's parents. Troy was the sceptic initially, but his parents spent time investigating and quickly realized that current organic and biodynamic principles were eerily similar to how previous generations of Kalleskes had farmed. No further discussion was needed. Moppa Shiraz is a go-to Barossa Shiraz. Their top Shiraz is Johann Georg which is from vines planted in 1875. Troy has also been tinkering with different styles and winemaking approaches since 2012. Parallax is an early-picked Grenache that is red fruited, crunchy and delicious. The Plenarius, a skin-contact Viognier that is effectively Kalleske's orange wine, is textural, savoury and a pleasure to drink. On the insistence of his cellar door crew, he made a batch of pet nat Grenache in 2022 and it is a dark-berried, frothy delight!

Torbreck Vintners

www.torbreck.com

Torbreck is one of the more recognized Barossa names in export markets, especially in the United States. Dave Powell is credited with establishing the Torbreck name with wines he crafted in the early years. The winery is now owned by Pete Kight and winemaking is in the hands of Ian Hongell. Working with old, dry-grown vineyards and multi-generational growers has always been at the heart of what Torbreck does. The wines all have great density and power and exude all the classic characteristics that speak of Barossa – warmth, earth, spice and fruit concentration – but still maintain elements of finesse and complexity. I think the wines have gone from strength to strength under Hongell's guidance, seemingly more focused on vibrant fruit purity. The Woodcutters Shiraz and Juveniles Grenache blend are lovely, easy-drinking wines and a wonderful entry to the Torbreck style. There are plenty of excellent wines in the Torbreck stable. The Struie is one of my favourites, made from fruit sourced in the Eden Valley. The Laird is the signature wine and is fantastic but the current price of A$800 at cellar door will no doubt mean that many will not get to experience it. If you want a taste of their top end Shiraz, the Factor is a more affordable route.

Agricola Vintners

www.agricolavintners.com

This is a new venture from Callum Powell, son of the infamous Dave Powell of early Torbreck fame. Callum was weaned on wine, having witnessed the meteoric rise of the Torbreck brand. Travel informed and refined his thinking. He visited Jean-Louis Chave where he learned about the concept of provenance and carrying the weight of a region on your shoulders. It is this ethos that has shaped what he is currently doing in the Barossa. He worked with his dad for a few years on the Powell and Sons project when he returned, but went out on his own. Agricola Vintners started as just barrels of Shiraz and while this has grown, he remains committed to that idea of one variety. His two wines are named after the towns from which the fruit is sourced, Ebenezer Shiraz, a richer, classically fleshy iteration of Barossa Shiraz and the more fine-boned, structured and savoury Flaxman Valley Shiraz. He is thoughtful, precise, relatively low intervention in the winery and comfortably opinionated. He adds sulphur just before bottling. 'I think what's much more important than making something that is "natural" is making something that is delicious and has this traceability of place,' he says. I have not met this kid, but I like his attitude and his wines. I will find a way to meet him soon.

Chris Ringland

chrisringland.com

Chris was very much a part of the success at Rockford in the early days. He now has his own 3.2-hectare site up in the Eden Valley. He still makes wines from the famous Hoffman vineyard in Ebenezer and has various other special projects. His wines are unashamedly big, concentrated and rich but he manages to coax finesse, complexity and length out of everything he does. He has retained that small batch attention to detail from his days as part of the Rockford Academy. Chris is a quietly spoken, lovely guy, generous with his time and thoughts on Barossa, and a pleasure to spend time with. Hoffman Vineyard Shiraz is a classic. His Randall's Hill Shiraz, from his Eden Valley property, is a rich, spicy, savoury delight.

Spinifex Wines

www.spinifexwines.com.au

Pete Schell and his partner Magali Gely have been in the Barossa for over 20 years. Spinifex was one of the first producers in Barossa to lean into making more restrained and elegant wines and although Pete would say he is now 'old new school' I consistently use his wines as examples of modern Barossa. Lola is a white blend of Semillon, Clairette and Ugni Blanc and this wine, coupled with his straight Clairette are eye-opening white wines from the Barossa. Both are fresh, textured and beautifully balanced. He is a strong believer in the future of different southern French varieties in the Barossa (see his commentary on Barossa grape varieties on p.98).

Papillon is a Grenache Cinsault and is so delicious I have dubbed it my ideal Monday to Thursday Barossa red. It is juicy, fresh and delicious, but with proper structure and complexity. The range at Spinifex is fantastic and shows a beautiful savoury, elegant side of Barossa. La Maline is fantastic and his regular bottling, labelled Syrah, is a delicious way to grasp the retrained nature of modern Barossa Valley Shiraz.

Small Fry Wines

www.smallfrywines.com.au

Owner Wayne Ahrens' great-great-grandfather came to South Australia from Germany in 1837 on what was the third ship of immigrants to South Australia. With such a long tradition in the region I quizzed him on why he doesn't fit the mould of a traditional Barossa producer. His answer was very simple. He attended Rootstock, Australia's first natural wine fair, in Sydney, and said that it was there that he had found his tribe. He is focused on low-intervention, low-input wines with a simple ethos – natural ferments, no-to-minimal adjustment, old oak and a soft hand in the cellar. Everything is fresh, lively and super fun to drink. Tangerine Dream is his skin-contact, orange wine made mostly from

Semillon and Pedro Ximenes with a splash of Riesling, Roussanne and Muscat. Starry Starry Night is 100 per cent Cinsault and an iridescent raspberry, tart cherry, mouth-puckering delight. Isolar is a Riesling–Roussanne blend. Why not? It works. This is a textured, savoury wine with a spine of classic, lemony Riesling acidity.

Organic vineyard at Small Fry Wines – Vine Vale, Barossa Valley.

Yetti and the Kokonut

yettiandthekokonut.com.au

David Geyer (Yetti) and Koen Janssens (Koko) formed a partnership in 2015 and they firmly fit the bill on non-traditional. Their focus is small batch, fun and eminently drinkable wines from the not so well known varieties. They do source grapes from other regions but the Barossa wines to try include El Doradillo which is made from old vine Doradillo, a Spanish variety that has a history in Australia. Fruit Basket rosé is sourced from the famous Stonegarden vineyard in Eden Valley. It is called fruit basket because of the blend of 14 different varieties: Muscat Blanc à Petits Grains, Muscat Rose à Petits Grains, Muscat of

Alexandria, Riesling, Sauvignon Blanc, Semillon, Pinot Blanc, Pinot Gris, Chardonnay, Gewürztraminer, Black Muscat, Grenache, Shiraz and Cabernet Sauvignon. The bottom line is that this is about style rather than the contents and it is exquisitely delicious. The Red Muscat is a really fun, dry red wine with vibrant classic Muscat aromas but is fruity, herbal and savoury.

Tim Smith Wines

www.timsmithwines.com.au

The winery was established in 2001 but Tim had years of experience working in the Barossa, Portugal, France and New Zealand before then. Tim is a straightforward, down-to-earth guy making really lovely, expressive and fairly priced wines. The three wines he makes under the Bugalugs label are the perfect entry into understanding Tim's approach. Bugalugs White is a textural blend of Clairette, Viognier, Grenache Blanc and Roussanne and both the Bugalugs Grenache and Shiraz are fantastic versions of modern, accessible Barossa. He does make a couple of classic cellar-worthy Reserve wines. The TSW Reserve Shiraz is mostly Eden Valley fruit and is rich and concentrated but with a spine of classic Eden Valley acidity. The TSW Reserve Mataro is sourced from a vineyard that he thinks was planted sometime in the 1870s.

Head Wines

www.headwines.com.au

Alex Head works predominantly with small growers in both Eden Valley and Barossa Valley. He makes a full range of classic Barossa wines, all of which are excellent, but the Grenache-based wines are standouts for me. The Old Vine Grenache is fragrant and textured with a gorgeous pure raspberry fruit. The Ancestor Vine Grenache is denser and more compact and concentrated with a darker fruit quality. This is a really good producer.

Tscharke Wines

www.tscharke.au

Owner Damien Tscharke is passionate about regenerative farming and spends a lot of time managing the health and biodiversity of his vineyards. Certified organic and biodynamic, he makes a really compelling range of wines from traditional classic Barossa varieties and has been experimenting with several alternative varieties. A Thing of Beauty Grenache is just that! An aromatic, medium-weight wine with seductive red berry fruit and a textbook savoury, spicy finish, it is modern, crunchy Grenache at its best. The Gnadenfrei White is 100 per cent Grenache Blanc and a perfect lens through which to view the future of white wine in the Barossa. Textured and savoury with seductive stone fruit and hay-like flavours, it is beautifully concentrated without being heavy. Tscharke makes a really cool Montepulciano that is pure fruited with a sort of wild, savoury edge.

Hayes Family Wines

www.hayesfamilywines.com

This relatively new producer was established in 2014. In addition to their estate Stone Well vineyard they work with multiple growers in the region, mostly with the classic varieties of Shiraz, Grenache, Mataro and Semillon. There are lots of top-notch wines in this stable but again, it was the Grenache that stood out. The Fromm Vineyard Grenache is ripe and concentrated with classic spice and savoury characters. The Estate Stonewell Block #2 Grenache is about as charming as Barossa Grenache gets. Ripe and concentrated with beautiful perfume and rich spice-laden fruit, it is also balanced, long and savoury. Really lovely stuff.

Arila Gardens Wines

www.arilagardens.com

Adam and Marie Clay purchased their 8-hectare site in Moppa in 2018 making Arila Gardens another relatively new producer. Adam Clay is not new to winemaking, having spent 10 years as a winemaker for Penfolds, with stints overseas in Italy, China and the United States. The Arila Gardens of Moppa range covers a broad selection of varieties, including the lovely G.S.M. (Grenache–Shiraz–Mataro), a Nero d'Avola and a Saperavi. The Arila Garden range features single-site wines that are based on a selection of only the very best fruit in any given vintage. The Sand Grenache is a standout.

Soul Growers

www.soulgrowers.com

This is a partnership started in 1998 by Paul Heinicke and Stu Bourne. They work with many growers across the region. Their single-vineyard wines represent the very best of what they do and the growers they source fruit from are top notch, generational farmers. Three Shiraz were standouts for me: Hoffmann, Kleinig and Hampel. All show classic Barossa warmth and richness with velvety old vine tannins imparting tremendous depth and complexity. It is hard to pick a favourite but the textural richness of the Hoffmann might just give it the edge.

Seppeltsfield

www.seppeltsfield.com.au

It is difficult to know where to start with this magnificent, historic Barossa Valley estate. Seppeltsfield was established in the Barossa Valley by Joseph and Johanna Seppelt. In 1850, Joseph Seppelt purchased 158 acres (64 hectares) of land from Hermann Kook for £1 an acre. The original intent was to farm tobacco. Later Seppelt generations focused more on grape growing and winemaking. Benno Seppelt was the second generation to run the estate and was quite visionary. In 1878 he started something remarkable that continues today: he laid aside a barrel of 1878 fortified wine (Port as it was called then) with the idea that it should not be bottled or released for 100 years. To visit the Centennial Cellar and try your birth year from barrel is about as special as it gets, and made even more remarkable by knowing that you will likely not be alive when it is released. Benno also designed a gravity-fed winery in 1888. Regarded as one of Australia's most successful wine dynasties, the Seppelt family kept ownership of all their wine interests, including Seppeltsfield, until 1985. B Seppelt & Sons, as it was then known, was sold, and languished through almost three decades of corporate ownership. The estate returned to private ownership in 2007. Warren Randall, with a group of investors, now owns Seppeltsfield and views himself as a custodian of its history and legacy. Obviously the fortifieds are magnificent, albeit in much smaller quantities these days, but they are again producing a range of excellent red and white wines. The Village range includes a fresh, crunchy red-fruit Grenache and brooding, dark-fruited Touriga. The single vineyard Shiraz wines use the background of the Barossa Grounds project and are labelled according to the 'grounds' that the sites are located in – Southing, Northing, Easting and Westing. All are well done and show, with broad strokes, some subregional variation. If you are in the Barossa and don't go to the Seppeltsfield, you have made a mistake.

Rusden Wines

www.rusdenwines.com.au

In 1979, Christine and Dennis Canute purchased a 16-hectare run-down vineyard planted on sand and clay in the heart of the Barossa

Valley in Vine Vale. This began a long, slow rejuvenation of the vineyards, the fruit of which was initially sold to local wineries. Little by little they started making wine, with the help of their son Christian, and in 2007 they built a cellar door. Rusden is now run by Christian and his wife, Amy. All fruit is grown and made on the estate. It is hard to go wrong here, which makes recommendations difficult. Wines that have recently captured my attention beyond his classic and delicious Black Guts Shiraz include Christine's Vineyard Grenache, from Grenache grown on sand in the middle of Vine Vale! What else is there to say other than pour me another glass of this fragrant seductress? The Rocky Valley Road Trousseau is a crunchy, medium-weight, juicy red that highlights Christian's curiosity about newer varieties in the Barossa. Chasing Daisies is a rich, textural, floral-scented blend of Grenache Blanc, Roussanne and Clairette, and the Wildwood Cinsault speaks volumes about how suited this variety is to the evolving climate in the Barossa Valley.

Hesketh Wine Company

www.heskethwinecompany.com.au

Jonathon Hesketh started the Hesketh Wine Company in 2006 and is now the owner of six separate estates grouped under the banner of The Usual Suspects Collective (www.usualsuspects.wine): Vickery Riesling, Ox Hardy Wines, Barratt Piccadilly Wines, Miss Zilm Clare Valley, Parker Estate Coonawarra and St John's Road Barossa. The cellar door is in Verdun in the Adelaide Hills but they make wines from several South Australian regions. The Barossa sourced wines to look for under the Hesketh label are the Grenache, a very interesting Negroamaro and a classically styled Shiraz.

An Approach to Relaxation

www.anapproachtorelaxation.com

This is an interesting venture by lapsed American Sommeliers Richard and Carla Betts. They purchased a magnificent old vine Grenache vineyard in the Vine Vale area of Barossa and make two wines only. Sucette, which is the Grenache and Nichon a white, predominantly Semillon blend. Both are delicious. The vineyard is owned now by Dr Dylan Grigg but they still get first access to fruit each vintage.

Other producers to seek out

First Drop (www.firstdropwines.com)
Try Mother's Milk Shiraz as an introduction and Fat of The Land Ebenezer Shiraz for classic, full throttle Barossa Shiraz.

Max & Me (www.maxandme.com.au)
This Eden Valley based producer is owned by Phil and Sarah Lehmann. The House Blend is a spot on Cabernet–Shiraz blend. The Springton Vineyard Grenache and the Estate Shiraz round out my selection to three picks.

Shobbrook Wines (www.shobbrookwines.com.au)
Tom Shobbrook was one of the earlier natural Barossa producers. The small production means wines are not easy to find but he has a few really interesting wines that are worth the effort. Poolside is a savoury, crunchy rosé. Tommy Ruff, Tommy Fields and his Seppeltsfield Syrah are also worth seeking out.

Massena (www.massena.com.au)
Moonlight Run Grenache–Mataro–Shiraz serves as a good introduction to the style of Massena wines. Stonegarden Grenache and Verto Shiraz are the top-shelf offerings.

Sons of Eden (www.sonsofeden.com)
Look for Notus Grenache, Zephyrus Shiraz and Romulus Old Vine Shiraz.

Tomfoolery (www.tomfoolerywines.com.au)
A solid producer of classic and contemporary Barossa styles. Fox Whistle Pinot Gris, Young Blood Grenache, Barda Negra Tempranillo and Black and Blue Shiraz are all worth checking out.

Teusner (www.teusner.com.au)
The top-shelf Albert Shiraz is fantastic. Also look for The G Grenache, Reibke Shiraz and Righteous Mataro.

Turkey Flat (www.turkeyflat.com.au)
First planted in 1847, since the 1860s this classic estate has been under the custodianship of the Schultz family. The Grenache is fantastic and

their top wine, the Ancestor Shiraz is made in minuscule quantities from the original Shiraz vines planted in 1847.

Vinya Vella (www.vinyavella.com)

This is Dylan Griggs venture. He purchased the Grenache vineyard from Carla and Richard Betts and now makes his own wine along with supplying fruit to the Betts and many other top producers. I have only tried the first vintage but it was a seductive beauty and I look forward to watching this evolve.

The Penfolds Story – 1844 to evermore!

Penfolds is Australia's best-known wine brand. While they do make wines from regions across Australia, they are fundamentally South Australian. The history dates to its foundation at Magill Estate in what is now a suburb of Adelaide. Christopher and Mary Penfold planted the first vines there in 1844 and established the Penfolds Wine Company. Mary retired in 1884, at which point Penfolds was producing one-third of the wine in South Australia. By 1907, it was the largest winery in South Australia. In 1948 Max Schubert was hired as the chief winemaker, marking the start of a period of experimentation and innovation that would eventually establish the global reputation of Penfolds. Schubert's legacy cannot be overstated.

The Creation of Grange

In 1950 Schubert was sent to France and Spain, ostensibly to learn more about Sherry and Port production. Fortified wines were the main wines consumed in Australia in those days. On a trip to Bordeaux he visited several estates, including Chateau Lafite Rothschild and Chateau Latour. It was here that he experienced Bordeaux wines of between 40 and 50 years old. This inspired him to try to make wines in Australia with similar age-worthy characteristics. He sourced Shiraz grapes from the Grange Vineyard at Magill and from a private vineyard just south of Adelaide at Morphett Vale. Combining his knowledge and new ideas from Bordeaux, he made his first experimental wine in 1951, which he named Grange Hermitage. It was never released commercially.

Over the next five years, he assiduously developed the Grange style. Working closely with Penfolds' scientist, Dr Ray Beckwith, he crafted a unique Shiraz based wine. He experimented with barrel fermentation at the end of vinification and maturation in American oak. In 1957 he was asked to show his efforts in Sydney to top management, wine aficionados and board member friends. Shockingly, the Grange experiment was universally disliked. Additional tastings in Adelaide netted the same result. One critic observed, 'Schubert, I congratulate you. A very good, dry port, which no one in their right mind will buy – let alone drink.'

He was ordered to stop making Grange. Experimental Grange vintages, already bottled and binned, were to be sold off to clubs as house wine. The remaining stock would be blended away. Grange was dead.

But Schubert was still determined. He took all the experimental Grange he could and stashed it out of sight in the underground cellars of Magill. From 1957 to 1959, the 'hidden Granges' were made without the knowledge of the Penfolds board. Max Schubert continued to source fruit and experiment in relative secrecy. Although management was kept away, friends and associates were occasionally brought in to taste the wines. News was filtering out about Schubert's unique Grange Hermitage. The Penfolds Board generously ordered production of Grange to restart, just in time for the 1960 vintage. In 1962 the 1955 Penfolds Grange won the first of 50 gold medals and many trophies. It is Australia's most famous wine.

One of the biggest mistakes I made as a young sommelier was trying Grange for the first time and wondering, out loud, what all the fuss was about: 'It's, big, rich and clunky. I don't get it.' I did feel compelled to buy a couple of bottles and put them away. In 1999 at a celebratory dinner, I poured 1981 Grange and 1983 Chateau Margaux. I was immediately embarrassed about my cocky ignorance and felt like penning apology notes to anyone I may have offended. They were very different wines, both magnificent. The Grange absolutely belonged at the same table and discussion as Chateau Margaux. It truly is one of the world's great red wines.

Post Schubert there have only been three chief winemakers: Don Ditter, John Duval and current chief winemaker Peter Gago. Gago has steered Penfolds through interesting corporate times. He has never wavered in his commitment to the quality of the wines and his role as custodian of Australia's most well-respected wine company and most famous red wine.

Wines to look for

- **Grange** – the current release will cost you A$850.00. What else can you drink from Penfolds while you are saving up to buy a bottle? Just about everything.

- **Bin 389** is a textbook Cabernet Shiraz blend that spends time in barrels previously used for Grange.

- **RWT** was created by John Duval when he was head winemaker to serve as a counterpoint to Grange. Grange is a multi-regional blend aged in American oak. RWT (Red Wine Trials) is 100 per cent Shiraz but from a single region (Barossa) aged in French oak. It is a fantastic wine that really needs a minimum of 10 years in bottle.

- **Yattarna** is the flagship white wine, a multi-region Chardonnay blend. The first vintage was 1995, and I feel it took time to find its legs. Now, I consider it to be one of the top Chardonnays in Australia.

- In the more affordable camp look for **Bin 311 Chardonnay**. Fruit is sourced from premium cool climate sites and shows delightful lime, peach and spice characters. **Bin 51 Riesling** is from Eden Valley and displays all the classic regional markers – lime zest, mineral and floral notes.

MOUNT LOFTY RANGES ZONE

This Zonal GI encompasses the regions of Adelaide Hills, Adelaide Plains and Clare Valley. While it can be used on a label, it is not common to find a wine labelled with this GI, producers generally opting for the better known names of either Adelaide Hills or Clare Valley. You do see the Adelaide Plains GI used from time to time. You feel that some of the Zonal GIs may have been set as a 'just in case measure' whereby a producer sourcing fruit from multiple regions can use the broader appellation. This makes sense for some Zonal GIs, but not for others.

ADELAIDE HILLS
(Peramagnk Country)

Mount Lofty is the highest point in the Adelaide Hills. It was named by Matthew Flinders in 1802, when he circumnavigated the coastline of Australia. A later explorer, Collet Barker, climbed it in 1831, providing sightings of the Port River, which would help Colonel William Light determine the place for the settlement of Adelaide in 1836.

According to some records, there were as many as 530 hectares of vines in the 1870s but they were all but gone by the 1930s. The removal of Imperial Preference, which had favoured Australian produce exported to the United Kingdom, was largely responsible for this demise but the challenges of cool climate viticulture and the lie of the land were also likely contributors. For several decades the land was used for dairy and beef cattle, sheep, fruit and vegetables. The rebirth of the Adelaide Hills started in 1976 with the founding of Petaluma by Brian Croser.

The 70 kilometre long, 30 kilometre wide Adelaide Hills GI is in the Mount Lofty Ranges, bordered on the north by Barossa and Eden Valley and to the south by McLaren Vale and Langhorne Creek. Adelaide Hills is the main GI and there are two subregional GIs, Lenswood and Piccadilly.

It is a region defined by elevation, which varies between 300 and 700 metres above sea level. Given the undulating nature of the topography, site selection is very important and, along with elevation, dictates what can and cannot be ripened. Most of the region is decidedly cool but there are warm pockets, which explains the diversity of grapes planted. Generalization about climate and suitable varieties is particularly dangerous in this region!

Pinot Noir and Chardonnay do exceptionally well here, and fruit sourced from the cooler sites often finds its way into the production of excellent sparkling wine. Shiraz plantings are increasing. The cool, sunny climate has helped Adelaide Hills develop a stellar reputation for Sauvignon Blanc and the regional expression has become somewhat of a benchmark for this variety in Australia. Grüner Veltliner is a more recent star with close to 20 producers now making at least one version.

The Adelaide Hills has become a hot spot for the natural wine movement. In a district called the Basket Range, a community of like-minded souls started making low intervention wines. Initially led by Anton von Klopper from Lucy Margaux, it became the spiritual home of the natural wine movement in Australia. All manner of producers from around the country are now making natural and lo-fi wines but this area remains a special place in the evolution of the movement. (See p. 129 for more on Australia's natural wine.)

Area under vine

3,960 hectares[29]

Climate

The region is very hilly, with a multitude of valleys and sub-valleys. Altitude and different aspects give rise to various mesoclimates but overall the climate is cool. Some west-facing slopes in the northern area are warm enough to ripen Cabernet Sauvignon. Most of the region is best suited to early ripening varieties.

29 Source: National Vineyard Scan 2020 and ABS

Soils

Quite varied but predominantly grey-brown or brown loamy sands. Some patches of sandy soils.

Varieties

Sauvignon Blanc, Pinot Noir, Chardonnay and Shiraz are the primary grapes but Riesling, Pinot Gris, Grüner Veltliner and small amounts of Nebbiolo, Barbera and Dolcetto are also grown.

Main wine styles

Sauvignon Blanc is the most planted white variety in the region and is often referred to as the benchmark for Sauvignon Blanc in Australia. The style tends towards ripe, tropical flavours of guava and passionfruit. Wines have crisp acidity with great length and intensity. The herbal notes tend to be background noise in the best examples.

Chardonnay here yields complex medium-weight wines with good natural acidity. As is reflected in other regions, oak use, lees work, and malolactic conversions are more carefully handled these days, leading to far better regional and site expression and more harmonious wines. A decent amount of Chardonnay, especially from the cooler sites ends up in the production of sparkling wine.

Adelaide Hills is the top region in the state for the production of high-quality Pinot Noir. The style is typically medium-bodied with ripe cherry and strawberry fruit, and soft tannins. A proportion of Pinot Noir ends up being used in the production of quality sparkling wines, the best and most classic of which are all traditional method and typically use Pinot Noir and Chardonnay to form the backbone. There is some Pinot Meunier in the region and that finds its way into several wines.

There are some very fine Shirazes now being made in the region. The cooler climate tends to give medium-weight wines with raspberry-scented fruit, pepper and savoury elements.

Grüner Veltliner is doing well in the region and is a sort of unique speciality. Wines are light- to medium-bodied with vibrant pear and citrus notes. Some examples do show the characteristic white pepper element. They do not have the same weight as the top Austrian examples but that likely has something to do with climate and possibly vine age.

Producers

Tappanapa Wines

www.tapanappa.com.au

This venture was started by industry legend and Adelaide Hills pioneer Brian Croser in 2002 after Petaluma was sold to Lion Nathan Group. The wines are now made back at the Petaluma winery, which Croser started in 1976 and bought back in 2014. Full circle indeed. Most of his wines are not made from Adelaide Hills fruit (see Wratonbully and Fleurieu entries) but the Chardonnay from his original Tiers vineyards has always been one of Australia's best and is still fantastic.

Shaw and Smith

www.shawandsmith.com

This venture was started in 1995 by Michael Hill-Smith MW and his cousin Martin Shaw. Michael was Australia's first Master of Wine so you knew from the start that the quality of wines would be top notch. Shaw and Smith Sauvignon Blanc is the benchmark for this variety in the region and beyond. It shows the very best of what this variety can do in Adelaide Hills. Vibrant, juicy and fresh, it shows tropical notes more redolent of passionfruit and guava than the herbal, gooseberry monotony of too many Sauvignon Blancs from Marlborough, New Zealand.

Their M3 Chardonnay is fantastic, and the Pinot Noir has hit its stride in more recent vintages. This is the very best winery to start with if you are trying to get a grip on what classic Adelaide Hills wines are all about.

BK Wines

www.bkwines.com.au

Brendon and Kirstyn Keys started this venture in 2007 and have quietly made a name for themselves by focusing on making pure, expressive wines from single vineyard sites, predominantly in the Adelaide Hills. They are very experimental and don't mind having a go at different styles, blends and techniques. Some wines are classic. Some are more fun, bordering on edgy. All are worth looking at. Swaby Chardonnay has always been one of my favourite wines, classically structured with texture, weight and layers of complexity. Gin Gin Clone Chardonnay and Yandra Chardonnay are also really good. The Ovum Grüner Veltliner spends a full year on lees and is savoury, textured, long and complex. Ramato is exactly that, a skin contact Pinot Gris that is structured and delicious. Skin n Bones is an extended skin contact Pinot Noir that is both vibrant and savoury. Great wines, lovely people and a fantastic place to visit if you are in the Hills.

Ashton Hills

www.ashtonhills.com.au

This pioneer Pinot Noir producer from the region was started by Stephen George in 1982. The site is at 570 metres above sea level in the Piccadilly subregion. Over the years George experimented with up to 26 Pinot Noir clones, ultimately settling on five key clones that now form the backbone of the Reserve and Estate Pinot Noirs.

He sold to Wirra Wirra (see p. 151) and is 'sort of' retired but you will still find him on the property if he is not in Burgundy. The Piccadilly Estate cuvée is the more accessible wine, typically delicious right out of the gate. The Reserve is a classic and rewards some patient cellaring.

Deviation Road

www.deviationroad.com

Hamish and Kate Laurie have quietly gone about crafting some of the best sparkling wines in Adelaide Hills and, for that matter, Australia. Kate honed her skills working in Champagne and her passion for traditional method sparkling wines is obvious from the minute you sit down to taste with her. The multi-vintage Altair Brut Rosé is a great place to start; a salmon-coloured citrus, red apple and raspberry charmer. Loftia Vintage Brut is fantastic and you simply have to try the Vintage Beltana Blanc de Blancs, a 100 per cent Chardonnay masterpiece. Tight and taut with electric acidity when released (as classic *blanc de blancs* should be), it unfolds into a complex, layered, lemon curd and toasted brioche flavoured beauty with a few years of patience. Really fantastic wines. Tasmania receives a lot of attention for sparkling wines, and for good reason, but a visit to Deviation Road delivers a vibrant reminder that Adelaide Hills has history and pedigree too.

Gentle Folk Wines

www.gentlefolk.com.au

Gareth and Rainbo Belton were marine scientists but decided to start their wine venture in 2012 after spending time in Basket Range helping James Erskine (Jauma), Alex Schulkin (The Other Right) and other early pioneers of the Basket Range wine movement. Starting out with just a few barrels they have carved out a boutique business making around 5,000 cases. Early wines were very 'natty'. Gareth once mentioned to me that, 'I got to a point where I didn't like my own wines.' He then started spending more time with Taras Ochota and tightened up what he was doing. The wines are now some of my favourites from the Basket Range. Rainbow Juice is a must; a textured, pale pink beauty. Vin de Sofa is a deliciously juicy light red – a wine to be gulped heartily. Preferably from a tumbler. The refinement in his red wines is obvious. Village Pinot Noir is the perfect entry into his world of delicately framed, aromatic wines. Monomeith and Little Creek are two single vineyard Pinot Noirs that show more depth and complexity but are still fragrant and delicately framed. Just perfect, and the wine styles mirror the name of the venture.

Ochota Barrels

www.ochotabarrels.com

I was at a casual dinner with a work colleague in Sydney many years ago and he grabbed my arm excitedly and said, 'Dude, you have to try this Grenache.' It was Ochota Barrels Fugazi Grenache. He poured me a glass and it stopped me mid-sentence. It was fragrant, medium-bodied, full of red fruit and pepper spice with a curious long umami-laced finish. It was such a departure from what I knew of this variety that I had to find out more. When I met owner Taras Ochota, he did to me what he did to most people in his orbit, and it was impossible not to fall in

Gamay vineyard planted by Taras on his property in the Basket Ranges, Adelaide Hills.

love with his easy charm. We tragically lost him in 2020 and it was and remains devastating. As I sit writing about him three years on, I still have to choke back tears. Aussie journalist and old friend Nick Ryan sums it up: 'In years to come when people write about the history of Australian wine, when it comes to my generation, Taras is who they will look to. At a time when Australian wine had come to be known internationally as prestigious, big, bombastic and overblown, Taras's wines were elegant, beautifully poised and immediately drinkable. He made the wine world reconsider Australian wine at an important time.'

His wife, Amber, a very accomplished winemaker in her own right, is carrying on the legacy with the help of Louis Schofield (Worlds Apart Wines) who helped Taras with multiple vintages prior to his passing. The wines are still magic. All the wines have some sort of musical connection, be it a band name, song title or lyric. And, yes, there are surfing references.

Most of the wines are from Adelaide Hills sourced fruit but the Grenache-based wines are from McLaren Vale. Fugazi is a must. This wine helped change perceptions of what is possible with Grenache and for some, what new Australian wine was. The Green Room is a lighter, juicier, Grenache-dominant wine that is perfect lightly chilled. Texture Like Sun is a blend of so many varieties that it is not worth listing and, in any case, that is not the point. It is about the style, which is a lovely, gently layered red wine. A Forest is a fragrant Pinot Noir, and look for his collaboration with Arizona winemaker Maynard James Keenan, Sense of Compression, which sees Grenache co-fermented with a touch of Gewurztraminer.

Worlds Apart Wines

www.worldsapartwines.com
This was established by Louis Schofield, who cut his winemaking teeth under Taras Ochota. He sources fruit from Eden Valley, McLaren Vale and Adelaide Hills. Hope Forest is a citrusy and savoury lightly skinsy (skin contact) Sauvignon Blanc from Adelaide Hills. Blue Eyes is an Adelaide Hills Gamay and is fresh and lively. A wine to chill, and drink with loud, slurping gulps – super delicious. A producer to keep an eye on, Schofield has a fantastic wine bar in Adelaide too, called the Hellbound Wine Bar (www.hellboundwinebar.com). Find time to visit.

Charlotte Dalton Wines

www.charlottedaltonwines.com.au
Charlotte Hardy (Dalton is her middle name) has been making wine for

over 20 years – I first came across her wines when she was Adelaide Hills based. She now has a winery and cellar door based in Port Elliot on the south coast of the Southern Fleurieu on the border of Currency Creek. She makes really interesting wines from classic varieties but most have a low intervention, cheeky bent. Her wines are from fruit sourced from several South Australian GIs but I have slotted her into Adelaide Hills based on several excellent wines she makes from the region. Her Love Me Love You Semillon is barrel fermented and aged on lees giving it a more textured, lemon curd character with length and complexity. One of the first wines I tried from her, it is still a favourite. She sources the fruit from a site in Balhannah in the Adelaide Hills. Also from Adelaide Hills fruit is her beautifully fragrant and elegantly structured A Change is Gonna Come Pinot Noir. Love Me Love You Shiraz is a delicious medium-weight, raspberry accented beauty. With many other lovely wines from fruit sourced in different regions this is a really good producer.

Murdoch Hill

www.murdochhill.com.au

Michael Downer's grandfather bought a farm that is now the home vineyard, although not planted to vines until 1998. This is very much a family-run business and one of the more exciting producers in the Hills, with a strong line up of Chardonnay and Pinot Noir plus a few fantastic Syrahs.

The regular bottling of Chardonnay and Tilbury are excellent, Pheaton Pinot Noir is my go-to in the line-up and Ridley Pinot x Three (a blend of Pinot Noir, Pinot Meunier and Pinot Gris) is a delight. Landau Syrah is lights-out delicious and walks a tightrope of density and concentration with elegance, fragrance and structure. It is one of my favourite cooler climate examples of the variety.

The Pawn Wine Co.

www.thepawn.com.au

Established in 2002 by Tom Keelan and his wife Rebecca Willson (of Bremerton in Langhorne Creek), this label focuses mostly on Adelaide Hills, with a few Langhorne Creek wines. There is excellent Grüner Veltliner and a very perfumed Chardonnay which is the result of the Entav clone they have in the vineyard. The Sangiovese is really good too as is the curious Maturana Tinta they make. According to Sarah Jane Evans MW this what they call Bastardo/Trousseau in Rioja. In this instance it yields a juicy, fresh berried, fun-to-drink red.

Unico Zelo

www.unicozelo.com.au

Brendan and Laura Carter are making exciting wines here. A lot of them. Wines are made in the same vein as Koerner. Although they are Adelaide Hills based, they also source fruit from the Riverland and Clare Valley, often blending different regions together. The results are great. Pastafarian is a Nebbiolo, Sangiovese, Merlot and Nero d'Avola blend from Adelaide Hills and Clare Valley and is a great introduction to what is affectionately called 'Smashable Reds'. These crunchy, juicy, fresh red wines are meant to be easy to drink and are ideal with food. Fresh AF is a Nero d'Avola–Zibbibo blend and is aromatic, vibrant and one of my favourites. There's plenty to try here.

Hahndorf Hill Winery

www.hahndorfhillwinery.com.au

This excellent producer has a tight focus on Austrian varieties. They were pioneer Grüner Veltliner growers and make one of the best versions in the region, and by extension, the country. Try the Gru Grüner Veltliner. It has the savoury white pepper spice that you see in top Austrian versions but also displays grapefruit and guava-like tropical characters. It is super delicious, and the whole range of Grüners is worth looking at. They have just debuted a field blend called Brother Nature. It is a blend of Pinot Blanc, Welschriesling, Grüner Veltliner, Riesling, Sauvignon Blanc, Chardonnay, Gewurztraminer, Savagnin, Muscat Blanc, Hárslevelű, Chenin Blanc and Muscadelle. But it really doesn't matter what is in the blend, it is all about the style; it is a delicious, super fun wine. There are also two must-try red wines – a Saint Laurent and a Blaufrankisch. In summary, a very cool producer making interesting wines from varieties that you are not expecting – very refreshing.

Some Basket Range producers to seek out

Lucy M Wines

www.lucymwines.com

Founder Anton von Klopper, who makes his wines on the Lucy Margaux Farm, was one of the early pioneers of natural wines in Australia and some see him as the Godfather of the movement. He is not an easy guy to get to know but my conversations with him have always been interesting. He is a gentle, thoughtful and passionate man who cares deeply about what he is doing. As natural wine was building steam, I will openly confess to struggling with the concept as well as some of the wines. I mention this because it was a Lucy Margaux wine that shifted my thoughts, the Wild Man Blanc, a skin contact Sauvignon Blanc (see opposite for more on Australian Natural Wine). It is an up and down ride for me with Anton's wines, but when they are on form, I love them. The Tête d'oeuf Sauvignon Blanc on skins, the Vino Rosato and La Sariette Pinot Blanc were all delicious and really stood out the last time I tried them.

Jauma

www.jauma.com

James Erskine is a lapsed Sommelier making a lovely array of wines. Most of his fruit is sourced in McLaren Vale but he is firmly entrenched in Adelaide Hills. Like Raindrops and Lilies are two lovely, lightweight, fragrant in style Grenache wines. Fujisan Chenin Pet Nat is a frothy, appley delight and the still Chenin from Blewitt Springs is vibrant, textured and savoury. Jauma is a great place to start if you are natural wine curious.

The Other Right

www.theotherrightwines.com

Minimal intervention wines are made here by husband and wife team Alex Schulkin and Galit Shachaf. Their new Multicoloured Sunrise is a delicious take on skin contact Pinot Gris. Bright Young Thing White and Bright Young Thing Red are perfect descriptions of the bottle contents. Fawn is their Chardonnay and Counting Stars is their skinsy, savoury version of Chardonnay.

Commune of Buttons

www.communeofbuttons.com.au

These low intervention wines are made by Jasper and Sophie Button. Look for the Basket Town Pinot Noir, ABC Chardonnay and Gloria Pinot Noir.

Basket Range Wines

www.basketrangewine.com.au

A pioneering property in the Basket Range area of Adelaide Hills, with 13 hectares planted to Pinot Noir, Merlot, Cabernet Sauvignon, Chardonnay, Petit Verdot and a small amount of Saperavi.

Natural and low-intervention wine in Australia

The emergence of natural wine certainly rattled the global wine cage. It seemed to have a particularly profound impact in Australia. Australia's early wine export success was predicated on vibrant, clean, varietally expressive and affordable wines. Technical proficiency in viticulture, winemaking and marketing laid the foundation for more than 20 years of export growth. At the same time, the domestic wine show system had a strong role in shaping wine styles within the parameters of what was deemed, at that time, to be varietally and/or regionally correct. Australian wine shows are interesting. They have evolved over time but for many years they shaped the look and feel of Australian wines with a very systematic and disciplined approach to judging. This was very important for a period of time as it served to give focus and direction and, to quote Len Evans, 'improve the breed'. Over time the parameters became didactic and intolerant. Creativity was stifled. A perception was forming that our wines, while technically correct and fault free, were lacking individuality and character. Blame cannot be laid solely at the feet of the wine show system in Australia, but it certainly had a hand in keeping the style boundaries very tight.

An attitude shift was fomenting before the first natural wines emerged. A younger generation that simply wanted to step outside these boundaries and see what else was possible, started to strike out and have a go. The early days of the natural wine movement in Australia started with the Natural Selection Theory, a group made up of Adelaide Hills-based winemakers James Erskine of Jauma, Anton van Klopper of Lucy Margaux (now Lucy M) and Tom Shobbrook of Shobbrook Wines, with Sydney artist Sam Hughes.

They did things differently. They hid amphorae of wine behind velvet drapes and played music to them. They danced, sang, and jumped on tables at trade tastings. James Erskine has opera training and is a very handy singer as it turns out. Journalist Christina Pickard says, 'Australia already had a number of small-scale producers that practised their own versions of traditional, low-tech winemaking. But they weren't as disruptive or ideological as the Natural Selection Theory. Thanks to the foundation laid in large part by the Natural Selection Theory, few corners of the wine world have been more profoundly affected by the natural wine movement than Australia.'

Australia's first natural wine fair also had an important role in the evolution of natural wine in Australia. Rootstock was the brainchild of Giorgio de Maria, Mike Bennie and James Hird. The first was in 2014 and the last was in 2017. It was a very important festival for bringing together aspiring natural and low intervention winemakers, but it was not just about wine. It brought together food and art from First Nations communities and served to broaden Australia's understanding of beer and sake, spirits and coffee, raw-milk cheese and heirloom livestock. It crowd-funded First Nations agriculture through Bruce Pascoe's Gurandgi Munjie project, and in the final year, as a way of dealing with waste, distilled the wine collected from the previous festival's spit buckets into a spirit. It was bottled and called Kissing a Stranger. I did not try it.

I certainly struggled with early natural wine experiences and still have limited tolerance for problematic wines. I am by no means a lover of technically perfect wines but brettanomyces, mousiness, excessive volatility and other microbial issues that marked many natural wines have never been appealing to me. These elements are tolerated and indeed enjoyed by some and that is fine. I feel that they confer a sameness in wine regardless of variety or origin and are equally as unappealing as the manipulated stamp of a heavy-handed winemaker. The late Taras Ochota summed it up as only he could in a text exchange which I am so happy I kept. He was not a fan of being labelled a natural wine producer. I quizzed him on this, and his response was: 'I am part of a sub-category of natural wines. It's the Beautiful Wine Movement. Gorgeously grown and made organically but clean and delicious. Brett, VA, spritz, aldehyde etc. that's just natural wine excuse shite.' Natural wine has evolved beautifully in Australia, and I love how it has affected our ideas on colour, clarity and varietal expression. Style is front and centre and the very best natural and low-intervention wines in Australia right now are delicious and exciting.

I have deliberately not segmented the natural and low-intervention wines in this book. I certainly mention it where needed but feel strongly that the complexity of Australian wine includes everything being produced so a separation was unnecessary. Many of the best natural and low-intervention producers are listed within the regional chapters and drawing a line in the sand as to who is working minimally is not something I wish to do. However, for the sake of quick reference, the following producers are my picks to pay attention to:

- Lucy M Wines www.lucymwines.com (p. 127)
- Jauma Wines www.jauma.com (p. 128)
- Commune of Buttons www.communeofbuttons.com.au (p. 128)
- Gentle Folk www.gentlefolk.com.au (p. 123)
- The Other Right www.theotherrightwines.com (p. 128)
- Basket Range Wines www.basketrangewine.com.au (p. 128)

- BK Wines www.bkwines.com.au (p. 122)
- Ochota Barrels www.ochotabarrels.com (p. 124)
- Vino Volta www.vinovolta.com.au (p. 279)
- Si Vintners www.sivintners.com (p. 262)
- Latta Vino www.lattavino.com.au
- Cobaw Ridge www.cobawridge.com.au (p. 206)
- Joshua Cooper Wines www.joshuacooperwines.com.au (p. 206)
- Small Fry Wines www.smallfrywines.com.au (p. 110)
- Yetti and the Kokonut www.yettiandthekokonut.com.au (p. 111)
- Patrick Sullivan Wines www.patricksullivan.com.au (p. 245)
- William Downie Wines www.williamdownie.com.au (p. 245)
- Eminence Wines www.eminencewines.com.au (p. 233)
- Harkham Wines www.harkhamwine.com.au (p. 70)

CLARE VALLEY
(Ndadjuri & Kaurna Country)

Clare Valley is located north-west of the Barossa Valley. Its history dates to 1840, when John Horrocks established Hope Farm and planted the first vines. Development of vineyard land was slow in those early years but by 1870 there were close to 600 hectares of vines.

The climate data is misleading and suggests a warmer region. The daytime temperatures during the critical ripening months can indeed be hot but the cooling breezes and consistently cold nights have a distinct moderating effect. Most vineyard sites sit at between 300 and 550 metres above sea level and this is an important factor in the shaping of the wine styles.

Clare has a deserved reputation for being one of Australia's premier Riesling-growing regions. There are actually far more red grape varieties planted than white.

Main wine styles

Classic Clare Valley Riesling is dry, with characteristic lemon and lime flavours and racy, crisp acidity when young. As it ages, complex characters of minerality and white pepper spice emerge. The very best sites can produce long-lived wines. Most benefit from 5–7 years of bottle age and can evolve for decades. The two best-known subregions for Riesling in Clare are

Watervale and Polish Hill but the variety is grown throughout the region.

The historically austere style is evolving making the wines easier to drink younger. Grosset attributes this to vine age in some cases. Working with a little residual sugar and dabbling with skin contact has also had an effect. Either way, you are met with a firm, laser-sharp backbone of acidity.

Clare Shiraz is typically full-flavoured with ripe blackberry, spice and mint characteristics. The strong diurnal temperature shifts allow for acid retention and a vibrant fruit quality.

Cabernet Sauvignon also does very well in Clare, displaying dark, rich, black fruit characters with firm but plush tannins. Often blended with Shiraz and sometimes a little Malbec.

Area under vine

5,060 hectares[30]

Climate

The temperature data in the Clare is often said to be very misleading due to the large diurnal shifts. Drops of temperatures from 35°C during the day to 13°C at night are common during main ripening months. Altitude and aspect create a multitude of meso- and microclimates. Protection from or exposure to cooling maritime breezes has an impact on which varieties do well.

Soils

There is a range of different recognized soil types, with underlying geology dating back over 500 million years. The Polish Hill River subregion has 10 million-year-old broken slate and ironstone soils and the Watervale subregion has underlying limestone soils.

Varieties

Riesling, Shiraz and Cabernet Sauvignon make up 80 per cent of the total plantings in the Clare Valley. While this is the varietal triumvirate that rules Clare, there are many other varieties planted. Most occupy under 100 hectares but are important in painting the full picture of Clare Valley's excitement. Time will tell but for me, so far, the interests sits with Grenache (one of the original varieties planted), Fiano, Nero d'Avola, Malbec, Sangiovese and Tempranillo. It is also home to Australia's first Assyrtiko plantings.

30 Source: National Vineyard Scan 2020 and ABS

Grosset's distinctive and dramatic Cabernet-based Gaia vineyard planted at 550 metres above sea level in the Clare Valley, South Australia.

Producers

Grosset

www.grosset.com.au

Jeffrey Grosset is a legend in Australian wine, one of the great Riesling producers in Australia and recognized globally for the quality of his wines. He is fastidious in everything he does and that shines through in his wines. A recent visit was less about tasting and more about discussing farming practices which are now A-grade certified organic and biodynamic.

Grosset Rieslings are a must. His Polish Hill Riesling is brilliant, with racy acidity, classic lime zest and mineral notes, it is a wine that needs cellar time. Springvale is from Watervale and while the racy Riesling elements are ever-present, the fruit is rounder and a tad softer. Both wines are essential for anyone wanting to understand the differences between the two famous Riesling districts in Clare. Grosset refers to them as hard rock and soft rock sites. Polish Hill is the hard rock site due to the iron-flecked blue slate. Watervale is the soft rock site, with underlying limestone soils.

Gaia is a middleweight, fragrant blend of Cabernet Sauvignon and Cabernet Franc. The vineyard sits at 550 metres above sea level. My first visit to this isolated, stunning site had me asking Jeffrey what the hell he was thinking. But clearly it works. It is one of the great Cabernet blends in Australia. He has recently experimented with newer varieties and the Apiana is a lovely lemongrass-scented Fiano, Nereus is a vibrant, fresh and floral Nero d'Avola.

Cordon-cut Riesling at Mount Horrocks. These grapes deliver rich, concentrated juice needed for the decadent and delicious Cordon Cut Riesling.

Mount Horrocks

www.mounthorrocks.com

Owner Stephanie Toole is Jeffrey Grosset's partner but does not sit in his shadow. She is making fantastic wines at her small production, single-vineyard focused estate. Also A-grade certified organic and biodynamic, there is nothing from Mount Horrocks that I can't recommend. The Cordon Cut Riesling has been her point of difference wine for years. It is a sweet Riesling made by cutting the vine in the latter stages of harvest and allowing the fruit to 'raisinate' on the vine (see photo). It is one of Australia's best sweet wines, and 2022 was the thirtieth vintage. The Watervale Riesling rivals Grossets as one of the valley's best examples. Her Semillon and Nero d'Avola are also worth seeking out. She is a fantastic producer but does not go about trying to garner accolades in the press or at international wine competitions. She just quietly goes about her business, crafting laser-focused, delicious wines.

Adelina Wines

www.adelina.com.au

This property is right next door to Wendouree and is run by Col McBryde and his wife Jen. Along with Mount Horrocks and Grosset, this is one of the few producers with organic certification in the Clare. The estate has old vine Shiraz (1915), Grenache (1940) and Pedro Ximenez (1915), combined with newer plantings of Shiraz, Malbec and Mourvedre. They have a negociant arm of the business where they source fruit from select growers in the Clare, McLaren Vale and Adelaide Hill. The Adelina Estate Wines are all from the property.

The Estate Field Blend – Shiraz, Grenache, Mataro, Ugni Blanc, Roussanne and Carignan – is awesome, as is the Estate Grenache. The Ruchioch Riesling is tight, taut and laser focused. The Shiraz Mataro has powerful fruit but with purity and restraint and a distinct iron-like minerality reminiscent of Wendouree wines. Col is a pleasure to spend time with. Frighteningly smart and very thoughtful, he is constantly tinkering with his farming practices and his approach to making the wines. In June 2023 Col won the Young Gun of Wine 'Vineyard of the Year', which speaks volumes about his commitment and focus. One of my favourite Clare Valley producers.

Vickery Wines

www.vickerywines.com.au

John Vickery has been instrumental in shaping the history of Riesling in Australia. He worked his first vintage back in 1951 and his career began at Leo Buring in 1955 at the Chateau Leonay winery. The focus was on Eden Valley and Watervale fruit. Without any modern-day processing, equipment, winemaking was quite a crude process, which shows true testament to his outstanding ability. Vickery's hallmark approaches were cool fermentation and careful handling, so it was in the latter years with the introduction of refrigeration and airbag presses that John was best able to capture the Riesling grape's fine delicate flavours. He is a living legend in the Australian wine business and was awarded the Order of Australia medal for 'service to the wine industry as an oenologist, particularly through the development of innovative methods for Riesling production'. The current wines are still focused on Clare Valley and Eden Valley fruit. The Clare Valley wines are the Watervale Riesling and the Reserve Watervale Riesling.

Wines by KT

www.winesbykt.com

Kerri Thompson is a gem. Having spent eight years working at the classic Leasingham Wines she went on to set up her own venture, which is primarily focused on her first love, Riesling. Her main vineyard source is the Peglidis vineyard owned by Bunny and Yvonne Peglidis. All the fruit for her Peglidis, Melva and Pazza Rieslings are from this site. This triumvirate of superb Rieslings should be your first point of call with her wines.

Wendouree

(no website)

One of Australia's great red wine producers, Wendouree has a storied history. Alfred Percy Birks and his brother planted the first vines in 1892, establishing A.P. Birks' Wendouree Cellars. In 1917, Alfred Birks handed over responsibilities to his son Roly, who extended the plantings in 1919, 1920 and 1940. After 53 years at the helm, Roly Birks retired in 1970, aged 77. He eventually sold to someone who could not maintain the property and it was left somewhat unattended. It has been in the custodianship of Tony and Lita Brady since 1974. The wines are amazing, but you can't just rock up to the door and try to buy them. They are only sold on a mailing list – and good luck getting on it. I have been fortunate to visit and taste several times and feel privileged every time. To say these are classic Clare red wines is, rather strangely, incorrect. The wines are classic Wendouree, such is the uniqueness of structure, character and flavour. All are brilliant. All need cellaring to show their greatness. The full range includes Shiraz, Shiraz–Malbec, Shiraz–Mataro, Malbec, Cabernet Sauvignon and Cabernet–Malbec. If I was to pick a favourite it would be the Cabernet–Malbec but I will happily drink any of the wines whenever offered. They also make a sneaky sweet wine, a super delicious Muscat of Alexandria.

Jim Barry Wines

www.jimbarry.com

This is an established producer whose wines I have been drinking for as long as I can remember. Peter Barry is the patriarch, having taken over from his father Jim. Sons Tom and Sam are being groomed and are basically running the show at present. Lodge Hill Riesling is a go-to everyday drinking wine. They were the first to plant Assyrtiko in Australia and it is a lovely, lemon scented, vibrant wine. The McRae Wood Shiraz has always been my favourite red in the Barry stable but I will never say no to the Armagh, their flagship Shiraz. It is ripe, concentrated and layered with flavour. A top shelf Clare Valley producer.

Miss Zilm Clare Valley

www.misszilmwines.com.au

Keeda Zilm spent nearly two decades winemaking in the Clare Valley before eventually taking the the plunge to establish her own label. She is part of the Usual Suspects Collective owned by the Hesketh Group. She makes really good Riesling and a delicious Pinot Gris. There is also a Fiano, and a Shiraz–Malbec but I have not tried either of them. A great producer that only recently popped up on my radar.

Koerner

www.koernerwine.com.au

Damon and Jono Koerner grew up in the Clare but are relative newcomers as wine producers. The focus here is lightness, freshness and vibrancy for both white and red wines. They work with traditional and newer varieties and all the wines are a pleasure to drink. The Clare Red Wine and Watervale Riesling are great starting points. The Rolle Vermentino is vibrant and lemony but with texture and savoury notes. Also try the Mammolo Sciacarello and La Korse. A really exciting producer that should be on your radar.

Pikes Wines

www.pikeswines.com.au

Andrew and Cathy Pike were founding partners of Pikes Wines in 1984 in partnership with Andrew's brother Neil. The Pike family goes back generations, producing authentic, handcrafted beverages in South Australia since 1886. Pikes Beer was first sold in 1886, followed by soft drinks and cordials from 1940, then Pikes wine from 1985 and beer again from 1996.

Although they are Riesling specialists they make a full range of classic and contemporary Clare wines. Pikes Traditionale Riesling is a blend of fruit from various vineyards across the region and is a go-to example of classic Clare Valley Riesling. The Merle Riesling, a reserve bottling of the best parcels of fruit from their own estate in Polish Hill, is one of the regions' best examples of the variety. They play with quite a few Mediterranean varieties, so experiment with their Fiano and Sangiovese. Their Los Companeros Shiraz Tempranillo is a fantastic melding of the fruit and spice of Shiraz and the savoury rusticity of Tempranillo. A top-shelf classic Clare producer.

Paulette Wines

www.paulettwines.com.au

This producer has been family owned and operated since 1983. Top Rieslings come from their Polish Hill River site. Try the whole range. The regular Clare Valley Riesling, Organic Riesling, Polish Hill River Riesling and the 109 Reserve Riesling are all great They also make the vibrant, frothy Trillians Sparkling Riesling, which is super delicious.

Naked Run Wines

www.nakedrunwines.com.au

Steve Baraglia is Barossa born and raised but is now the senior wine-maker at Pikes. In late 2005 Steve and his wife Laura purchased a small vineyard in Sevenhill with Riesling, Shiraz and Cabernet Sauvignon. Their ethos is small production and low intervention. Attention to detail is obvious. The First Riesling, from their own site, is fantastic. The Hill 5 Shiraz–Cabernet is rich and full bodied but with textbook clarity and purity of fruit that defines the best Clare reds. The limited release Cabernet–Malbec is an absolute beauty and while it will most likely be hard to find, get a bottle if you can. This is a top small batch producer.

Andrew Kenny Wines

www.kennywine.net

In 2020 Victoria and Andrew Kenny found a run-down vineyard in the Auburn subregion, which they are slowly converting to organic practices. They also deal with small growers in Adelaide Hills and Polish Hill River. They make small batch wines from single vineyard sites. The Kabi Polish Hill River Riesling is drop-dead delicious. It captures the structure and racy acidity that defines the Polish Hill River district, but being off-dry, the palate is broader and more seductive; a chalky, pine–lime delight. This is a new producer to pay attention to.

FLEURIEU ZONE

This Zonal GI covers the regions of McLaren Vale, Langhorne Creek, Currency Creek, Kangaroo Island and Southern Fleurieu.

MCLAREN VALE
(Kaurna Country)

In 1838, senior surveyor John McLaren was commissioned to map areas south of Adelaide and did so down to what is now Sellicks Hill. It is likely, though not confirmed, that the region took its name from him. The first winery established in South Australia was Chateau Reynella (1838) in McLaren Vale but while Barossa and McLaren Vale share similar timelines for development they grew quite differently. Barossa has a distinct German history while McLaren Vale was initially settled and developed by British, and later Italian, immigrants.

McLaren Vale has 30 kilometres of coastline. No matter where you are, you can either see, smell or feel the ocean and this is a crucial element to understanding the DNA of the region. The vast majority of the vineyards sit at 50–150 metres above sea level, so major elevation is not a key factor, but the hillsides and breezes afford all manner of meso- and microclimates.

Water management is an important factor in Australian vineyard regions in general, but McLaren Vale has been a leading light in this area. It was the first region in Australia to manage its underground water source so that it is self-replenishing. It also built the first and largest water reclamation network so that 100 per cent of the irrigation water is from a sustainable resource rather than river water. In addition, a third source of water was developed by using treated, reclaimed grey water from Adelaide.

Diversity is what makes McLaren Vale one of Australia's more compelling regions. While Shiraz is still the most planted variety, at 54 per cent, the varietal mix is shifting. The region was swift to take positive strides in dealing with a changing environment and started the search for different varieties. It is important to note that this was not inspired by any market driven forces: it was about the future. The region is looking at varieties that hold their natural acidity and freshness, given the predictions on climate change.

Area under vine

7,308 hectares[31]

Climate

The climate is distinctly Mediterranean, with warm summers, mild winters and relatively low growing season humidity. Rainfall accumulation is mostly in the winter months. Breezes come down from the ranges of Mount Lofty and in from Gulf St Vincent.

Soils

Soils are extremely varied; this is one of the most geologically diverse wine regions on earth. There are more than 40 different geologies, ranging from 15,000 years old to 550 million years old. There's a veritable patchwork quilt of different soil and underlying geology, with various types of red and brown loam, yellow clay, distinctly sandy soils and some limestone (see McLaren Vale geology map).

Varieties

Shiraz, Cabernet Sauvignon and Grenache are the dominant red varieties, in that order. Chardonnay, strangely, is the dominant white variety but I am willing to bet that this will not be the case long term. Fiano, Vermentino, Tempranillo, Nero d'Avola, Aglianico, Barbera, Montepulciano and at least a dozen others are on the rise and point to a very exciting future.

31 Source: McLaren Vale Grape Wine and Tourism Association.

Main wine styles

McLaren Vale Shirazes have similar weight to those of the Barossa Valley but the structure and texture is different, with slightly grippier tannins and more lifted acidity. A range of subregional styles exists but there is a common thread of dark chocolate, blueberry and spice characters. Wines are typically medium to full bodied with vibrant, pure fruit in the best examples.

Cabernet Sauvignon shines in the cooler sites and in cooler vintages. Wines are full-bodied with ripe, soft tannins and classic blackcurrant/blackberry aromas and flavours.

Grenache is grown in several parts of the region and there are many old vines dating back to the late 1800s and early 1900s. Grenache is the shining star of McLaren Vale. Better vineyard management combined with experimentation and attention to detail in the winery has uncovered a much broader range of styles than many thought imaginable. The very best examples capture the ethereal, fragrant, red fruited elements of the variety, combined with present but gentle tannins and the hallmark white pepper spice. Over the past several vintages, Grenache has commanded the highest price per tonne of any variety picked in the region.

Tempranillo and Sangiovese are the two most planted of the emerging varieties. Both produce a range of styles but definitely lean more towards medium bodied, fresh and vibrant.

Nero d'Avola is one of the more promising varieties for the future. Styles can range from medium to full bodied but the best capture the floral elements of the variety and are not heavily extracted or too oaky.

The ocean influence in McLaren Vale. Wherever you are in the region, you can either see it, smell it or feel its effect.

There are some fun, easy-drinking Chardonnay-based wines in McLaren Vale but with due respect to the producers crafting solid examples, if you wanted to drink top-notch, regionally distinctive Chardonnay in Australia, McLaren Vale would not be on the list.

Of all the white varieties in the region, Fiano and Vermentino are the two that will form the significant part of the future of McLaren Vale white wines. Perfectly suited to the climate, the wines styles are lively, fresh and vibrant, with lemon-scented fruit and delicious natural acidity. The added viticultural management bonus is that these varieties don't require as much water to grow. Locally caught squid or the delicately fleshed King George Whiting, salad, bread and a chilled bottled of McLaren Vale Fiano or Vermentino – what else is needed? White Rhône varieties will also be part of the white wine style shift in the region. Grenache Blanc, Roussanne and Grenache Gris are shaping delicious, textured wines. See more on white Rhône varieties at Yangarra Estate, below.

Producers

Yangarra Estate Vineyard

www.yangarra.com

The history of this premier McLaren Vale estate dates to 1946 when the first Grenache vines were planted by Frederick Arthur Smart. The focus at Yangarra is single-vineyard and estate wines using southern Rhône varieties. Grenache and Shiraz are mainstays with Roussanne, Carignan, Terret Noir, Vaccerese, Bourboulenc, Picpoul Noir, Clairette Blanc, Grenache Blanc, Grenache Gris and Counoise. Certified organic and biodynamic in 2012, regenerative vineyard practices are at the core of the Yangarra philosophy. It is now owned by American company Jackson Family Wines, a move which seems to have benefited both. Yangarra has never made better wines than they are currently; there is so much to be excited about here. Grenache is vitally important and aside from the regular bottling, the Ovitelli, Hickinbotham and High Sands bottling are a wonderful snapshot of what is going on with this variety in McLaren Vale. Try them side by side if you get the opportunity. The white wines are on fire at present. Ovitelli Blanc is a ceramic egg fermented blend of Grenache Blanc, Roussanne, Clairette, Piquepoul and Bourboulenc. It has weight and texture but is simultaneously light on its feet. Lemony and floral, it has a lovely mineral-edged, savoury finish; a deliciously appropriate white wine that has its finger pointing directly to the future success of white varieties in Australia's warmer regions. The Roux Beauté Roussanne drives that message home with distinction.

SC Pannell Wines

www.pannell.com.au

Stephen Pannell grew up surrounded by wine. His parents started Moss Wood in Margaret River, before purchasing Domaine Pousse d'Or in Volnay. Steve was the chief red wine maker at Hardys and has worked

Yangarra at dawn. A serene home for the Rhône varieties they specialize in.

all over the world, including Aldo Vajra in Barolo, Chateau Mouton Rothschild, Domaine Dujac and Domaine Comte Lafon. He is one of Australia's best and most thoughtful winemakers, and whenever I talk to him, I learn something. Grenache is important here and he makes several. Basso Garnacha is the juicy, early drinking version, while the single vineyard McDonald Vineyard Grenache and Smart Vineyard Grenache are both fantastic. In 2021 he bought a 9.5 hectare vineyard in Blewitt Springs, which has 3.3 hectares of over 100-years-old Grenache vines. I look forward to the first release of that. Koomilya is his benchmark Shiraz. There are three bottlings: GT Block, JC Block and DC Block. It's a toss of the coin or a matter of personal preference as to which is better but all three are in the running for the best Shiraz wines in McLaren Vale.

Bekkers Wines

www.bekkerswine.au

This small production, high-quality estate was started by Emmanuelle and Toby Bekkers. Toby and Emmanuelle make the wines together now, but Toby has a strong background and reputation in viticulture. They make a Grenache, a Syrah and a Grenache–Syrah at present. All three are top notch. Most wines are sold on a mailing list but you can find them in select retail stores and restaurants around the country and in a few export markets. In 2020 they purchased the historic 20-hectare Clarendon Vineyard Estate. It is a steeply terraced site perched above the village of Clarendon that was originally planted between 1842 and

1848. All manner of trials and tribulations were attached to the vineyard, but the long and short of it is that it had fallen into disuse, so it needed some attention. I visited the site with Toby in 2022 and his excitement about it is palpable. They have ripped out some vines and are doing restorative work on the remaining ones – retraining, grafting, etc. Grenache, Shiraz, Cabernet Sauvignon and Cabernet Franc will be the focus. The first vintage release will be 2022. It is a stunning vineyard site and make no mistake, it is steep! I am excited to see what the Bekkers shape from it.

Hickinbotham Clarendon Vineyard

www.hickinbothamwines.com

The first vines were planted in 1971 by Alan David Hickinbotham, son of Australia's first wine science lecturer at the famous Roseworthy Agricultural College, Alan Robb Hickinbotham. This 186-hectare property of rolling hillsides remained under Hickinbotham family ownership for more than 40 years until it was purchased by the American wine company Jackson Family Wines in 2012. The vineyard has been farmed according to organic and biodynamic practices since 2019. The wines are made by American Chris Carpenter who heads to Australia several

Hickinbotham Clarendon vineyard – perfectly situated in the elevated environment of the Clarendon hamlet in McLaren Vale.

time a year. It is a pleasure spending time with Chris. He has a blue-chip background making wine in the Napa. He crafts some of the very best Cabernet Sauvignons in the region: Lokoya, La Jota and Cardinale to name a few. But he is like an excited schoolboy when you get him talking about Hickinbotham. He loves the property, and it has been great to watch the wines evolve under his guidance. I am particularly fond of the Trueman Cabernet Sauvignon but you cannot go wrong with any of the wines at present: Brooks Road Shiraz, The Revivalist Merlot, The Peake Cabernet–Shiraz, a gorgeous Cabernet Franc called The Nest and the recently released varietal Malbec.

Battle of Bosworth Wines

www.battleofbosworth.com.au

Joch Bosworth and his wife Louise Hemsley-Smith have been farming organically for longer than anyone in McLaren Vale. Their wines represent some of the best value in the region, given the high quality across the board. Puritan Shiraz is a vibrant blackberry spice bomb that is made without the addition of sulphur. The Cabernet Sauvignon is a great introduction to the vibrant, grippy style of this variety in McLaren Vale and their Touriga Nacional is concentrated, perfumed and charming. A delightful, family-run estate doing it right. If you catch Louise on the right day, she just might have some of her delicious scones at the ready.

D'Arenberg

www.darenberg.com.au

When I think of this producer I think of history, experimentation, innovation, and approachability – it is a McLaren Vale icon. Chester Osborn is the face of the winery and one of the more charismatic, quirky and lovely people you will meet in the Australian wine business. The Cube, their newish cellar door experience centre, captures the spirit of the place and provides an insight into Chester's iconoclastic character. 'Designed to entice and excite the senses', it is too complicated to explain here so you will just have to pay a visit. There is a dazzling array of wines. It is not possible to mention them all, but favourites include d'Arry's Original Grenache–Shiraz blend, Dead Arm Shiraz, Derelict Vineyard Grenache and Hermit Crab Viognier–Marsanne. There is plenty to explore. A visit to the Cube is a must if you are in the region: it is so much more than your regular cellar door experience. And visit the men's restroom. Just do it.

Paxton

paxtonwines.com

David Paxton was an early adopter of biodynamic farming practices and had fully converted by 2004. Paxton are making great examples of modern McLaren Vale wines. Freshness and vibrancy are key here. The early picked NOW Shiraz is all stainless steel fermented, a juicy, fresh version of a classic variety. I love the Graciano and their Tempranillo, not often exported, shows why there is quite a lot of this variety planted in the region. Quandong Farm is their top Shiraz; lifted, perfumed and delicious.

Oliver's Taranga

www.oliverstaranga.com

After six generations of self-proclaimed stubborn, competitive growers, winemaking duties and general management of this winery now fall on the shoulders of Corrina Wright, but this is still very much a family-run business. They also sell fruit and are perennial winners of contracts to supply Shiraz to Penfolds for Grange. The wines include those in the classic, rich McLaren Vale style typified by their flagship HJ Shiraz but they were also early adopters when it came to planting new varieties. There is delicious Fiano and Vermentino, a lovely iteration of Mencia and a delicious rosé made from the same grape. A family with tremendous grape growing history in the region is making lovely wines top to bottom. In June 2023, Oliver's Taranga went into partnership with Mike Press Wines to buy the Gemtree winery. This is an interesting development that will make them significant landholders in McLaren Vale.

Noon Wines

noonwinery.com.au

This family-run estate was established by David Noon in 1976. His son Drew Noon MW and Drew's wife Raegan now operate this property. Winemaking duties have been under Drew's guidance since 1996. They produce small batch handmade wines, all of them red. Attention to detail is obvious. 'Light wines. It's just not us!' says Noon. 'My heart is in producing full-bodied reds.' His statements might lead you to think you will be getting clunky old-school wines, but Drew Noon does not make clunky wines. His wines are powerful, rich and concentrated, but they are balanced. The High Noon Rosé is a delicious, strawberry-scented wine in a minerally, full-flavoured style. Noon Eclipse is mostly Grenache with a small amount of Shiraz and Graciano. It is layered, spicy and savoury with mouthfuls of ripe strawberry and mulberry flavours. He sources fruit from Langhorne Creek for his Reserve Shiraz and Reserve Cabernet Sauvignon.

Coriole

www.coriole.com

Coriole was started by the Lloyd family in the 1960s. Shiraz is the dominant variety in their vineyards, and they are custodians of some of the oldest Shiraz vines in the region. However, they were also curious about other varieties quite some time before it became the trendy talking point. They pioneered the planting of Sangiovese in 1985, Fiano in 2001 and Piquepoul in 2010. Those two whites are fantastic and a good place to start. The Chenin Blanc is also superb and has the capacity to age beautifully for 10–15 years. The Sangiovese, which qualifies as old vine now, is a treat, with cherry, dried flowers and a touch of cinnamon spice. The Lloyd Reserve is their flagship Shiraz made from the old vines. A rich, powerful, classically structured wine, it is best cellared for 5–10 years. There is a long family tradition of olive oil production (see Lloyd Brothers below) so be sure to get some if you visit.

Lloyd Brothers

www.lloydbrothers.com.au

The Lloyd Brothers, David and Matthew, are third generation South Australian vignerons. Their grandfather started planting vines and making wine in McLaren Vale in the 1960s. David owns and operates Lloyd Brothers Wine and Olive Company, and they use fruit from Matthew's Adelaide Hills vineyard. Olives have been a strong venture for this side of the Lloyd family and indeed this crop was the primary focus of the estate for many years. The estate is home to the first commercially planted Kalamata olive grove in South Australia. In terms of vines, it is planted to Shiraz Grenache and a small amount of Mourvèdre. General Manager Sam Temme helped David establish the wine brand from 2006–2010 and rejoined the team in 2020. He is an industry veteran whose wealth of global experience is helping fine-tune the future of the Lloyd Brothers brand. The estate grown Shiraz–Grenache and Shiraz–Grenache–Mourvedre are both delicious. A slightly off-the-radar producer but one to keep an eye on over the next few years.

Hither & Yon

www.hitherandyon.com.au

Brothers Richard and Malcolm Leask are behind what was originally intended to be a small venture that they dubbed their 'bottle project'. From this small beginning in 2001 it has grown to become one of the many exciting McLaren Vale producers. Regenerative farming is at the heart of the Hither & Yon philosophy. The Petit Blanc is a dry Muscat that is a perfectly perfumed aperitif wine. The Aglianico Rosé is citrusy and savoury. I really like the Carignan, though it needs a little cellaring to be at its most charming. The Grenache Touriga is a fennel-tinged, fresh cherry and berry delight. There are so many good wines to enjoy here.

Samuel's Gorge

www.gorge.com.au

Established by winemaker Justin McNamee in 2003, Samuel's Gorge is located on a ridge in an old shed built in 1853. His focus is Grenache, Shiraz, Mourvèdre, Graciano and Tempranillo. Justin is a charming, articulate guy who loves the region. He has an opinion or two on most things related to McLaren Vale which makes him a pleasure to spend time with. His raspberry-scented, savoury and textural Grenache has always struck a chord with me. The Graciano is a beauty too, medium-weight, perfumed and floral, and full of juicy red fruit character. A great producer, making small batch wines with attention to detail.

Ministry of Clouds

www.ministryofclouds.com.au

Bernice Ong and Julian Forwood are the charming and engaging duo that started Ministry of Clouds in 2013. This is an excellent producer from top to bottom. They do make Riesling from Clare and Chardonnay from Tasmania but the bulk of what they make, and their collective heart, lies in McLaren Vale. Their estate grown Picpoul is a lip-smacking, rather than lip-stinging delight. Full of crisp, lemony acidity, it has a ripe pear quality that you don't typically see in the Languedoc versions of this variety. It clearly shows how wonderfully suited to McLaren Vale this native southern French variety is. They make a delicious Grenache–Carignan blend and their Blewitt Springs single vineyard Shiraz shows why this district of the Vale has everyone excited. It is fragrant, lifted and beautifully balanced. The first wine I ever tried from Ministry of Clouds was their Tempranillo–Grenache blend and it remains a favourite. McLaren Vale Tempranillo has a lifted, floral character which works beautifully with the spice and red fruit of carefully grown Grenache. Lovely people, making excellent wines.

Brash Higgins

www.brashhiggins.com

Brad Hickey is a lapsed American sommelier who visited Australia and fell in love: with a woman and the country. His primary fruit source is their organically certified Omensetter Vineyard, but he does work with purchased fruit from the Riverland. His Amphora Project wines were my introduction and I still love them. There's a Nero d'Avola (labelled NDV) and the Riverland-sourced Zibibbo (labelled ZBO). The Chenin is from a Blewitt Springs site and is luscious and delicious with a distinct saline savouriness. These are exciting, well-made, distinctive wines.

Thistledown Wine Company

www.thistledownwines.com

Masters of Wine Giles Cooke and Fergal Tynan have very quickly established themselves as top-flight Grenache producers. They work with fruit from the Barossa and Adelaide Hills but it is their McLaren Vale Grenache-based wines that have captured and held my attention. The array of modern Grenache is dazzling, and seems to get better each vintage. Vagabond, She's Electric, Sands of Time and This Charming Man are all 100 per cent Grenache sourced from McLaren Vale and I struggle to pick a favourite. OK, Sands of Time is my favourite … today. The Walking With Kings Roussanne–Grenache Blanc is a complex, textured beauty that you can accidentally drink too much of. This fantastic producer needs to be on your radar.

Ox Hardy Wines

www.oxhardywines.com.au

Andrew Hardy is respected fifth generation winemaker with nearly four decades of experience in Adelaide Hills, Clare Valley, Coonawarra and McLaren Vale. The great-great-grandson of Thomas Hardy, who is considered the father of the South Australian wine industry, he has also worked vintages in California, Oregon and Bordeaux. Ox Hardy is his own brand started in 2018, but it is a sort of full-circle family story centred on the Upper Tintara Vineyard and Winery. Originally purchased by Thomas Hardy in 1870, the site fell into disuse in 1923, although it remained in the Hardy family's hands. Andrew has stepped back into this site and with the 2018 vintage made wines for the first time in 95 years using the original gravity-fed slate fermenters. I like the story behind this winery and Andrew is a very accomplished winemaker. The Ancestor Vines Shiraz is his flagship wine and is made from Shiraz vines planted by Thomas Hardy in 1891. The regular bottling of Shiraz from the Upper Tintara site is super delicious and a lovely, blueberry-scented, structured example of modern McLaren Vale Shiraz. The Fiano is delectable and juicy from vines planted in 2011.

Angoves Family Winemakers

www.angove.com.au

This fifth-generation family has interests in the Riverland (see p. 174) and owns vineyards in McLaren Vale as well as sourcing fruit in the region for a varied collection of wines. Their Warboys Vineyard is organic and biodynamically farmed. This is their showpiece site and is home to their newly renovated cellar door. There are three Warboys Vineyard wines, Shiraz, Grenache and a Shiraz–Grenache blend. I have been tasting this range for a few years and feel that each vintage, the wines have got better. The Grenache is my favourite (what a surprise) but all three are great. The other McLaren Vale wines fall under the Family Crest series and the Wild Olive Organic series, all of which are mid-priced and represent excellent value. This is a company that has done the hard yards investing in conversion to certified organics in all their vineyards and continues to make farming practices a priority. They also have a project in Tasmania but I have yet to try those wines.

Poppelvej

www.poppelvej.com

Established in 2016 by Danish brothers Jens and Uffe Deichmann, the winery takes its name from the street they grew up on. They use natural fermentation in the winery, with no additives and minimal/no use of sulphur. These are distinctive natural wines and Poppelvej is a producer to keep an eye on. Some wines teeter on the precipice of too funky for me but there are several that I really like. Irresistible Impulse is a briny, savoury Sauvignon Blanc, the Æ (Æventyr) is a concrete egg fermented Gewurztraminer and the Rookie Grenache is a spot-on version of light-weight, fragrant Grenache. It will be interesting to follow the progress of Poppelvej.

Wirra Wirra Vineyards

www.wirrawirra.com

This is a much-loved winery in the region. The inspiration and legacy of founder Gregg Trott seemed to linger for decades. There were some changes at the winery in 2022 and there is now a new CEO and head winemaker. It appears these changes will be positive for the estate, but I have not tried any of the wines made by the new winemaker. In circumstances such as this I am generally cautious about recommending wines, but the history and quality of this estate and the calibre of the new winemaker gives me confidence to say that this is still a producer that should be on your list of McLaren Vale wineries to experiment with. I will, however, refrain from specific wine recommendations in this instance.

LANGHORNE CREEK
(Ngarrindjeri Country)

First planted in the 1850s, Langhorne Creek is located 70 kilometres south-east of Adelaide on the shores of Lake Alexandrina, between the Bremer and Angas Rivers. The original settlers were drawn to the area due to its fertile alluvial soils, and grape growing soon became part of the agricultural mix. This is one of Australia's oldest wine-producing regions and there are several sixth generation grape-growing families of note: Pott's family at Bleasdale, Folletts from Lake Breeze, Case family of Kimbolton and the Adamses from Brothers in Arms, who are custodians of one of the oldest Cabernet Sauvignon vineyards in the world – planted in 1891 and still producing today.

The climate is moderated by the Lake Doctor, the local name for the cooling breezes that come directly off Lake Alexandrina. The driving force of these winds is the Southern Ocean and the impact is significant. It cools down the growing season daytime temperatures and mitigates winter frost.

Cabernet Sauvignon and Shiraz are the signature grapes and while varietal versions exist, many in the region feel that the blend of these two classic varieties is the best expression of true Langhorne Creek red wine. This style tends to be full-bodied with soft, ripe tannins, black fruit flavours and spicy oak character. Most are totally delicious as young wines but can also age gracefully. Paradoxically, Verdelho, while not extensively planted, has become a regional speciality with several wineries producing delicious versions. These wines are light-bodied, fresh and juicy and typically made to be consumed young.

Area under vine

6,069 hectares[32]

Climate

Onshore southerly winds blow directly in from the Southern Ocean across Lake Alexandrina. Referred to as the Lake Doctor by locals, these southerly winds also decrease summer temperatures and increase the relative humidity. Most of the rainfall occurs in winter and spring. Irrigation is common.

Soils

Predominantly deep, fertile, alluvial sandy loams that vary in colour from red-brown to dark grey, with patches of black, self-mulching clays. All soil types promote vine vigour, which leads to generous canopies and cropping levels.

Varieties

Shiraz and Cabernet Sauvignon are the two most planted varieties. Combined, they represent just under 70 per cent of vineyard plantings. Merlot and Chardonnay are the other two major varieties. Malbec and Verdelho have a history in the region and there's a small amount of Grenache planted. As is the case in many areas in Australia, Langhorne Creek has been tinkering with Mediterranean varieties. Lagrein, Montepulciano, Tempranillo, Dolcetto, Fiano and Vermentino are all showing promise.

32   Source: National Vineyard Scan 2020 and ABS

Main wine styles

There are plantings of Cabernet Sauvignon dating back to the 1850s in Langhorne Creek. This is the signature variety of the region. Rich and ripe, with soft tannins, it is often blended with Shiraz.

Shiraz here is typically rich and full flavoured with soft tannins, blackberry, chocolate and liquorice characters. It is often blended with Cabernet Sauvignon.

Although not extensively planted, Langhorne Verdelho has developed a reputation as a regional speciality. Light-bodied, juicy and fresh, these wines are meant for early consumption.

Producers

Bleasdale Wines

www.bleasdale.com.au

This is the region's most historic estate. Frank Potts purchased land in 1850, primarily for farming, and planted Shiraz and Verdelho a few years later, thus establishing Bleasdale, the first winery in the region. The Potts' Catch Verdelho, a fresh, juicy wine with tropical fruit character, is a good place to start. The flagship Frank Potts is a Cabernet-dominant blend with some Malbec, Petit Verdot and Merlot. While totally drinkable young this is a structured wine that definitely benefits from a few years in the cellar. Bleasdale has been growing Malbec since the late 1800s and produced the region's first straight varietal version in 1961. The current iteration is called the Generations Malbec and I have always loved it; a vibrant mouthful of spiced mulberry with plenty of structure to hold your attention.

Matala Vineyard

www.metala.com.au

Guy Adams (Brothers in Arms) is now the custodian of the oldest family-owned Cabernet Sauvignon vines on the planet, planted in 1891 by his great-great-grandfather. While there are only 14 rows of the original Cabernet Sauvignon, this estate now has 200 hectares, mostly planted to Cabernet and Shiraz. The Semper Fidelis is the wine made from the old Cabernet vines and worth seeking out.

Brothers in Arms

www.brothersinarms.com.au

The Adams family has a long history in the region and established the Brothers in Arms brand in 1998. The regular bottlings of the Cabernet Sauvignon and Shiraz–Cabernet are always delicious and a great introduction to the style of Langhorne Creek red wines.

Bremerton Wines

www.bremerton.com.au

Established in the mid-1980s by the Willson family, Bremerton has been under the steady hand of winemaker Rebecca Willson for decades. This is one of the region's star performers. The Verdelho was the first wine I ever tried at Bremerton, and I still love it. The Coulthard Cabernet is a silky, fragrant and medium-bodied expression of the variety, and it is also worth seeking out some of their Special Release wines. Fiano, Vermentino and Barbera are of particular interest.

Other producers

Langhorne Creek has been a sourcing region for many established wines made in nearby regions, especially McLaren Vale. Below is a list of notable producers sourcing quality fruit from Langhorne Creek.

Wolf Blass (www.wolfblass.com). See box below.

Noon Winery (www.noonwinery.com.au)

McLaren Vale based Drew Noon sources fruit for his Reserve Shiraz and Reserve Cabernet Sauvignon from the Borret family vineyards. These two excellent wines are right up there with the best expressions of those varieties in the region.

The Pawn Wine Co. (www.thepawn.com.au)

Owner Tom Keelan is married to Rebecca Willson from Bremerton wines. He is mostly focused on Adelaide Hills under this label but also makes a a zippy Fiano from Langehorne Creek fruit and it is worth seeking out.

Wolf Blass and Langhorne Creek

Wolfgang Blass moved to Australia, from Germany, in 1961 and established his Wolf Blass wine brand in 1966. Wolf Blass was quick to recognize the quality of fruit available in Langhorne Creek and the region holds a strong place in his heart. He made his very first wines with fruit from Langhorne Creek, including the well-known Grey Label Cabernet Shiraz. Australian red wines tended to be loaded with heavy tannins, but Wolf pursued a softer, more approachable style. In the 1970s, he won three consecutive Jimmy Watson Trophies for his Black Label Cabernet–Shiraz containing Langhorne Creek Cabernet.

CURRENCY CREEK
(*Ngarrindjeri Country*)

The Currency Creek wine region is located south of the city of Adelaide.

It stretches from the coastal village of Port Elliot in the west to Lake Alexandrina in the east. Vines were first planted here in 1969.

Area under vine
1,032 hectares[33]

Climate
The maritime climate is similar to that of Margaret River. It is slightly warmer than Coonawarra and Langhorne Creek.

Soils
Rolling sandy hills with a sub-soil of cracking clay.

Varieties
Cabernet Sauvignon, Shiraz and Merlot.

33 Source: National Vineyard Scan 2020 and ABS

Main wine styles

Shiraz and Cabernet Sauvignon dominate the plantings in this region but it is the latter that is the star, producing a ripe, rounded style akin to Coonawarra. Shiraz is medium to full bodied. These are small wineries, with small production and wines that are quite hard to find. Most are sold locally.

Producers

Try the Finniss River Shiraz from **Salomon Estate** (www.salomonwines. com) and **One Paddock Currency Creek Winery's** (www.onepaddockcur-rencycreekwinery.com.au) the Purging Ostrich Shiraz and Purging Ostrich Merlot. Charlotte Dalton has established a winery and cellar door in Port Elliot. See **Charlotte Dalton Wines** entry in Adelaide Hills (p. 126).

KANGAROO ISLAND
(Ngarrindjeri Country)

This is the third largest island off the coast of Australia. With stunning native flora and fauna, pristine beaches and fantastic local produce and seafood, there is nothing not to like about Kangaroo Island. There were some early attempts at viticulture but none was particularly successful. Jacques

Lurton, from the Lurton family in Bordeaux, purchased land and developed his Islander Estate brand in 2000. This seemed to draw attention and there are now several very cool wineries on the island. Joch Bosworth and Louise Hemsley-Smith from Battle of Bosworth recently purchased 60 hectares and are now producing a few wines under the Springs Road label.

Main wine styles

Cabernet and Shiraz dominate the plantings at present but there are so many delicious, refreshing wines. This is an exciting place. Small production is an issue so access to a good cross-section of wines will be a challenge for the foreseeable future. A place I will be watching closely.

Area under vine

144 hectares[34]

Climate

There is a distinctly maritime climate with strong south-easterly winds from the Southern Ocean. The average summer temperature is 25°C, which is considerably cooler than Adelaide. There is a certain amount of humidity but it stays relatively dry during the critical ripening months. There are no real extremes of climate, which leads to an even ripening season. Harvest dates compared to McLaren Vale are much later.

Soils

Soils are varied across the island. Sand, loam and clay, generally overlaying limestone. Some soils are similar to Padthaway.

Varieties

Cabernet Sauvignon, Shiraz, Merlot, Cabernet Franc, Malbec, Chardonnay and Sauvignon Blanc.

34 Source: Wine Australia

Producers

Islander Estate Vineyards (www.iev.com.au) has lots to choose from but the Estate Sauvignon Blanc and Shiraz captured my attention recently, along with their flagship wines – The Investigator Cabernet Franc and The Independence Malbec. **Springs Road** (www.springsroad.com.au) is

Battle of Bosworth's venture. There is a deliciously fresh Chardonnay and the Little Island Red is a fragrant, juicy, middleweight Shiraz. **Bay of Shoals** (www.bayofshoalswines.com.au) has vineyards first planted in 1993 that overlook the Bay of Shoals. There is a strong white wine line-up: try the Pinot Gris, Sauvignon Blanc and Riesling.

SOUTHERN FLEURIEU
(Peramangk and Ngarrindjeri Country)

A stunningly beautiful peninsula extending south of McLaren Vale, directly facing the Southern Ocean. The viticultural potential of this area was noted by Dr John Gladstones in his book *Viticulture and Environment* and reiterated in *Wine, Terroir and Climate Change*: 'At least in climatic terms, this region has arguably the best conditions in all of South Australia for table wine production.' There were grape-growing efforts as early as 1876, but all manner of issues beset the area. By the early 1900s there were basically no vineyards.

Area under vine

490 hectares[35]

Climate

The climate here is strongly influenced by the Southern Ocean. Temperature is a 1–2°C warmer than Adelaide in the winter but 3–5°C cooler in the summer months. Rainfall is predominant in the winter months. Spring frosts generally are not an issue.

Soils

Soils are generally sandy-clay loams over clay and limestone. Some sites are planted on gravelly clay over limestone.

Varieties

Chardonnay, Sauvignon Blanc, Merlot, Shiraz and Pinot Noir.

35 Source: National Vineyard Scan 2020 and ABS

Main wine styles

Fragrant, mid-weight Chardonnay and Shiraz, aromatic Sauvignon Blanc (sometimes blended with Semillon) and herb scented Merlot are made here. Tapanappa Wines Foggy Hill Pinot Noir shows clearly that there are sites on this peninsula where Pinot Noir thrives.

Producers

Tapanappa Wines – Foggy Hill

www.tapanappa.com.au

Brian Croser AO planted Pinot Noir here in 2003. The Foggy Hill Vineyard, part of Tapanappa Wines Distinguished Sites, sits on a north-west facing slope 300–350 metres above sea level, one of the highest points on the Fleurieu Peninsula. The coast is only 8 kilometres from here and the cooling effects of the Southern Ocean are obvious. Croser is one of Australia's most respected and fastidious wine professionals and had long searched for a place to craft quality Pinot Noir. It appears that he has found it here. Both Foggy Hill and Definitus Pinot Noirs are worth seeking out; intense and focused expressions of a variety that is clearly suited to this unique site.

Minko Wines

www.minkowines.com

This small, family-run estate was established in 1993. The Cabernet Merlot blend is excellent, and they make a fresh, juicy Pinot Gris and a savoury, citrusy Savagnin.

Mt Billy Wines

www.mtbillywines.com.au

Originally planted by John Edwards in 1992, the No Secrets Vineyard on the property is the source for the Soliloquy Syrah. Fruit from the Barossa, McLaren Vale and Clare Valley is used for a series of other wines.

THE LIMESTONE COAST

The Limestone Coast is a large, zonal GI that incorporates Coonawarra, Padthaway, Wrattonbully, Robe, Mount Benson and Mount Gambier. Tidswell Wines was the sole winery that did not sit within the boundaries of any of the specific regions so used Limestone Coast GI. But they have now closed down, after 25 years in business. There are many wines on the market that are blends of wine and/or fruit from two or more of these regions that opt to use the Limestone Coast GI on their labels. The Limestone Coast is the second largest grower of grapes in South Australia.

COONAWARRA
(Boandig Country)

Coonawarra was first planted in the 1880s but the region struggled from 1890 to 1945. Most of the wine during this period was distilled into brandy. In the 1930s the government structured a vine-pull scheme offering money to convert vineyards to dairy land. In spite of this, there were some classic wines produced in the 1930s and 1940s but a real resurgence of interest started in the 1950s. Today, Coonawarra is one of Australia's great red wine producing regions.

Consistent cloud cover and ocean breezes combine to make it quite cool. The famous crumbly red topsoil known as *terra rossa,* a unique, cigar shaped strip of land, defines the region's wines. The strip is 27 kilometres long and 2 kilometres wide and consists of a thin top layer of iron-oxide red soil over free-draining limestone subsoils. These in turn sit over a water table, which is relatively close to the surface. All these factors combine to make this region suited to classic red wine production with Cabernet Sauvignon at its heart. The wines are full of character and finesse; medium-bodied with classic regional signatures of cassis and mint.

Main wine styles

Coonawarra is the pre-eminent producer of Cabernet Sauvignon in Australia. Wines are medium- to full-bodied with cassis, blackberry, plum and dark cherry flavours, and firm but plush tannins. The very best versions can age gracefully for decades.

Which is best: 100 per cent Cabernet or Cabernet with the addition of other varieties? There has been a tradition of varietally labelled 100 per cent Cabernet Sauvignon but that has evolved. Sue Bell from Bellwether Wines asserts that for now, climate change is benefiting the quality of Cabernet Sauvignon: 'We were always a region on a knife edge with ripening. A cooler vintage resulted in too much greenness, but a warmer season was amazing. Twenty years ago I was working out how to get green seeds out of fermenters, or jumping for joy the years we ripened them, waiting for skin and seed tannins to ripen after fruit flavours. These days I rarely need to worry about that, canes always lignify [go brown] and seed/skin tannin is correspondingly ripe with fruit flavours.'

Shiraz has a long history in the region and was, in the early days, the most planted red variety. The style is medium bodied with spice and raspberry-toned fruit. Coonawarra has a tradition of Shiraz–Cabernet blends and there are many delicious versions.

Merlot does not have a long tradition in Coonawarra but has been a very successful blending partner for Cabernet Sauvignon and makes interesting, elegant varietal wine.

Riesling has a decent history in Coonawarra and several producers have been making it for decades. Wines are generally dry with classic lemon and lime notes and typically more fleshy than Clare or Eden Valley Rieslings.

As with Riesling, there is a tradition of Sauvignon Blanc production in Coonawarra, albeit in small quantities.

Area under vine

5,784 hectares[36]

Climate

The maritime influence is quirky but pointed in Coonawarra, given that the region is about 100 kilometres inland. There is an upwelling of the Bonney Current off the coast during the latter part of the ripening period. This is a key factor in moderating the climate (see box, below). Consistent cloud cover contributes to a reduction in temperature. Winters are cold and summer night temperatures are cool during the latter part of the ripening period.

Soils

This is a flat region with famous *terra rossa* soils of thin iron-oxide based topsoil over limestone.

Varieties

Cabernet Sauvignon and Shiraz are the main varieties but Merlot, Chardonnay, Cabernet Franc, Riesling and Sauvignon Blanc are also grown, and there is increasing interest in alternative varieties.

36   Source: National Vineyard Scan 2020 and ABS

Producers

Wynns Coonawarra Estate

www.wynns.com.au

This is Coonawarra's most important and historic producer. John Riddoch moved to the Coonawarra region in 1861. In 1890 he established the Coonawarra Fruit Colony. He offered allotments to colonists, and the planting of fruit trees and vines began in 1891. By 1897, 89 hectares of vines were being cultivated by the colonists and 52 hectares by Riddoch. The famous triple-gabled winery and surrounding vineyards were built in 1891 and named Chateau Comaum. Ultimately, the business was not successful for various situational and financial reasons and fell into a period of disuse. The winery was destined to become a wool shed until it was purchased by Samuel Wynn and his son, David, in 1951. A history of quality wine followed. It is now owned by Treasury Wine Estates. Sue Hodder has been the chief winemaker since 1998 and has steered it through ups and downs of corporate ownership with a steadfast focus on quality, so that today the wines are the best they have ever been in the history of the estate. The Black Label Cabernet Sauvignon is the very best wine to taste if you want to understand the character of Coonawarra Cabernet. I would also argue that it is the best value, regionally expressive Cabernet Sauvignon you can find anywhere on the planet. John Riddoch Cabernet Sauvignon and Michael Shiraz are the jewels in the crown. Wynns Coonawarra Estate wines are a must try but Treasury Wine Estates does not sell Wynns wines in the US at present. I am not sure what the logic behind this decision is since this is one of Australia's most important producers.

Balnaves of Coonawarra

www.balnaves.com.au

The Balnaves family has a history in the region dating back to 1855. The first Balnaves vineyards were planted in 1975. The Balnaves brand, however, didn't start until 1990. Today it is a very high quality, family-run estate making a full range of classic Coonawarra wines. The Blend is a wonderfully balanced and aromatic wine comprising Cabernet Sauvignon, Cabernet Franc and Merlot. The Tally Reserve is the their flagship 100 per cent Cabernet Sauvignon and one of the very best expressions in the region. Excellent wines, and a lovely family, worth getting to know.

Bellwether

www.bellwetherwines.com.au

Sue Bell is a treat, one of the great personalities in the region. She makes wonderfully detailed wines with fruit from several regions (Tasmania, Wrattonbully, Heathcote and Riverland) but the Bellwether Estate is based in Coonawarra and the region is lucky to have her. Ant Series

Cabernet Sauvignon is a vibrant, juicy and fragrant expression una-dorned with new oak; very pure. Bellwether Cabernet Sauvignon is a lovely fragrant wine that has power and intensity with pure fruit and elegance. This is a wine for the cellar but can be drunk on release.

The Bonney Upwelling

Sue Bell from Bellwether Wines explains: 'It is different every year ... timing, location and temperature, but is usually centred around Robe. It is something the fishermen have known about forever, as it brings up nutrients from deep down in the ocean that tuna in particular love. In 2023, the tuna fleet is based in Robe not Carpenters Rocks, where it is typically centred. It moderates our cli-mate, so we don't get the warmer weather that regions around Adelaide get. It also seems to be buffering the impacts of climate change so we are changing slower, meaning Coonawarra will be successful with Cabernet Sauvignon for longer. Our region has a fascinating maritime influence. The cold current each summer season keeps us cool.'

Majella Wines

www.majellawines.com.au

Brian Lynn (Prof Lynn as he is called) is a classic old school Australian wine personality. Never without a smile on his face, he is always a breath of fresh air. There are lots of wines to choose from here. The Musician is a lovely Cabernet Shiraz blend, The Malleea is a more premium version of the same blend but only made in good years. The Sparkling Shiraz is a ripe blackberry, spicy plum and raspberry flavoured mouthful of frothy deli-ciousness. His Cabernet Sauvignon is classic and ridiculously well priced.

Bowen Estate

www.bowenestate.com.au

Doug and Joy Bowen have been refining the wines at this small estate for over 40 years. I don't get to see the wines very often, but I always buy them when I do. Coonawarra is not my go-to place for Chardonnay, but Bowen Estate makes a lovely medium-weight version. The Cabernet Sauvignon is classic, and I really like the Shiraz as it shows cooler cli-mate characteristics of raspberry, pepper and spice. Coonawarra Shiraz is delicious but tends to sit in the shadow of Cabernet Sauvignon in this region. This is a great example and shows that Coonawarra Shiraz, at its best, belongs on the same table.

Penley Estate

www.penley.com.au

The wines at this estate have never been better than they are right now. Penley had always been a solid producer that was a safe bet for classic Coonawarra wines. In 2016, Kate Goodman took over the winemaking duties and the rapid elevation of quality and interest is nothing short of astonishing. The classic wines are more precise and refined and she has been tinkering with different techniques and varieties. The entry-level Phoenix Cabernet Sauvignon is stupidly good value for money. Helios is a textbook, age-worthy, top-end version. The Francis Cabernet Franc is a lovely Coonawarra flavour detour. Giliam Light Dry Red is a fresh, vibrant Cabernet–Merlot–Shiraz blend. She is also making a Piquette and an amphora-fermented Chardonnay. This is a really exciting winery that needs to be on your radar.

Parker Coonawarra Estate

www.parkercoonawarraestate.com.au

This excellent estate was purchased by the Jonathan Hesketh Group in 2013. Andrew Hardy consults on the winemaking and the wines have never been better. The Parker Terra Rossa Cabernet Sauvignon is textbook Coonawarra with great density of fruit, firm, grippy tannins and classic blackcurrant and cedar characteristics. The Parker Estate First Growth is the flagship wine and is a cellar-worthy beauty.

PADTHAWAY
(Ngarrindjeri Country)

Padthaway is part of the Limestone Coast zone. It is located north of Coonawarra, with its south-eastern boundary butting up against Wrattonbully. Vineyards were first established by Seppelts in 1964, subsequently followed by Lindemans, Hardys and Wynns. The Padthaway wine region was given GIC status in 1999. There is a history of major companies owning land and/or sourcing fruit from Padthaway. More recently there's been an increase in the number of private producers.

Main wine styles

Cabernet Sauvignon and Shiraz are the two most planted varieties, which makes sense given that the overall temperature is similar to, albeit a tad warmer than, Coonawarra. What is curious is that the region has a reputation for white wines, specifically Chardonnay, which currently represents 22 per cent of plantings. This reputation is likely a holdover from the early days when Lindemans was sourcing from the region and promoting a very well-made Chardonnay which became quite popular. It is only recently that Padthaway has made the move to become more than simply a source for good quality fruit for the larger wine companies. Large companies are still a major part of what drives the wine economy – Penfolds routinely sources premium fruit for its top wines here and pays handsomely for it. The emergence of growers making their own wine has given the region more of a focus on quality over quantity. Chardonnay from the region is delicious and while I don't put it among the elite regions for the variety in Australia the grapefruit-citrus tang and ripe stone fruit flavours are really appealing. There is one fantastic sparkling wine made from Chardonnay too (see recommendation below).

Cabernet Sauvignons are similar in weight and style to Coonawarra but with a little more flesh and softer tannins.

Shiraz does sit in the shadow of Cabernet in this region the same way as it does in Coonawarra but I really like the medium-weight, red fruited savoury spice the best examples display.

Area under vine

4,160 hectares[37]

Climate

Although inland, the lack of any mountain ranges means that it has a mostly maritime influenced climate. It is similar to Coonawarra but slightly warmer overall. Water availability is a limiting factor, so irrigation is essential.

Soils

These are predominantly brown, sandy loam over red-brown clay over limestone. There are some classic *terra rossa* type soils very similar to Coonawarra but with more variable depths and some stony influences.

Varieties

Shiraz, Cabernet Sauvignon and Chardonnay are the main varieties. Sauvignon Blanc, Pinot Gris and Malbec are also grown and there is some dabbling in Mediterranean varieties.

37   Source: National Vineyard Scan 2020 and ABS

Producers

At present there are only two cellar doors operating full-time – Browns of Padthaway and Farmers Leap. There are several properties that are by appointment only. Plenty of interesting wines are made by companies not based in the region. Below is a list of wines and wineries to look for from this region.

Padthaway Estate

www.padthawayestate.com.au

A great estate making tight, focused wines, this is home to the Eliza and Landaire wines. Eliza Vintage Blanc de Blancs and Vintage Rose are traditional method wines and are both totally delicious. The press they use is a custom-built version of the traditional Champagne press. Under the Landaire label, try the Vermentino. It is a good example of the evolving style of this variety in Australia. The Graciano is also worth sampling.

Farmer's Leap Wines

www.farmersleap.com

Grapes were first planted on the estate in 1993 but the Longbottom family has a history of farming in the Padthaway region that goes back four generations. The Brave Shiraz is a single vineyard wine from the estate in a medium- to full-bodied style with lovely dark raspberry and spice notes. Pillar Box Red is the entry level Shiraz–Cabernet–Merlot blend, with an affordable and easy drinking style.

Bryson Wines

www.brysonwines.com.au

The Morambro Creek that bisects the Bryson vineyard gives its name to the line of premium wines from the estate, which was established in 1994 by the Bryson family. The Bryson Barrel Select is a separate bottling of premium blocks of Shiraz and Cabernet Sauvignon and a flagship wine that is made in great years. It is a rich, full-throttle style but with a spine of juicy acidity that keeps your interest alive. There are essentially three main labels made at the estate. Morambro Creek, Jip Jip Rocks and Mt. Monster. Under the Morambro Creek label, both the Cabernet Sauvignon and the Shiraz are classic examples of the Padthaway style. The Jip Jip Rocks wines do use fruit from other regions as well as Padthaway. The Shiraz, Cabernet Sauvignon and

Shiraz–Cabernet are all Padthaway-sourced wines, extremely well made and represent tremendous value for money. Mt. Monster wines are all made using estate fruit and represent excellent value for money.

Penfolds

Penfolds sources premium fruit from Padthaway for many wines in its stable, and pays top dollar for it. While this changes from wine to wine and from year to year, top quality Padthaway fruit has shown up in the following wines: Bin 707 Cabernet Sauvignon, Grange (Shiraz), Koonunga Hill and St Henri Shiraz.

WRATTONBULLY
(Ngarrindjeri Country)

Farmers looking for grazing land were the original settlers in this region in 1842, and today the area is still known for prime lamb, beef and pasture seed productions. Although the first grapes were planted in the 1960s, the area didn't receive much interest until the 1990s. Since then, the undulating hills, a modicum of elevation (45–145 metres) and classic *terra rossa* soils have captured the attention of several well-known producers from other regions. The underlying limestone is a theme, not just for viticulture, here. The World Heritage-listed Naracoorte Caves are located in the Narcoota Range.

Sandwiched between Coonawarra to the south and Padthaway to the north, the region shares similarities with both in terms of climate and soils but Coonawaara and Padthaway are basically flat, this region's character and wine styles benefit from the undulating hills of the Narcoota Range

Main wine styles

Cabernet Sauvignon and Shiraz combined make up almost 70 per cent of the region's planted area. This is a red-wine dominant region. Cabernet Sauvignon is the variety many producers hang their hats on. The style is in a similar vein to Coonawarra Cabernet Sauvignon but there are differences. Perhaps it is down to the power of suggestion but you get the sense that the elevated sites lend a hand in delivering a different quality of tannin, balance of acidity and clarity of fruit. Shiraz here is medium-weight, red-fruited and savoury and this region is home to one of the very best Merlots produced in Australia.

Area under vine

2,727 hectares[38]

Climate

Wrattonbully shares the curious 'inland' maritime climate of both Coonawarra and Padthaway but the hills in the region seem to mark a point of difference. Cool nights and warm days are typical during the growing season. The elevated sites create air flows which give a measure of protection against spring frost.

Soils

The classic *terra rossa* soils evolved as a result of sedimentary clays on ancient flood plains and marine landscapes. The best sites are red loam over limestone and loam over clay.

Varieties

Cabernet Sauvignon, Shiraz, Chardonnay, Merlot and Pinot Grigio.

38   Source: National Vineyard Scan 2020 and ABS

Producers

Terre a Terre

www.terreaterre.com.au

This is a project started in 2003 by Xavier Bizot and his wife Lucy, who happens to be Brian Croser's daughter. The vineyard is named Crayeres and there are several really interesting wines. The Sauvignon Blanc is a barrel-aged, textural, lime blossom scented version with lovely structure. The Cabernet Franc is aromatic and charming on the nose, with serious structure and depth. They also make wines under the Terre a Terre label from the family vineyards in Piccadilly Valley in the Adelaide Hills.

Tapanappa Whalebone Vineyard

www.tapanappa.com.au

Brian Croser purchased this vineyard in 2002. Originally named Koppamurra Vineyard, the name was changed to Whalebone after an ancient whalebone was discovered in the Crayeres vineyard when it was first planted. The Cabernet Shiraz is a lovely iteration of this classic Australian blend and the mint-scented, leafy and floral Merlot–Cabernet Franc had me thinking Right Bank Bordeaux when I first put my nose in the glass. This has more fruit weight on the palate and different tannin structure but is a fragrant, complex delight.

Mérite Wines

www.meritewines.com

This estate was established in 2000 by Mike Kloak and Colleen Miller. Mike has done a lot of work with clones of Merlot, recognizing that the historic problem with this variety in Australia was the original plant material. They are now a top producer with a laser focus on Merlot, making some of the best Merlot in Australia. There are several wines to suggest here, including the Shiraz–Malbec and a straight Cabernet Sauvignon, but you must try the single vineyard Merlot. Beautifully structured, aromatic, plummy and textured, it restores one's faith in this variety in Australia.

Smith & Hooper Wines

www.smithswinestore.com.au

This is a Wrattonbully venture from Yalumba's Robert Hill-Smith. The solid selection of characterful wines includes an excellent and well-priced Merlot and a Cabernet–Merlot blend. The Reserve Merlot is a bit more serious and age-worthy.

ROBE
(Buandig Country)

James Halliday is noted for stating, in his 2014 edition of the *Wine Atlas of Australia*: 'In a perfect world, Robe would have joined forces with Mount Benson, making a single GI; however, viticultural politics rather than soil and/or climate considerations resulted in a long stand-off before Robe made its application.' It is certainly not the only GI in Australia beset with politics during its formation. Robe is a charming port town famous for its crayfish (lobsters). If you are there at the right time of year, there is no better place to feel the impact of the cooling currents of the Southern Ocean, an element that is critical in shaping the growing conditions of the Limestone Coast regions.

Area under vine

677 hectares[39]

Climate

Climate is distinctly cool and maritime with the influence of the Southern Ocean on one side and three lakes on the other. The growing season is long, cool and relatively dry.

Soils

The wide variety of soil types includes classic *terra rossa* and sandy loam in the limestone ridges. There is calcareous sand on the coastal dunes.

Varieties

Cabernet Sauvignon, Chardonnay, Sauvignon Blanc, Merlot and Shiraz.

39 Source: National Vineyard Scan 2020 and ABS

Main wine styles

Cabernet Sauvignon and Shiraz make up over half of the total plantings in the region. Robe has been a consistent source of fruit for many larger producers, most notably Treasury Wine Estates. The vast majority ends up in Penfolds wines.

Producers

Karatta Wines

www.karattawines.com.au

Established in 1997 by Peg and David Woods, this remains the most prominent independent producer in the region. Their Field Blend White is light, lively and delicious and the Great Cabsy, an early harvest, co-ferment of Cabernet Sauvignon and Shiraz is a medium-weight, fresh take on a classic Australian red style.

MOUNT BENSON
(Buandig and Ngarrindjeri Country)

This area is just north of Robe, with its regional boundary stretching further inland. Both regions are quite new to grape growing with no record of plantings prior to 1989. It is very much a maritime-influenced region due to its proximity to the Southern Ocean.

Area under vine

541 hectares[40]

Climate

Cool maritime climate, strongly influenced by the Southern Ocean. Growing season temperatures can be 2–3°C cooler than Coonawarra. Bud break is typically 10–14 days earlier than Coonawarra but harvest dates are around the same time. The growing season is long, cool and dry.

Soils

Mostly *terra rossa*.

Varieties

Cabernet Sauvignon, Shiraz, Chardonnay and Sauvignon Blanc.

40   Source: National Vineyard Scan 2020 and ABS

Main wine styles

Cabernet Sauvignon is the signature variety in the region. The cool, maritime climate shapes a distinctly fragrant, medium bodied version of this variety. Charming and elegant and not as weighty as Coonawarra, many examples have a lifted herbal note without being green and stemmy. Sauvignon Blanc in this region can be delicious and makes a great pairing with the abundant local seafood.

Producers

As is the case in many smaller regions, producers here do source fruit from nearby regions. The recommendations are focused on fruit from Mount Benson

Cape Jaffa Wines

www.capejaffawines.com.au

Sauvignon Blanc is a star here, while the Upwelling Cabernet Sauvignon gives a great lens into the style of this variety in Mount Benson. They also make wines from fruit sourced in Robe and Wrattonbully.

Norfolk Rise

www.norfolkrise.com.au

The Make Waves Syrah is a medium-weight, red fruited charmer and I particularly like the Fair Winds Cabernet Franc, which is lifted and herbal but with crunchy red fruit.

MOUNT GAMBIER
(Buandig Country)

Mount Gambier was first planted in 1982 and received its GI status in 2010, so it is a relatively new region. The southern section of the region ranks as one of the coolest in South Australia. The landscape of the Mount Gambier region is dominated by several physical features. The town sits on a coastal plain, underlain by limestone with relic beach dune systems illustrating the advance and retreat of sea levels during the last Ice Age. Volcanic activity in relatively recent geological times in the South of the region, saw the development of volcanic cones and craters, within which sits Blue Lake, a distinct tourist feature.

Area under vine

270 hectares[41]

Climate

The climate is cool due to the south facing coastline. One of the cooler climates in South Australia.

Soils

The limestone subsoils are scattered with igneous rock from volcanic activity. There are volcanic loam soils in some of the areas.

Varieties

Pinot Noir, Cabernet Sauvignon, Chardonnay and Sauvignon Blanc.

41 Source: Wine Australia

Main wine styles

Pinot Noir has developed a reputation here and Chardonnay quality is on the rise. The future for this region seems to be resting on these two varieties. Wineries are small, with small production, making wines quite hard to find. Most are sold locally.

Producers

Caroline Hills

www.carolinehills.com.au

Cabernet Sauvignon was the first variety planted on the estate, in 1988. Gradually, more vineyards were added, and the estate now has Pinot Gris, Pinot Noir, Cabernet Franc and Merlot. The Pinot Gris is textural but with a crisp spine of acidity. The Tezza Pinot Noir is a medium-weight, strawberry-scented wine that is quite delicious.

Herbert Vineyard

www.herbertvineyard.com.au

The Pinot Gris is excellent and there is a really lovely, fragrant and fine-boned Pinot Noir. Delicious wines.

LOWER MURRAY ZONE

The Riverland is the only region that sits within this zone.

RIVERLAND
(Meru Country)

Along with Riverina and Murray Darling, the Riverland is one of the key areas that supply the industry with affordable varietal wines. Plantings of the main varieties, Cabernet, Chardonnay and Shiraz, are driven mostly by market demand but there are many producers, albeit on a much smaller scale, working with alternative, warmer climate varieties such as Sangiovese, Nero d'Avola, Montepulciano and Vermentino. The lack of major disease pressure also allows for ease of organic, and in some cases biodynamic, vineyard practices. While the image of this region has historically been one of large volume production (and this certainly exists) there is a really captivating alternate scene that has developed and given rise to some very interesting wines that challenge the preconceived notions. Home to just under 1,000 wine grape growers with more than 21,000 hectares under vine, it is responsible for a third of the national crush. The Riverland's influence and importance to the national wine industry flows far beyond this.

Its unique character within the Australian wine story is unparalleled and and while the region is noted for innovative large-scale production, there is increased interest and investment in boutique, premium wines. When talking about its contribution in terms of scale, diversity, export value, return on investment, and innovative viticultural understanding and practice, the Australian wine industry would quite simply be far less valuable, profitable or viable without the Riverland.

Area under vine

22,030 hectares[42]

Climate

This is a classic continental climate, with long, hot, sunny days and cool nights. Low rainfall and high evaporation rates mean irrigation is essential. Summers are dry, with low disease pressure.

Soils

These are quite varied but there are two main types. River valley soils are made up of sandy loam over clay. On higher ground it is windblown sand over lime and clay, known locally as Mallee soils.

Varieties

Cabernet Sauvignon, Shiraz and Chardonnay are the main varieties, but there are 85 different varieties grown with success in the region. Many newer 'alternative varieties' have been planted since the early 2000s. There are too many to list here but there is real excitement with the following: Bianco d'Alessano, Vermentino, Montepulciano, Nero d'Avola, Mencia and Touriga.

42   Source: National Vineyard Scan 2020 and ABS

Main wine styles

The historic theme with the wines in the Riverland has been approachable, affordable varietal wines that have been made to be drunk young. Virtually all classic varietal wines offer a fantastic price/quality ratio. Cabernet Sauvignon, Shiraz and Chardonnay are the 'fighting' varieties that established the region as a source of affordable, easy-drinking wines. These three combined represent 65 per cent of vineyard plantings, so they remain the engine room of the region, but changes are afoot. The last decade or so has seen a radical shift in attitude, and plantings of different varieties. These varieties are quietly reshaping the look and feel of the wines from this region. As is the case in several areas in Australia these varieties, mostly southern Mediterranean in origin, have been planted with an eye to the future. Climate change is the driving force behind the search for more suitable varieties; varieties that produce contemporary wines that are fresher, livelier and more suited to our lifestyles and the food we eat.

Producers

There are several large volume traditional producers whose wines are worth seeking out to get a true sense of the wine styles that set the standard for the region decades ago. All of them are dabbling with newer varieties but their bread is buttered on the strength of their more traditional wines.

Angove Family Winemakers

www.angove.com.au

This is a large operation, but it is a fifth-generation, family-run business and the attention to detail shows. The company has been through the laborious and costly process of getting organic certification. They started conversion in 2007 and now all their vineyards in the Riverland are certified. It is at least 30 per cent more expensive to farm this way and there is a natural drop in vineyard yields during that certification process. There is not much elasticity on price for Riverland wines, which means that they can't just charge 30 per cent more for their wines, but they converted because it was the right thing to do. They are hyper conscious of the impact on the environment and have many good environmentally driven initiatives – lightweight bottles, strict recycling, rehabilitation of indigenous flora and fauna to name just a few. It is good to see a larger producer doing it right. The Angove Organic series is solid top to bottom with standouts being Rosé, Pinot Grigio and Shiraz. The Naturalis line of wines is also great, especially the Sauvignon Blanc and Chardonnay. They have a lovely property in McLaren Vale too (see p. 150).

Oxford Landing

www.oxfordlanding.com

Under the umbrella of Yalumba this has always been a go-to producer for easy-drinking, affordable, perfectly correct varietal wines. It was established by Robert Hill-Smith's father, Wyndham Hill-Smith in 1958. They are committed to sustainability, and in 2007 kicked off a revegetation project. They purchased 600 hectares of unused farmland next to the vineyard and focused on the replanting and regeneration of native flora and fauna. Over 200,000 native trees and shrubs have been planted in a dedicated conservation area. They also use lightweight bottles, recyclable cartons and recycle 100 per cent of the winery wastewater: another larger producer that is doing it right. There is a full array of classic varieties in the stable, with my favourites being Cabernet Sauvignon, Sauvignon Blanc, Pinot Grigio and Merlot.

Banrock Station

www.banrockstation.com.au

This is another solid producer with a full range of classic varieties. Banrock Station has always put the health of the environment front and centre. Their ethos is stated clearly on their website: 'Every drop of Banrock Station goes into conserving the planet. Over the last 20 years, we've contributed to over 130 projects across 13 countries, from maintaining our wetlands in the Riverland to protecting the turtles in the Great Barrier Reef to supporting polar bear and orangutan rehabilitation, and we are continuing to support causes that are important for you and the environment. Our most recent commitment to partner with Landcare Australia will result in 100,000 native trees & shrubs being planted each year. We've humbly given $6 million to conserving this planet!' Their new Eco Flat Bottle is a really cool initiative. It is made from Australian-sourced 100 per cent recycled PET plastic and is 84 per cent lighter than a standard glass bottle. The net result is a significant reduction in transport-related emissions. Try the Eco Bottle Pinot Grigio and Cabernet Sauvignon.

Ricca Terra

www.riccaterra.com.au

Ashley Ratcliff used to be the vineyard manager at Oxford Landing so knows his way around the Riverland. He and his wife Holly purchased their first vineyard in 2003 and took time developing it. Ashley says: 'Our vision was to make wine from grape varieties that were best suited to Australia's warm and dry climate. Chardonnay, Cabernet Sauvignon and Merlot quickly made way for Nero d'Avola, Montepulciano, Tinta Barroca, Fiano, Vermentino and many other Mediterranean grape varieties.'

Along with many other producers, Ricca Terra Farms is reshaping conventional thoughts on what the Riverland can, and maybe should, be. There are so many exciting wines, and the single varietal Vermentino, Fiano, Grenache Blanc and Arinto (the first in Australia) are all fantastic. Juicy June is a Negroamaro–Grenache blend, while Bullets Before Cannonballs is an unconventional blend of Tempranillo, Lambrusco, Lagrein and Shiraz. It is gulpable and delicious. He also makes an excellent Montepulciano and a Nero d'Avola. Terra do Rio is the new label dedicated to the Portuguese varieties he has planted. He also sells fruit to a dazzling array of cool producers in other regions. This is one of the best producers for exploring new varieties in the Riverland.

Delinquente Wine Co

www.delinquentewineco.com

Delinquente makes small batch, minimal intervention wines from Southern Italian grape varieties. Con-Greg Grigoriou grew up in the Riverland and his love for the region is obvious when he says: 'The Riverland is where I grew up, so to me it's incredibly special. The hugely open, bright blue sky; the heat rising up off the road and the red dirt. But then, the lush, calming, cooling Murray River, giving life and sustenance to the people, plants and animals that live near it. The river is peaceful like nowhere else I know – the constant, slow and steady flow of the water moving downstream is pretty meditative. It's a special place.'

He sources fruit from organic vineyards in the region and makes seriously delicious wines, with fun, funky wine names and outlandish labels to match. Try them all: Screaming Betty Vermentino, Pretty Boy Nero d'Avola Rosato, Roxanne the Razor Negroamaro Nero d'Avola, Roko Il Vagabondo Montepulciano and Tuff Nutt Bianco Pet Nat. One of my favourite Riverland producers.

919 Wines

www.919wines.com.au

Established by Eric and Jenny Semmler, this is another producer working with alternative varieties and has been doing so for a long time. The 919 Reserve wines are all single varietal from their own vineyards and from fruit they purchase from Whistling Kite. Look for the Gros Manseng, the Touriga or the Tempranillo.

Starrs Reach Vineyard

www.starrsreach.com.au

Starrs Reach Vineyard has been owned and operated by the Mason Family since 2010 and while this is a relatively new venture into viticulture, the family dates back five generations in the Riverland. Their sustainably farmed, 175-hectare vineyard has extensive plantings of Grenache and Mataro with Chardonnay, Shiraz, Cabernet Sauvignon, Merlot, Colombard, Sauvignon Blanc and Durif making up the balance. A new producer on my radar, they are making really good wines with a focus on single vineyards. The vibrant, cherry-scented, juicy and savoury Grenache is a standout. There's an excellent Grenache-based rosé too.

Byrne Vineyards

www.byrnevineyards.com.au

In 1960, Eric and Romla Byrne purchased a property near Devlin's Pound near Waikerie. The Byrne family has interests in other regions, but has a storied history in the Riverland. In 1995 they purchased the Scott's Creek Vineyard, which was originally planted by Penfolds in 1970. This is another larger producer with a strong focus on sustainability and land management. Among many great initiatives, they reserve 12 hectares of native land for every 1 hectare that they farm. This amounts to 17 square kilometres of natural carbon sink made up of wetlands and bushlands. They produce a series of wines under various brand names. The Sidney Wilcox Old Vine Zibibbo is a delicious, fragrant, peach bomb and the unique Vine Dried Shiraz is intense and concentrated but balanced and fun to drink.

Mallee Estate

www.malleeestate.com.au

Mallee Estate was established by Peter and Eleni Markeas. Family owned and operated, the first vineyard was planted in 1969 and the Mallee Estate wine brand was established in 1998. There is a great line-up of wines under the Mallee Estate label. The Cabernet Sauvignon, Shiraz and Tempranillo are all great. They have a range of varietal wines under the 230 Strong Men label but I have yet to try them. A really solid, independent producer.

Whistling Kite Biodynamic Wines

www.whistlingkitewines.com.au

Owners Pam and Tony Barich have nurtured Whistling Kite Vineyard for almost 50 years. Certified organic in 1997 and certified organic/biodynamic in 2007 the estate works with traditional and alternative varieties. Their Gros Manseng was the first alternative Riverland wine I had ever tried, and I still love it. There is a delicious Mencia Rosé and a perfumed, apricot-flavoured Viognier.

FAR NORTH ZONE

This zone exists for the region of Southern Flinders Ranges GI (*Nukunu Country*), a region that is planted predominately with Shiraz, most of which is sold to Barossa Valley winemakers. **Bundaleer**, a Shiraz producer, is the most notable regional producer, but I have never tried the wines.

PENINSULAS ZONE

This zone captures the fruit grown in the Southern Eyre Peninsula GI (*Nawu Country*). Its maritime climate and patches of classic *terra rossa* soils mean that it is suited to both Shiraz and Cabernet Sauvignon. **Boston Bay Wines** (www.bostonbaywines.com.au) makes a very good Riesling and zippy Sauvignon Blanc here.

8

VICTORIA

In the 1880s Victoria was Australia's largest wine producing state. Phylloxera was discovered in Geelong around 1875 and had affected several regions by 1900, most notably Geelong and Rutherglen. The discovery of gold around the same time essentially shut the door on wine production in many areas. The ensuing years saw a few diligent producers continue to grow grapes and make wine until the 1970s saw the start of renewed interest. You will see this mirrored in several of Victoria's most famous regions.

Victoria is tucked into the south-eastern corner of the Australian mainland and although it is the second smallest state it is home to more individual wineries than any other state in Australia. It has many diverse regions. The warm-climate regions span the northern and western rim of Victoria, Murray Darling, Swan Hill and Rutherglen. The vast majority of the state's other regions, with a few exceptions, are noticeably cooler. The net result of this regional climate diversity is that Victoria can produce virtually every imaginable wine style – fine sparkling wine, a broad array of white wine styles, high quality Pinot Noir, savoury Shiraz, perfumed, mid-weight Cabernet blends and the historic fortified wines.

The GIs of Victoria

Victoria is one of Australia's smaller states, home to 6 zonal GIs, 21 regional GIs and 2 subregional GIs. That's almost as many as South Australia, which is responsible for close to 50 per cent of Australia's annual production.

Port Phillip zone

This zone incorporates the regional GIs surrounding Port Phillip Bay; Yarra Valley, Mornington Peninsula, Geelong, Macedon and Sunbury.

Central Victoria zone

This includes the regional GIs of Bendigo, Heathcote, Strathbogie Ranges, Upper Goulburn, Goulburn Valley and its subregion of Nagambie Lakes.

North East Victoria zone

This captures the regional GIs of Rutherglen, King Valley, Alpine Valleys, Beechworth and Glenrowan.

Gippsland zone

An oddity in that it is a zonal GI with a regional GI of the same name.

Western Victoria zone

This encompasses the regional GIs of Henty, Pyrenees, Grampians and its subregion of Great Western.

North West Victoria zone

Captures the Victorian side of the Murray Darling and Swan Hill regional GIs.

PORT PHILLIP ZONE

James Halliday fittingly describes the regions of Port Phillip zone as the dress circle of Melbourne. All the regions are an easy drive from Melbourne so day trips are possible and if you want to understand regional Australian Pinot Noir, there is no better place to start.

YARRA VALLEY
(Woiworung Country)

The Yarra Valley, like many regions in Victoria, had its early viticultural history halted in the late 1880s due to the Gold Rush and, in some cases, phylloxera. The resurgence of interest started in the 1970s and this region is one of the pioneer areas for the development of modern Pinot Noir in Australia.

Climate and soils in this region are varied. The topography is a complex mix of hills and valleys. Aspect, elevation and exposure can change

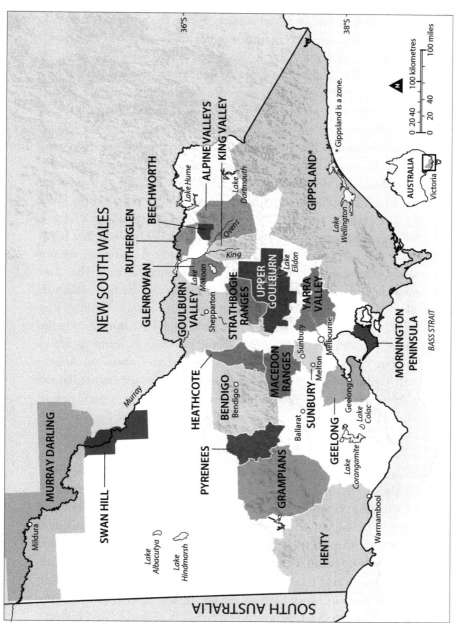

Map 4: The Geographic Indications of Victoria

in the space of several hundred meters. While the climate is noted as being cool overall and two main soil types are referenced (see below), much is site dependent.

As a result, several classic varieties do well, and many new varieties are being planted. Although this is generally a cool climate region, red varieties amount to 65 per cent of total plantings. Chardonnay and Pinot Noir are the modern era stars, grown in many sites across the region. Cabernet Sauvignon has a storied history in the region and the many examples sit alongside the very best of Australia. Despite various safeguards, phylloxera was discovered in the region in 2006. It is moving slowly, which has allowed viticulturists some time to plan. Losing older vine premium sites and the inherent attributes they bring to a wine is a challenge. You can't replace that. Additionally, the financial burden is significant. It takes time to replant, and it is costly. A grafted vine from a nursery costs about six times as much as an ungrafted one. The silver lining is that it is providing an opportunity to rationalize how vineyards are planted and to rectify any planting errors of the past. Reimagining aspect, row orientation, spacing, density, etc., will have long term benefits, as will addressing the need to plant different varieties to adjust for climate change. Nebbiolo, Mencia, Grenache, Trousseau, Aligote Gamay, Grüner Veltliner and several other varieties are being planted with the future in mind. Planting of new vineyards is also occurring in sites deemed too cold in the past, and the Yarra has space for that.

Main wine styles

Chardonnay is the most planted white variety and the second most planted variety overall. Styles vary depending on fruit source. Chardonnay is grown on some very diverse sites but styles are generally fine, textural and restrained. The signature character of classic Yarra Chardonnay is that it typically displays a white peach character. Fruit sourced from the coolest sites also ends up being used for top-quality sparkling wine production.

Pinot Noir is one of the premier red varieties of the region. Given that it is planted in many parts of the region it is hard to pinpoint the Yarra style of Pinot Noir, although it is typically perfumed and mineral, ranging from quite light-bodied to more medium weight and textural. As with Chardonnay, fruit from the coolest sites is often used in high-quality sparkling wine production.

While Pinot Noir might be the variety you are thinking of when you first visit the Yarra, you leave realizing that its Cabernet Sauvignon-based blends are world-class. Site selection is critical for the Cabernet-based wines as some parts of the valley are too cool to ripen the variety consistently.

Site selection is important for Shiraz too. This is a great place to look for cool climate expressions of the variety, which are medium-bodied, raspberry-scented and savoury. Many producers in the Yarra choose to label the wines Syrah.

Although not extensively planted, several producers are crafting lovely expressions of Nebbiolo, with Luke Lambert possibly making the best version in the country.

Area under vine

2,840 hectares[43]

Climate

Differences in altitude and aspect lead to substantial variation in mesoclimate. Even the warmest sites in the Yarra are relatively cool. There is a typical annual rainfall of 1,160 millimetres, but only 200 millimetres of that falls between October and April

Soils

Although there are two main types there is a multitude of micro-site complexity. The grey-brown sandy loam with a mix of rocky clay subsoil is derived from the ancient sandstone of the Great Dividing Range. The younger red soils are of volcanic origin.

Varieties

Chardonnay, Pinot Noir, Shiraz and Cabernet Sauvignon are the main varieties. Sauvignon Blanc, Nebbiolo and many newer varieties are being trialled, such as Mencia, Grenache, Trousseau, Aligote Gamay and Grüner Veltliner.

43 Source: National Vineyard Scan 2020 and ABS

Producers

Yering Station

www.yering.com

This is one of a cluster of historic estates that has the word Yering in its name. Vines were first planted by the Sottish Ryrie brothers in 1838.

Yering was the name given to the land by the Woiworung people, who were original custodians of the land in this region. In 1850, Swiss-French immigrant, Paul de Castella purchased the site and increased the vineyard by 20 hectares, sourcing vines from around the globe, including some from Chateau Lafite. This marked the start of 'proper' grape growing and wine production. The property changed hands multiple times in the early to mid-1900s. The Rathbone family purchased Yering Station in 1996. A stalwart Yarra producer with a full complement of classic styles ranging from solid to exceptional. The regular Yering Station bottlings are a great introduction to the Yarra Valley. The Pinot Noir and Shiraz–Viognier are both excellent and don't miss the Cabernet Sauvignon, which is a mid-weight, aromatic and pure expression of the variety. The Reserve wines are only made in the best years and the Shiraz–Viognier typically captures my attention.

Yarra Yering

www.yarrayering.com

Established in 1969 by Dr Bailey Carrodus, this is one of the region's iconic producers. He passed away in 2008 and the winery is now owned by Ed Peters and Reid Bosward who also own Kaesler in the Barossa. Winemaking is in the hands of the immensely talented and thoughtful Sarah Crowe. The 70 hectares of vineyards are all dry grown and the approach is quintessential old-school small batch. I have had a fondness for these wines ever since the first sip of No.1 Dry Red Wine passed my lips. The wines are about depth, balance and lightness of touch. I had not tasted through a full line-up of wines since Sarah took over but did so in April 2022, sampling all the top wines from three vintages: 2015, 2017 and 2019. It was a privilege to be given this snapshot of Sarah's approach. These might just be the best wines that have been made at Yarra Yering. This may be seen as heretical by the traditional devotees of this estate, but I believe it to be true. The No.1 Dry Red Wine is the most famous bottling and is still a must-try wine. Predominantly Cabernet Sauvignon, it includes varying splashes of Merlot, Malbec and Petit Verdot. No.2 Dry Red Wine is predominantly Shiraz, with a tiny amount of Viognier and, more recently, a small amount of Mataro. No.3 Dry Red Wine is all native Portuguese varieties of which Touriga Naçional and Tinta Cáo make up most of the blend with some Tinta Amarela, Tinta Roriz, Alvarelhão and Sousáo. Those three are the flagship wines at Yarra Yering. The other wine that resonates with me is the Agincourt Cabernet Malbec.

Yeringberg

www.yeringberg.com.au

Yeringberg is a historic winery, vineyard and farm. It has been owned and operated by the de Pury family since 1863. The fourth generation, Sandra and David de Pury, now run the business. A visit is like stepping back in time, and there are several lovely wines. The red blend is just called Yeringberg and comprises Cabernet Sauvignon, Cabernet Franc, Merlot and Malbec. It is a balanced, medium-bodied gentle reminder of Cabernet Sauvignon's elegance and grace. The Shiraz is spicy, restrained, and full of dark, raspberry fruit. The Marsanne–Roussanne is a textural, honeysuckle-scented white wine with a lovely savoury finish. Lovely people and wonderful wines.

Mount Mary Vineyard

www.mountmary.com.au

This is another well-established estate where the flagship wine is Cabernet based, a reminder that while the recent narrative on Yarra is all about Pinot Noir, Cabernet is the variety with the longest history and pedigree. John and Marli Middleton established Mount Mary in 1971. It remains a family-owned, single vineyard estate, now run by third generation family member Sam, who is making some of the Yarra Valley's best wines. The Pinot Noir is really good, but of the classic wines, the Quintet, to this taster's palate, is a thing of beauty. It is a magnificent blend of Cabernet Sauvignon, Merlot, Cabernet Franc, Malbec and Petit Verdot. Medium bodied, with fragrant herbal notes, red and black fruits and silky tannins, it is so wonderfully balanced when young that it is hard to put it in the cellar even though that is exactly what you should do: and keep your hands off it for 10 years. This is one of Australia's best Cabernet-based blends. The white partner is Triolet, a blend of Sauvignon Blanc, Semillon and Muscadelle. Production of this amazing, textured white is small but it is worth seeking out. In response to the changing environment they planted southern French varieties in 2008. There are three white varieties, Marsanne, Roussanne and Clairette, and four reds, Grenache, Syrah, Mourvèdre and Cinsault. These grapes now see their way into a white blend called Marli Russell RP1 and a red blend, Marli Russell RP2. I have not had them but look forward to seeking them out on my next visit to the Yarra.

Mac Forbes

www.macforbes.com

Mac Forbes is a charming, smart, thoughtful winemaker whose career I have watched for the last 20 years. Experimentation and constant refinement are his driving passions. Chardonnay and Pinot Noir form the backbone of his wines but he is always tinkering with varieties, viticulture, site selection, planting densities, new winery techniques, old winery techniques, new blends, old blends. He is less concerned about varietal expression than terroir. He wants to make wines that speak to the sites they are grown on. Accordingly, his flagship wines are labelled with the vineyard and/or district they are grown in. His Pinot Noirs are delicate, fine-boned and perfumed. Woori Yallock Pinot Noir has always been a favourite but the Villages blend is a great introduction to the Mac Forbes style. His Chardonnays are tight, taut and restrained and typically bristling with acidity and a vibrant energy. They definitely repay your patience with a few years in the cellar. His EB (Experimental Batch) wines are always a treat. This is a range that sits aside from the core Mac Forbes offering and gets yearly input from the vintage crew as to what they should 'play' with. Every year is different but always fun and (nearly always) delicious. Do not miss his line-up of Rieslings. He sources fruit from the Strathbogie Ranges and bottles with varying degrees of residual sugar, the labels indicating the approximate grams per litre, sort of ... RS54, RS20, RS8, etc.

Giant Steps Wine

www.giantstepswine.com.au

This winery was started by the tireless Phil Sexton in 1997. The primary focus has always been on single vineyard Chardonnay and Pinot Noir. The winemaker from 2003 to 2021 was Steve Flamsteed (Flammo) and his wines just seemed to get better every vintage. He has handed the reins to Melanie Chester and if the first vintage of her wines is any indication, that trajectory continues. There is not a bad wine in this line-up, so it's just a matter of which site or style you prefer. The Yarra Valley cuvées of both the Chardonnay and Pinot Noir are well-priced and delicious. LDR (Light Dry Red) is a blend of Shiraz and Pinot Noir and is ridiculously easy to drink. I have always had a soft spot for Applejack Vineyard Pinot Noir and the Wombat Creek Vineyard Chardonnay. You can't go wrong with any of the wines though, so just go ahead and experiment.

The elevated Giant Steps Applejack vineyard is an ideal site for restrained Chardonnay and Pinot Noir.

Oakridge Wines

www.oakridgewines.com.au

This winery was established in 1978 and pioneered using fruit from the Upper Yarra. Head winemaker Dave Bicknell has legend status among Australian winemakers. Bicknell is fastidious and his attention to detail is obvious. His Chardonnays have long been admired and he was one of the early adopters in making more restrained, tight, taut, flinty styles by picking earlier and employing a very reductive winemaking approach. To get a sense of the style, try the Vineyard Series wines, either the Willowlake or Hazeldene Chardonnays. The 864 bottlings represent the single site series of wines and represent the best wines. The 864 Funder and Diamond Chardonnay is a drop-dead stunner. It has power and density of fruit but is detailed, complex and layered with a vibrant spine of lemony acidity. The range of Pinot Noirs is exceptional too. Look for the 864 Henk Vineyard Aqueduct Block Pinot Noir and the Vineyard Series Henk Pinot Noir. This is a top-shelf Yarra Valley producer at the top of its game.

Gembrook Hill

www.gembrookhill.com.au

This is a beautifully situated site in the upper Yarra Valley. The land was purchased in 1983 by Ian and June Marks. Their son Andrew Marks is

A classic Upper Yarra Valley vineyard site. Elevated, cool-climate sites like this are sought after for the character and quality of the fruit.

making the wines these days. The Sauvignon Blanc is one of the best in the valley and a wine I always buy if I see it in a restaurant or a wine shop. The Chardonnay and Pinot Noir are excellent too. Production is small, so wines are not easy to find but they are worth the effort.

Hoddles Creek

www.hoddlescreekestate.com.au

Owned and operated by the d'Anna family, this estate was established in 1997. The property had been in the family since 1960 but had never been planted to grapes before. This is an upper Yarra Valley winery with a focus on estate-grown single vineyard wines. Most production is Pinot Noir and Chardonnay, but there is also a small amount of Merlot, Cabernet Sauvignon, Sauvignon Blanc, Pinot Gris and Pinot Blanc. I don't typically get overly excited about Pinot Gris or Pinot Blanc but the Hoddles Creek versions are delicious. The 1er Pinot Noir and 1er Chardonnay are both excellent.

Denton

www.dentonwine.com

This is a perfectly situated property. If you get a chance to visit, it is the ideal spot to view the lower part of the Yarra Valley. Planting began in 1997 and there are now 32 hectares in total, with a range of different varieties. The best sites are planted with Chardonnay, Pinot Noir and

Nebbiolo. This is probably one of the best sites for Nebbiolo in the valley. They also tinker with some different styles. The Yellow Under Flor is a Chardonnay aged in barrel under flor yeast. It is a really cool, savoury style. The Orange and the Yellow are additional Chardonnay versions that see some flor ageing. If you like the character of Fino Sherry then these are fun wines to explore.

Timo Mayer

(no website)

Timo grew up in the Württemberg region of Germany, where his family has been making wine for more than 400 years. Now firmly entrenched in the Yarra, he makes small-batch wines on his Bloody Hill property, named so because it is 'bloody steep'! The Bloody Hill and the Dr Mayer Pinots are both fantastic. He makes a Nebbiolo from fruit he sources from De Bortoli's Dixon Creek vineyard. He also does a 100 per cent whole cluster fermented Cabernet Sauvignon. This is a fantastic line-up of wines made by one of the valley's real characters. To say Timo is unique just doesn't quite capture it. I don't know how to explain him fully so just find a way to meet him. You will be happy you did and you will leave with a story or two to tell.

Luke Lambert Wines

www.lukelambertwines.com.au

Luke makes fantastic, small-batch wines and not one of them is Pinot Noir. He sources fruit from the Denton vineyard. All wines are hand-picked, wild yeast fermented and bottled without fining or filtration. All are matured in large, old French and Slavonian oak foudres. Oaky flavours are not part of the picture here. I love his Black Label Syrah, which is fragrant, spicy, savoury and full of dark raspberry character; one of the best cooler climate Syrahs you can find. But his passion is Nebbiolo, and it shows. His Nebbiolo is amazing, maybe the best in the country. In 2017 he bought his own block of land in Glenburn, just north of the Yarra Valley, and planted 2 hectares of Nebbiolo. The vineyard is called Sparkletown. I can't wait to see those wines in a few years.

Dominique Portet

www.dominiqueportet.com

It is hard to imagine anyone with a better wine pedigree than Dominique Portet. His father, Andre Portet, was the *régisseur* (vineyard and winery manager) at Château Lafite Rothschild. Dominique studied Oenology at Montpellier University of Oenology and then worked in the Médoc, Rhône Valley, Provence and with Champagne giant Moët et Chandon. In 1976 he moved to Australia, founding renowned sparkling wine house Taltarni in the Victorian Pyrenees and Clover Hill in Tasmania. He moved to the Yarra Valley in 2000 to start Dominique Portet winery. He says of this move, 'I found fragrance and structure. Most of all the structure reminds me of Bordeaux. The Yarra has a charm, a beauty that engulfs you.'

His son, Ben, is gradually taking the reins and the wines are fantastic, top to bottom. There is the excellent tart, lemony vintage traditional method Blanc de Blancs and the delicious Brut Rosé NV. His Sauvignon Blanc is barrel aged and is super delicious; long, complex and full of melon and grapefruit flavours. Of the reds the Cabernet-based wines really stand out. The Fontaine Cabernet Sauvignon is a pure fruited, aromatic middleweight that is ridiculously good value. The Dominique Portet Cabernet Sauvignon and the Cabernet Malbec are both fantastic fragrant, elegant wines with layers of depth and complexity.

Ben Haines Wines

www.benhaines.wine

Ben is based in the Yarra Valley and while many of his wines are from fruit sourced in the region, he does make wines from other nearby regions. Although he is not a 'natural' producer per se the winery is very much low intervention, making precise and focused wines. His top Pinot Noir, appropriately named One for the Loves Pinot Noir is a silky textured, fragrant wine with gorgeous cherry fruit, spice and herbal characters. The Something About Sunday Chardonnay is from fruit sourced at the Denton Vineyard. It is an exuberant lemon- and peach-flavoured beauty that typically takes a couple of years in the bottle to show its best. He makes a top-flight Syrah and a regular bottling from fruit sourced in Grampians. Both these wines are top notch and worth seeking out.

Bobar Wines

www.bobarwines.com.au

Tom and Sally Belford started Bobar in 2010. The winery is tucked into a quiet section of the Yarra Glen district, and most of their fruit is sourced from Steeles Creek and Dixons Creek vineyard sites. Production is low intervention and small batch, with some really lovely, expressive wines. There is a delicious, textural Viognier where the inherent perfume of the variety is beautifully counterbalanced with a savoury tang from a week or so on skins. The Chardonnay was similarly textural with broad savoury notes, juicy acidity and a lovely phenolic grip that added dimension. The Syrah is a beautifully aromatic, medium-weight wine with the classic cool-climate character of raspberry, pepper and smoked meat. It reminded me of the Syrahs of French producer Hervé Souhaut when I first stuck my nose in the glass. The biggest revelation was an absolutely drop-dead delicious Gamay made using fruit sourced from the Roundstone vineyard planted in 1995. A great line-up of wines, made by a charming, thoughtful and down-to-earth couple.

Jayden Ong

www.jaydenong.com

This small, family-owned and operated winery produces wines under four labels. One Block wines are single block, single vineyard wines. My picks in this line-up are the Pinot Noir Gembrook, a delicately framed, light and fragrant delight and the Sauvignon Blanc Gladysdale, which has texture and weight. It sees a few months in old barrels and has a lovely lime blossom aromatic component. The La Maison de Ong line is all about premium Yarra Valley reds. The standout here is the Hermit Syrah, a mid-weight, fragrant beauty, loaded with dark raspberry and spice. Moonlit Forest is a range of unfiltered wines, most of which are made with fruit sourced in other regions. Jayden Ong Wines are made and bottled by Jayden Ong. There are two single vineyard ranges including the Yarra Valley GI's highest altitude vineyard 'Forest Garden', which is close planted over rocky soils, with vines dry-grown at nearly 700 metres above sea level on a south-facing slope, and 'Chestnut Hill', planted over heavy grey clay loam in 1985, and dry-grown at 280 metres on a north-east aspect. Both the Pinot Noir Chestnut Hill and the Chardonnay Chestnut Hill are fantastic. This very good producer also has a fantastic cellar door and bar in Healesville.

Thousand Candles

www.thousandcandles.com.au

This is a large and historic property covering 445 hectares of land. The farm is made up of vineyards and pastures for raising beef. Not just any beef – it is all grass-fed Waygu, the majority of which is full-blood Tajima Waygu. It is some of the best beef I have eaten anywhere, not just in Australia. Preservation of native bushland is a focus too. It is a stunning property and to be on the ridge overlooking the vineyards at sunset is positively mesmerizing. Stu Proud was the original viticulturist when the project was started in 2010 and is a mine of information on grape growing and soil health. I will spare you the details of the early days of Thousand Candles but suffice to say that under Stu's guidance the property is now on track with a more realistic and sensible focus. Stu is also the chief winemaker and has assembled a great team. The Gathering Field range serves for the entry level bottlings and the Pinot Noir–Shiraz blend in this series is a delight, full of crunchy fruit, savoury and delicious. The Gathering Field Nouveau is, as you would expect, juicy, lively and fresh. The Gathering Field Red Blend (Cabernet Sauvignon, Cabernet Franc, Merlot and Malbec) is a lovely fragrant, medium-weight reminder of the elegance of Cabernet-based blends in the Yarra Valley. The wines under the Thousand Candles label represent the best blocks of fruit of the vintage. The Single Vineyard Syrah is a spicy, blueberry-scented beauty and the Single Vineyard Pinot Noir is a leafy, earthy middleweight with a core of strawberry and cherry fruit. I am happy to see the trajectory this property is now on.

Peyten & Jones

www.pj.wine

Yarra Valley born and raised, Ben Peyten and Troy Jones have created a really cool vibe with their cellar door, which is very conveniently located across from the Four Pillars Gin distillery (more on that later). They are making a range of low intervention, fun, playful wines here, but whether by design or accident (it can be hard to tell with these two) some of their wines drift from playful into serious. The Peyton & Jones label definitely sits in the serious camp. The Hollow Bones Pinot Noir is a fantastic wine made with fruit sourced from a site situated 230 metres above sea level. Under the VV label, the Sangiovese is a wine to look for. There are some fun wines under the Skin Contact labels. Wild Ride is a skin-contact Verdelho that augments the apricot character of the variety with an interesting savoury overlay. The Freaks and Wonders Shit Show Mataro spends eight months on skins and is an interesting mix of vibrant blue fruit and savoury, earthy characters.

If you don't cross the street and visit Four Pillars Gin, you have made a mistake. This distillery was established in Healesville in 2015. It is owned by a group with a wine background and as such the visits are tailored to wine geeks. This is not a gimmicky side visit while in wine country: they are making world-class gin. A refreshing gin and tonic after a day of wine tasting is the perfect way to relax and reset the compass.

De Bortoli

www.debortoli.com.au

De Bortoli is a fourth-generation family that started out in the Riverina and now has vineyards in the Yarra Valley. Leanne De Bortoli and her husband Steve Webber manage the Yarra Valley estate, producing a full range of Yarra Valley classics and a collection of other wines that dance on the edge of alternative. The Lusatia Chardonnay and Pinot Noir are both sourced from the Lusatia Park vineyard and are excellent, especially the fragrant and detailed Pinot Noir. The Melba Amphora Cabernet Sauvignon is really good. Fermented and left on skins for 120 days in 1,000 litre amphorae, it is super-savoury, complex and textural. with an earthy, menthol character. Riorret (terroir spelled backwards) is a range of single site Chardonnays and Pinot Noirs that never disappoints. PHI is in the same vein but with the addition of other varieties, one of which is a lovely Gamay.

Salo Wines

www.salowines.com.au

This is a project started by Dave Mackintosh and Steve Flamsteed. Steve was the head winemaker at Giant Steps for many years and Salo is a small production side-project that started in 2008. They make one wine – so refreshingly simple. This Full Moon Chardonnay is sourced from a site in the Gladysdale area in the upper Yarra Valley. It is tightly woven but has a gorgeous lemon meringue pie character. It is a wonderfully layered and complex wine.

MORNINGTON PENINSULA
(Boon Wurrung Country)

Although there were small-scale vineyards in this region in the late 1800s, most had disappeared by the early 1900s. The serious replanting didn't resume until 1972. The Mornington Peninsula is located directly south of Melbourne, on a slender peninsula jutting out into Bass Strait. The climate is strongly influence by the ocean but aspect and site play a major role in shaping the wines. What is consistent is wind. It is generally blowing from one direction or the other. Chardonnay and Pinot

Gris do very well in the region, but over 50 per cent of the vineyard land is planted to the region's signature variety, Pinot Noir.

Phylloxera has not been found in the region and there are strict control measures in place. However, growers are researching and experimenting with rootstocks. The region is in the process of a 10-year study on suitable rootstocks for Pinot Noir. A wise move.

It is very hard not to be charmed by this region. Beautiful beaches, abundant local seafood and charming cellar doors, can all be found within a 45-minute drive of Melbourne. This proximity to Australia's second largest city generates an obvious tourism boost not only from city residents but also from international visitors. Land prices continue to increase, which ultimately translates to high wine prices overall. Thankfully, wine quality in the region is commensurately high.

Area under vine

1,100 hectares[44]

Climate

The climate is strongly maritime overall as no vineyard site is more than 7 kilometres away from the ocean. Individual site climate is very important. Humidity is relatively high. Frost is rare, due to consistent winds.

Soils

These are quite varied and complex but can be loosely broken into three groups: yellow and brown soils over friable, well drained clay in the Dromana area; red volcanic based soils around Red Hill and Main Ridge; more sand-based soils in the northern area near Moorooduc.

Varieties

Pinot Noir, Chardonnay and Pinot Gris are the main varieties but some Shiraz is also grown.

44 Source: Mornington Peninsula Wine

Main wine styles

Chardonnays from this GI have a very distinctive style, with typical flavours of melon, citrus and fig. Pinot Noir is the most planted variety in the region. Wines are light- to medium-bodied, with delicate cherry–strawberry fruit notes, a firm spine of acidity and soft tannins. The cool climate here is ideal for Pinot Gris. The best examples are light- to medium-bodied with stony, mineral notes and vibrant fruit. Shiraz from the region is medium weight in a cool climate style with the accent on red fruit and spice rather than richness.

Producers

Main Ridge Estate

www.mre.com.au

Established in 1975 by Nat and Rosalie White, this is the region's most iconic producer. At 230 metres above sea level, it is one of the oldest, coolest and highest altitude vineyard sites on the Mornington Peninsula. The 2.8 hectare site sits on rich, red volcanic soils and is planted to Pinot Noir, Chardonnay, Pinot Meunier and Merlot. The Pinot Meunier, when they make it, is an absolute delight; delicately framed, focused and pure. The Half Acre Pinot Noir is the most noted wine they make, and it is truly exceptional. It has long been considered one of the best Pinot Noirs in Mornington and in Australia. Andrew Caillard MW calls this estate the Grand Cru vineyard of the Mornington Peninsula. There's no argument about that from me.

Moorooduc Estate

www.moorooducestate.com.au

Dr Richard McIntyre planted the first vines on this estate in 1983. It is a small, family-run estate with a determined focus on Pinot Noir and Chardonnay. Daughter Kate McIntyre became a Master of Wine in 2010 and is also involved in the business. The single vineyard wines are all fantastic. Chardonnay and Pinot Noir both come from the McIntyre and Robinson sites, while the Garden vineyard is planted entirely to Pinot Noir. The Estate Chardonnay is a vineyard blend, principally from McIntyre with a little Robinson. The Estate Pinot Noir is typically equal parts McIntyre, Robinson and Garden vineyards. Both wines are a great place to start exploring this producer.

Yabby Lake

www.yabbylake.com

Tom Carson has been at the helm of the Yabby Lake winemaking team since 2008. He spent 12 years at Yering Station and a couple of forma- tive years working at Coldstream Hills with James Halliday. To say he knows his way around Pinot Noir would be an understatement. The Yabby Lake Pinot Noirs are fantastic, but they also make delicious Chardonnay, compelling, savoury Syrah and a small amount of Pinot Gris. The single vineyard wines are perennially brilliant and when a particular parcel of fruit from within the single vineyards looks exceptional, it gets vinified separately and bottled under the Single Block label. Excellent wines top to bottom.

Crittenden Estate

www.crittendenwines.com.au

Garry Crittenden is a pioneer in the Australian wine industry. He was the first vintner to see the potential of the Mornington Peninsula. Son, Rollo, is now in charge of the winemaking. This estate offers a broad range of wines from a cross-section of varieties. Not all are from Mornington Peninsula. The Morning Peninsula estate wines are mostly focused on the classic varieties of Chardonnay and Pinot Noir.

Stonier

www.stonier.com.au

Brian Stonier was one of the first vignerons in the Mornington Peninsula. He planted Chardonnay in 1978 and followed it up with Pinot Noir in 1982. The winery was owned by Accolade but they sold it to Circe in 2022. I have always admired and appreciated the regular bottling of Stonier Pinot Noir. It is an affordable example of the Mornington Peninsula Pinot style. The Reserve Chardonnay is a textured, complex wine and the W-WB Single Vineyard Pinot Noir is excellent. Fruit is sourced from the Windmill vineyard and is 100 per cent whole bunch fermented.

Hurley Vineyard

www.hurleyvineyard.com.au

Kevin Bell and Tricia Byrnes planted the Hurley Farm in 1998 and 1999. This is a Pinot Noir only producer that sells out quickly! It is not a winery that I knew about until recently but everything is really good. I will make a point of visiting when I am next on the Peninsula. The approach here is organic viticulture, non-irrigation, low yields and teasing out the best expression of a vineyard site. Production is small, with attention to detail. The single vineyard designated wines are Lodestone (1.4 hectares), Hommage (0.8 hectares) or Garamond (1.2 hectares).

The estate wine is a blend of sites. Of the single vineyard wines, I have only tried the Lodestone bottling which is perfumed, pure and packed with gorgeous cherry and strawberry scented fruit. Textured, layered and complex, it is a lovely wine. Apparently, this site is the warmest and the wines are correspondingly the richest. If that is the case, I am excited to try the rest of the line-up. This is a winery now on my radar and it should also be on yours.

Paringa Estate

www.paringaestate.com.au

In 1984, Lindsay McCall bought an old north-facing orchard with the intention of clearing it and planting Shiraz. This was not exactly the conventional wisdom in 1984. He sought advice but was told Shiraz wouldn't ripen in the cool maritime climate of the Peninsula. He did not listen and went on to plant Shiraz in the warmest part of the site. Why was he so doggedly determined to make Shiraz? He had tried a bottle of Seville Shiraz from the Yarra Valley a few years earlier and it was his epiphany wine. Today, they make a full range of excellent estate wines from Riesling, Pinot Gris, Chardonnay and Pinot Noir. And of course, there is an outstanding Shiraz. I like stubborn people like Lindsay McCall.

Kooyong and Port Phillip Estate

www.portphillipestate.com.au

Both estates are owned by the Gjergja family and all wines are made at Port Phillip Estate. Kooyong is a 40-hectare vineyard planted in 1996 to Pinot Noir and Chardonnay, with a small amount of Pinot Gris and Shiraz. Port Phillip is made up of two vineyard sites. Red Hill, planted in 1987, is a 9-hectare vineyard predominantly planted to Pinot Noir and Chardonnay. Balnarring, planted in 1997 is an 11-hectare site and is also planted to Pinot Noir and Chardonnay. All wines are estate grown, made and bottled. The single vineyard bottlings of Kooyong wines have always been impressive. Favourites for me are Faultline Chardonnay, Ferrous Pinot Noir and Meres Pinot Noir, though to be honest, they are all good. Both the Morillon Chardonnay and Morillon Pinot Noir from Phillip Estate are fantastic. The winery, which serves as the cellar door and is home to their top-notch restaurant, is an architectural landmark, an impressive and very stylish limestone rammed-earth structure.

Ten Minutes by Tractor

www.tenminutesbytractor.com.au

Martin Spedding started this venture back in 1997. He began by working with three family-owned vineyards in Main Ridge area – Judd, Wallis and McCutcheon – all ten minutes by tractor apart. Since then, additional new vineyards have been added. I have liked the wines from when I first tried them around 2008. They have become incrementally better with each vintage and now I rank Ten Minutes by Tractor as one of the finest producers on the Peninsula. The 10X bottlings are all solid and a great introduction to the style of Ten Minutes by Tractor wines. The three original sites, and in particular the Pinot Noir bottlings, are where my heart lies. It's a toss-up between McCutcheon and Wallis as to a favourite but to choose really would be splitting hairs. The restaurant on site is exceptional, so plan on going for a long, leisurely lunch and compare several bottlings side by side.

Ocean Eight

www.oceaneight.com.au

The Aylward family originally established Kooyong Estate in 1997. They sold in 2004 to turn their attention to a couple of vineyards on either side (bay and ocean) of the Peninsula for Ocean Eight, 17 hectares of vineyards planted to Pinot Noir, Chardonnay and Pinot Gris. Owner and winemaker is Mike Aylwood. He loves freshness and acidity, and his wines reflect this in their taut, bristling and vibrant nature. These are food wines built to be on the table with a variety of dishes. The Pinot Gris is deliciously easy to drink, and both the estate Chardonnay and its Pinot Noir counterpart are excellent.

Dexter Wines

www.dexterwines.com.au

Tod Dexter and his wife Debbie purchased and started planting their vineyard site in 1987. Tod was the winemaker at Stonier for the next 10 or so years and was selling fruit from their site to the winery. Eventually they decided to break out and make their own wines. The small site has a total of 4 hectares of Chardonnay and Pinot Noir from vines that are now over 30 years old. The regular bottlings of Chardonnay and Pinot are lovely wines and in exceptional years they do a Black Label bottling of both varieties. A great producer and a cool guy.

GEELONG
(*Wathaurong Country*)

In the early days of viticulture and wine production in Victoria, Geelong was one of the most important areas. In 1861 there was 225 hectares of vines and by 1870, that had almost doubled to 440 hectares. Many of the original vineyards were established by Swiss immigrants. Phylloxera was discovered around 1875 and the government, likely facing pressure from other regions that had been devastated, ordered all vineyards to be pulled out. Replanting started slowly again in 1966 and increased at a steady pace through the 1990s. This region has not developed at the same rate as Yarra Valley or Mornington Peninsula but there are several notable producers making some of Australia's top wines. Aside from the physical beauty of the region, there are no corporate entities involved in wine production. All the estates are family owned and operated.

There are no official subregions according to the GI regulations, but it is accepted locally that there are three quite distinct areas: the Bellarine Peninsula, Moorabool Valley and the Surf Coast/Otways.

Main wine styles

Pinot Noir is the flagship variety. The history and reputation of the wines made at Bannockburn and By Farr set the standard for the region. Site and vintage are all-important in dictating the style but in general, top quality Geelong Pinot Noir walks an interesting tightrope of richness, structure and intensity with fragrance and delicacy.

Chardonnay tends towards stone fruit and citrus characters, with the weight and texture balanced by firm acidity in the best vintages.

Shiraz from Geelong sits between classic cooler and warmer climate styles. Wines are red fruited and savoury with spice and herbs.

Area under vine

780 hectares[45]

Climate

Overall, the region is cool climate due to the dual influences of Port Phillip Bay and Bass Straight. The Moorabool Valley is influenced by warm winds. The

45 Source: Wine Geelong www.winegeelong.com.au

Bellarine Peninsula is distinctly maritime, with the constant influence of the Southern Ocean. The Surf Coast is also heavily influenced by the Southern Ocean but receives higher rainfall totals due to the proximity of the Otway Range

Soils

Primary soil across the region is red-brown clay over a hard clay base. Underlying limestone subsoil is common and has an influence on several notable vineyard sites. A type of black, cracking Biscay clay is also common.

Varieties

Pinot Noir, Shiraz and Chardonnay are the main varieties. Cabernet Sauvignon, Pinot Gris, Riesling and Sauvignon Blanc are also grown, and Viognier, Marsanne, Albarino, Fiano, Tempranillo, Grenache, Nebbiolo and Gamay are being experimented with.

Producers

Wine by Farr (By Farr and Farr Rising)

www.byfarr.com.au

Established in the Moorabool area in 1994 by Gary Farr, and now mostly run by his son Nick, this estate has been producing some of Australia's best Pinot Noir for decades. There are six different soil types across the estate vineyards. Rich red and black volcanic loam and limestone are the two main types, along with quartz gravel through a red volcanic soil, ironstone (called buckshot) in grey sandy loam with a heavy clay base, volcanic lava rock and some sandstone-based soils. The complexity of soils is key in shaping the distinctive wines. Gary began honing his craft at Bannockburn (with yearly vintages at Domaine Dujac) in the late 1970s so there is no real surprise that he would make great wines from the outset at his own estate. There is excellent Chardonnay and a delicious Viognier but you really should get stuck into the Pinots! A side-by-side tasting of Farrside by Farr, Tout Près and Sangreal is a heck of an exploration of not only this estate and the Geelong region but also of top-flight Pinot Noir in Australia. This is one of the country's top wine producers.

Bannockburn Vineyards

www.bannockburnvineyards.com

Established in the early 1970s by Stuart Hooper, this is a pioneer producer in Geelong. Early wines were influenced by Stuart Hooper and Gary Farr. Stuart passed away in 1997 but the estate has remained in the Hooper family's hands. The winemaker since 2015 has been Matt Holmes. There is excellent Chardonnay and Pinot Noir. The Bannockburn Serré, a high-density planted Pinot Noir, has ranked with the best examples of the variety in the region.

Lethbridge Wines

www.lethbridgewines.com

Ray Nadeson and Maree Collis established Lethbridge Wines in 1996 and you'd be hard pressed to find a more charming, intelligent couple in the wine business. Their flagship vineyard in Lethbridge is sustainably farmed and 'informed by organic and biodynamic practices'. The property has quite the selection of varieties: Pinot Noir, Shiraz, Viognier, Merlot, Sangiovese Brunello, Gamay and Chardonnay. These great wines range from the classically styled and structured to contemporary, cutting edge and playful. Mietta Pinot Noir is delicious. The Hillside Haven Pinot Noir is a bottling from a granite soil site and is perfumed, elegant and layered. I also really like the Hugo George Sangiovese–Merlot and the Indra Shiraz.

Scotchmans Hill

www.scotchmans.com.au

Established in 1982, Scotchmans Hill was a pioneer on the Bellarine Peninsula. Cornelius Kirkcaldy Pinot Noir, Cornelius Kincardine Chardonnay and Cornelius Sauvignon are the flagship wines for this estate. The Mount Bellarine line is a great place to start to get an understanding of this estate.

Mulline Vintners

www.mulline.com

Mulline Vintners is a collaboration between Ben Mullen and Ben Hine. Their first vintage was 2019 and they are solely focused on Geelong. I have only tried four of the wines they make. The Portarlington Chardonnay from the Bellarine Peninsula is medium weight, tight and taut with a savoury, lemony character. The Pinot Noirs I tried were all excellent, especially the two Bellarine Peninsula wines. Drysdale is a fragrant up-front delight and the Portarlington is tighter, more compact and savoury. I am really excited to try more from these guys.

SUNBURY
(Woiworung Country)

This is a relatively small region with a long history of viticulture, dating back to 1858. The climate is moderated by cold winds from which there is little protection as the region is relatively flat. The region is known for the production of elegant, long-lived Shiraz. Craiglee is the most famous producer in the region.

Area under vine

101 hectares[46]

Climate

The cool climate is accentuated by consistent winds that sweep across the plains. The nearby Macedon Ranges to the north and the ocean to the south also contribute to the cooling influence.

Soils

Typically dark, old infertile loamy soils. Some alluvial terraces with free-draining sandy loam.

Varieties

Chardonnay and Shiraz.

46 Source: Wine Australia

Main wine styles

Shiraz is the hallmark grape of the Sunbury region. The cooler climate shapes a very distinctive, peppery, savoury, raspberry-toned style. The best wines have the capacity to age, as the story about Craiglee will attest (see opposite). Sneakily delicious Chardonnay can be found here. Wines are elegant and structured with a firm backbone of acidity as you would imagine from this cool climate.

Producers

Craiglee Vineyard

www.craigleevineyard.com

If you only ever try one wine from this small region it simply has to be Craiglee Shiraz. Vines were planted here in 1864 but production ceased in the early 1920s, largely due to economics and changing tastes. Pat Carmody's family purchased the property, which was then a sheep grazing site, in 1961. Several bottles of 1872 Craiglee Shiraz were tasted at a dinner in Melbourne in 1972. This was an award-winning wine in its day, having garnered medals in international competitions. The wine was, by all accounts, remarkable and one of the attendees visited Craiglee and convinced Pat that vines needed to be replanted on the property. Pat believes that his legacy is to produce wines capable of ageing the way that 1872 Craiglee Shiraz did. The current style of Craiglee Shiraz is medium-weight, liquorice and cherry scented. This is a Shiraz that must be tried at some point in your wine tasting excursions. Craiglee Chardonnay is also fantastic and is a wine that can age gracefully.

Hairy Arm Wine Co.

www.hairyarm.com

This is a group of Melbourne-based winemakers and industry consultants. The company was started by Steve Worley in 2004. They make a collection of excellent, single-site wines from Sunbury, Heathcote and the Yarra Valley. Look out for the Hairy Arm Sunbury Shiraz, a medium- to full-bodied wine with rich, dark raspberry fruit and a lovely savoury finish.

MACEDON RANGES

(Dja Dja Wurrung, Taungurung and Wurundjeri Woi Wurrung Country)

Small vineyards and wineries were established in this region in the 1840s and 1850s but, like many regions in Victoria, production had all but ended by 1915. Virgin Hills was planted in 1968 and a slow, steady viticultural revival continued for the next three decades.

The region sits at the southern end of the Great Dividing Range. Altitude ranges from 300–800 metres above sea level. This is one of the coolest regions in mainland Australia. The dual effects of the cold winds and altitude push the average temperatures down even in the key ripening month of January. The south-east section of the region is the coolest, with the north-west being marginally warmer. All manner of mesoclimates are spread across the region so site selection is critical. Protection from wind and spring frost, maximizing sunshine hours and detailed canopy management can make the difference between ordinary and top-quality wines. This is a region that is positively bristling with energy and excitement at present. World-class Chardonnay and Pinot Noir is made here, along with vibrant Riesling, Sauvignon Blanc and sparkling wines. These classics combined with some of the more thrilling 'low intervention' and 'natural' wines, which I tried on a 2022 visit, mean that this is not only a region to watch but a must-visit when in Victoria. Although the region is only a one-hour drive from Melbourne it doesn't quite see the tourist traffic of Yarra Valley and Mornington Peninsula.

Main wine styles

Some of the very best Pinot Noirs produced in Australia come from this region. Generally, these are light- to medium-bodied, full of cherry and strawberry flavours, with juicy acidity and great length, depth and complexity.

Chardonnay is made in an elegant style, with citrus, nectarine flavours and a crisp backbone of acidity.

A decent proportion of the Chardonnay and Pinot Noir grown in the region ends up in the production of high-quality sparkling wine. Many producers in the region dabble in sparkling wine production.

Riesling is a variety that clearly excels in the cooler climate of Macedon. Granite Hills has been the beacon for many years. In contrast to the typical lemon and lime notes you get from Clare and Eden Valley Riesling, Macedon Rieslings tend to show a more rounded fruit character with apple and stone fruit and often display tropical notes of guava and passionfruit in their youth.

Some of the most exciting low intervention wines I tried during a 2022 visit came from Macedon. These included skin contact whites, orange wines, alternative varieties and unusual blends. These provide a lovely contrast with the classic varieties and styles and give this already appealing region an additional gloss.

Area under vine

250 hectares[47]

Climate

This region is one of the coolest overall climates on the mainland of Australia. Altitude and wind are key factors that shape the cool temperatures. Site selection important. High vineyards located at 650–800 metres altitude on the Great Dividing Range from Mount Macedon to beyond Trentham have the coldest hours during the ripening period. Central vineyards can be cold with air down-flowing from surrounding ridges. Western vineyards on the north-western side of the Great Dividing Range have somewhat milder summer nights and warmer days as some are sheltered from cold westerly winds. Vineyards south of Mount Macedon are warmer due to the closeness to the ocean. Northern vineyards are exposed to northerly winds, and have the lowest amount of cold degree hours.

Soils

Soils are quite diverse across the region. The underlying geology of the region is 400 million years old, from the Ordovician period. Sandstone and shale predominate. There are granite outcroppings in the Cobaw Range with sandy, stony shallow loam. The are some volcanic soils in the south-east.

Varieties

Pinot Noir, Chardonnay, Riesling and Sauvignon Blanc are the main varieties. Also grown are Gewurztraminer, Pinot Gris, Merlot, Cabernet Franc, Tempranillo and some Italian varieties, including Lagrein.

47 Source: Wine Australia

Producers

Granite Hills

www.granitehills.com.au

Granite Hills is a classic, historic Macedon producer that has been crafting beautiful wine for over 50 years. Situated 550 metres above sea level with granite boulders strewn across the landscape, it is a spectacular property. The distinctively cool site is planted with an array of varieties.

The Gamay is fresh and juicy, there is an elegant and slightly herbal Grüner Veltliner and the Shiraz is spicy and medium weight. The Rieslings from this producer are lights-out brilliant. The 1971 Block Riesling is one of my favourite examples of this variety from Australia. Laser focused, vibrant and pure, with chiselled citrus and apple fruit characters, this is an electrifying Riesling.

Cobaw Ridge

www.cobawridge.com.au

Alan and Nelly Cooper, who established the estate in 1985, have a compelling line-up of wines that lean towards the natural and low intervention. The skin-contact Chardonnay is a fantastic example of the style. Il Pinko is a rosé made from Syrah and is a perennial favourite, savoury, textured and complex. There's some tannic grip too; it is almost like a light red masquerading as rosé. The Syrahs from Cobaw Ridge are fantastic, full of dark raspberry, violets and savoury character. The Lagrein is also a beauty. Find these wines: it is a little gem of the Macedon Ranges.

Joshua Cooper Wines

www.joshuacooperwines.com.au

Josh is Alan and Nelly's son and struck out on his own in 2012 with a single barrel of wine. He says, 'My wine operation is based around a négociant system, sourcing from sensitive and conscientious growers with great vineyard sites in the Macedon Ranges and across Central and Western Victoria.' His Macedon wines are really good. Doug's Vineyard Pinot Noir is beautifully textured, long and complex and I have always like the Ray-Monde Vineyard Pinot Noir, which sits just outside the Macedon GI boundary (but who really minds). It is a fantastic wine. The Spring Rosé is Pinot Noir based and Spring Pinot Noir is the best way to acquaint yourself with Josh's style of Pinot. The fruit is from Doug's and Ray-Monde vineyards.

Bindi Wines

www.bindiwines.com.au

Originally purchased in the 1950s as part of the larger grazing farm Bundaleer, Bindi is a 170-hectare farm. The first vines were planted in 1988 with subsequent plantings in 1992, 2001 and high-density plots in 2014 and 2016. Total plantings of vines are now at 7 hectares. Bindi is a tight family affair run by Michael Dhillon and wife Wendy. A more

In an effort to push quality boundaries, Michael Dhillon has been experimenting with close planting of vines at Bindi for almost a decade.

charming and engaging couple you would be hard pressed to find. They are always tinkering, with an eye to improvement and it shows. Every year the wines get better which seems impossible as the wines have been fantastic for decades.

Bindi Chardonnays, especially the Quartz bottlings are restrained, beautifully structured and compact wines that expand on the palate with layers of flavour and texture. Whenever I am afforded the opportunity to try the full line-up of Pinot Noirs side by side, it inspires excitement and a touch of anxiety as I feel compelled to pick a favourite – a pointless ambition. And to complicate matters there are new, close-planted sites that will be available soon. Putting those new wines aside, Dixon, Block 5, Kaye and Original Vineyard are the Pinot Noirs I know best. In 2022 I tried the 2021 Block 5 Pinot Noir in situ with Michael. My notes say: 'perfume, texture, layered and complex. Everything I want from Pinot Noir is here. Unbelievable wine. Perfect Pinot. This is the best young Pinot Noir I have ever tried from Australia.' Yes. That good.

Shadowfax Wines

www.shadowfax.com.au

This is a Geelong-based producer that purchased two sites in Macedon, Little Hampton at 730 metres above sea level and Straws Lane at 800 metres. They make a great range of different varieties but it was the Pinot Noirs that captured my attention. The Macedon Range Pinot

Noir is a blend of the two sites and a delicious place to start. The Little Hampton Pinot is a tad richer than the Straws Lane but both are firmly structured with layers of flavour and beautiful acidity and length. These are really good wines.

Curly Flat

www.curlyflat.com

This producer burst on the scene in the early 1990s and garnered accolades from the outset. I have always liked these wines despite feeling that there was some unevenness from time to time. Matt Harrop took the reins in 2017 after 19 years at Shadowfax and the wines have never been better. A cheeky White Pinot (a rosé) and an easy drinking Pinot Gris are always worth a try as is the sneakily good Chardonnay, but it is the Pinot Noirs that shine. The Estate is a blend of sites and then there are the Central and the Western cuvées which are sourced from specific blocks on the estate. All are worth trying but the Western, which is particularly perfumed and charming strikes a chord with me.

Hanging Rock Winery and Vineyard

www.hangingrock.com.au

The estate was established in 1983 and they make a range of wines from both Macedon and Heathcote. Hanging Rock is a noted traditional method sparkling wine producer. Look for their NV Cuvée, which is a blend of several vintages and labelled with Roman numerals indicating the succession of releases. The current release is their eighteenth and labelled XVIII

Lyons Will Estate

www.lyonswillestate.com.au

This boutique, family-run estate was started by Ollie Rapson and Renata Morello. They don't buy or sell any fruit, everything they make is from their own vineyard sites. I have not tried their Chardonnays or Pinot Noirs but if their flinty, mineral and textural Riesling and absolutely delicious, red fruited, crunchy Gamay are an indication, I am sure they are excellent.

Dilworth and Allain

www.dilworthandallain.com.au

This is a small, mostly négociant-style business that also makes a few limited production wines. Not all fruit is from Macedon but there are a couple of interesting bottlings worth a look. The Franklinford Dolcetto is delicious and the Coupe de Foudre Pinot Noir is all Macedon fruit in an easy-drinking, approachable style.

Place of Changing Winds

www.placeofchangingwinds.com.au

Rob Walters found a site that sits at around 500 metres elevation, on the southern edge of the foothills of Mount Macedon, planting the first vines in 2012, with more in 2018. Chardonnay and Pinot Noir are the focus. Unfortunately, I have not had the wines from this estate but the reviews from people I trust are excellent, which is why I have included this producer. I plan to rectify my lack of experience with these wines the next time I am in the region.

CENTRAL VICTORIA

This is an expansive GI zone that sits on the northern foothills of the Great Dividing Range. The regions of Bendigo, Heathcote, Goulburn Valley, Nagambie Lakes, Strathbogie Ranges and Upper Goulburn all sit within this zone. The climate is mostly continental, with warm days and cold nights.

GOULBURN VALLEY AND NAGAMBIE LAKES
(*Ngurraiillam Country*)

The establishment of this region is inextricably linked to the creation of the Tahbilk estate (see entry under Tahbilk). Phylloxera ultimately heralded the end for the smaller producers in the region. Tahbilk survived and when the Purbrick family purchased the property in 1925, it was the only operating winery in the region. The late 1960s saw some replanting, with the establishment of Mitchelton. Nagambie Lakes is an official subregion and forms a system of lakes, billabongs, lagoons and streams. It is a cooler area and while viticulture exists in the broader Goulburn GI, this subregion is where most of the real action is. The area is well suited to viticulture and the patches of sandy soils are the reason that the old, pre-phylloxera vines still exist at Tahbilk.

Main wine styles

This is mostly a full-flavoured red wine region with a few distinctive white wines. Shiraz is the most planted variety of any colour. Wines are richly coloured and flavoured, with some stunning old-vine bottlings from Tahbilk standing the test of time and ageing gracefully for decades.

Cabernet Sauvignon also does very well in the region. The best come from cooler sites, and cooler vintages tend to yield the best examples.

Marsanne is an interesting legacy of what was likely a shotgun approach to planting. It has thrived here, especially at Tahbilk, where you will find the single largest planting of Marsanne on any estate in the world.

Viognier seems to have found a comfortable home in the region, producing fragrant medium-weight wines.

Area under vine

1,265 hectares[48]

Climate

The climate is distinctly warm, with the inland valley floor experiencing warm days but cool nights. The heat is moderated by lakes, creeks and billabongs connected to the Goulburn River. Growing season rainfall is not generous but access to water for irrigation is generally not an issue.

Soils

These are quite varied but fall into three loose groupings: red and brown sandy clay loam, yellow-brown clay loam and gravelly quartz sands.

Varieties

Shiraz, Cabernet Sauvignon, Marsanne, Viognier.

48   Source: National Vineyard Scan 2020 and ABS

Producers

Tahbilk

www.tahbilk.com.au

This is one of Australia's most historic estates. In 1860, a syndicate was formed to raise money to establish what was to be the Tahbilk Vineyard Proprietary. Within two years 80 hectares of vines had been planted, and by 1875, Tahbilk was producing around 70,000 cases of wine. As in many other regions in Victoria phylloxera put an end to virtually all the smaller vineyard sites but Tahbilk survived and when the Purbrick family purchased the property in 1925 it was the only winery still operating. There are pre-phylloxera Shiraz vines planted in 1860 here. Marsanne was also planted in the 1890s but the oldest vines on the estate now were planted in 1927. Marsanne is the best place to start at Tahbilk. The regular release is fresh, vibrant and easy to drink. The Cellar Release is aged for several years before release and the 1927 Vines bottling is a wine that repays years of cellaring. The 1860 Vines Shiraz is a classic. While it has the richness of fruit and weight of other warmer climate areas in Australia, the flavour profile is different; more iron-like and mineral, with peppery notes.

Mitchelton

www.mitchelton.com.au

Mitchelton was established in 1969 and now has a dazzling array of wines. Many are sourced from outside the region but of the estate wines, the Estate Single Vineyard Shiraz and Single Vineyard Marsanne are both solid.

HEATHCOTE
(Dja Dja Wurrung and Taungurung Country)

This region is north of the Great Dividing Range with elevations of between 180 and 360 metres above sea level. The original plantings of vines started after the Gold Rush in the 1860s but most were wiped out by phylloxera. The warm days are moderated by consistently cool nights, but this is a region for classic full-flavoured wines. The southern boundary butts up against the northern section of Macedon Ranges but the regions could not be more different.

The specific Cambrian soils are prized in this region. With a reputed age of 500 million years, it is well drained but with water holding capacity deeper down. The most planted and revered variety from Heathcote is Shiraz.

Main wine styles

The warmth of the region makes it suited to full-bodied red wine production and that is what informs the overall style of the region. With concern about the general warming trend, there are producers working with different varieties (see notes on the Chalmers Colbinabbin vineyard, p. 214).

Shiraz is the most planted variety in the region. It represents over 50 per cent of Heathcote's annual crush and essentially established the region's red wine reputation. Full-bodied, dense and richly textured, classic Heathcote Shiraz has the weight and power of Barossa Valley Shiraz. However, the fruit profile is different; there are similar black-berry and spice characters but Heathcote Shiraz typically displays an earthy, iron-like minerality. At its best, it creates remarkable wines with concentration and intensity. Many Heathcote producers have built their reputations on it. Climate change may indeed force a long-term rethink. Many producers are working hard to craft fantastic wines and the very best examples manage to balance fruit concentration, tannin and acid structure with increasing alcohol levels. I have had plenty of mid-range Shirazes from Heathcote that do leave me wondering about the future. It strikes me that trying to achieve balance with alcohol levels routinely clocking in at 15–16% abv must raise questions as to whether this is the best variety to be broadly planted in the region. For sure, there are many great examples of Shiraz in the region, but there are also plenty of wines that are overripe, one-dimensional and heavy. Discussions of a different varietal mix in the vineyards must be had.

Cabernet Sauvignon from the region is rich and full-flavoured, in a black fruited style. It works well in Cabernet–Shiraz blends too.

Grenache only represents about 4 per cent of plantings (2021) but you have to wonder if this might increase in the years to come given the changing environment.

Area under vine
1,840 hectares[49]

Climate
Overall, this is classic continental climate, with warm to hot days and cool nights. Individual site altitude and aspect creates important variation. The altitude ranges from 160–320 metres above sea level. The northern vineyard sites tend to be warmer (1.4–1.8°C overall) than sites in the south.

Soils
The exceptional soil of the region is the famous Cambrian Greenstone. It is a 500-million-year-old, decomposed, Cambrian era rock, giving a fine, structured red soil over textured, red calcareous soils. It has excellent drainage but

49   Source: National Vineyard Scan 2020 and ABS

has the bonus of good water retention capacity. There are a range of other soils beyond the classic Cambrian Greenstone.

Varieties

Shiraz, Cabernet Sauvignon and Grenache are still the main varieties but Viognier, Tempranillo, Nebbiolo and Sangiovese are becoming more and more important.

Producers

Jasper Hill Vineyard

www.jasperhill.com.au

Established by Ron and Elva Laughton, Jasper Hill's first vintage was 1982. This is the benchmark producer in the region. All the wines are estate grown and bottled. The first vines went into the ground in 1975 and they have never used synthetic chemicals. The vines are neither grafted, nor irrigated. Pruning and harvesting are both done by hand. You get the picture. This attention to detail is reflected in the wines. Their famous Georgia's Paddock vineyard is planted to Shiraz (12 hectares) and Riesling (3 hectares) and there is a hectare each of Semillon, Nebbiolo and Viognier. Georgia's Paddock Shiraz should be the starting point if you want to understand the classic character of Shiraz in Heathcote. Although rich, full-bodied and concentrated the wine never comes across as overbearing, especially when given a few years of bottle age. There is an underlying, iron-like minerality running through a core of black, spice-scented fruit. This top-notch producer should be your first port of call in Heathcote.

Syrahmi

www.syrahmi.com.au

Adam Foster established his brand to focus on Shiraz, Grenache and Mourvedre. His first release was a 2004 Shiraz. The grapes for Syrahmi Shiraz are sourced and selected from single vineyard sites each year but not always the same sites. The different batches of Shiraz each vintage are processed separately and are then graded and selected for either Syrahmi, Demi and in some years La La. Syrahmi and La La are always single clone, single vineyard wines. Demi is a blend made up of multiple clones and vineyards. Demi Shiraz was the first wine I'd tried and it is still a consistent favourite. Adam manages to tame the richness and concentration that defines Heathcote Shiraz and always produces balanced, fragrant and exciting wines.

Tellurian Wines

www.tellurianwines.com.au

This family-owned and operated vineyard and winery is certified organic. Shiraz is at the core of what they produce but they have an array of southern Rhône varieties planted too: Grenache, Mourvèdre, Carignan, Marsanne, Viognier, Roussanne and Grenache Gris. There is also some Fiano and Nero d'Avola, which is smart of them given the changing conditions in the region. The Pastiche Shiraz is very good and maintains a lovely balance of earthy spice and concentrated dark fruit. I really like their peachy, floral and textural Viognier and the Nero d'Avola is a lovely vibrant, fragrant iteration of this native Sicilian variety.

Chalmers Heathcote Vineyard

www.chalmers.com.au

This site was purchased in 2008 and the first vines were planted in September 2009. The inaugural Chalmers Heathcote wines were produced from the 2011 vintage, coinciding with the launch of the Montevecchio range. The site, near Colbinabbin, is planted to 24 different varieties, primarily of Italian origin. While they make a range of really interesting wines for their own labels, some fruit is sold to other winemakers. This is a space to watch, not just because there is a large range of exciting wines from alternative varieties. Rationalizing what varieties Australia is growing is an increasingly important discussion. Chalmers is ahead of the curve.

Munari Wines

www.munariwines.com

This is a family-owned vineyard founded in 1993, a really solid producer known for richly textured Shiraz. Look for the Lady Pass Shiraz and the Beauregard Shiraz. They make a cheeky, fresh lemony Garganega from fruit sourced at the Chalmers vineyards. They also grafted their Merlot and Malbec vines over to Sangiovese. The first vintage of this wine, called Next Chapter, was 2021. I have not tried it yet but am keen to do so.

Wild Duck Creek Estate

www.wildduckcreekestate.com.au

Wild Duck Creek Estate is a small multi-generational family-owned winery that established its reputation on the backs of rich, ripe, concentrated and classically structured red wines made mostly from Shiraz. The Reserve Shiraz is a deep, dark, brooding version of warm climate Shiraz. Duck Muck is a predominantly Shiraz red blend that certain collectors adore, and is hard to find.

M Chapoutier Australia

www.mchapoutier.com.au

This famous and historic northern Rhône estate has various interests in different regions in Australia. The Heathcote wine is La Pleiade Shiraz, a joint venture with Ron and Elva Laughton from Jasper Hill. They planted a vineyard on the Jasper Hill property near Georgia's Paddock using Australian Shiraz clones and imported French clones.

Greenstone Vineyards

www.greenstonevineyards.com.au

Greenstone Vineyards was established in 2003 by David Gleave MW from Liberty Wines in the UK, Alberto Antonini from Poggiotondo in Tuscany and Australian viticulturist Mark Walpole. They recognized the 40-hectare site as being well suited to Shiraz and Sangiovese. I have had many excellent bottles of the Sangiovese when the wines were still made in the Heathcote region. Greenstone was sold to a Melbourne-based businessman in 2015. He also purchased the Yarra Glen property in the Yarra Valley. The Greenstone wines are now made at this winery. I have not tasted the wines since the move to the Yarra Valley.

Sanguine Estate

www.sanguinewines.com.au

Tony and Linda Hunter first planted their vineyard in 1997 and gradually added vines each year. Sanguine Estate now has 22 hectares under vine. Shiraz is the focus, and the Reserve d'Orsa Shiraz is their flagship wine. They recently partnered with famous Australian test cricketer Alan Border to produce the first vintage of a limited release wine called Maiden Tonne. Cricket fans will see the play on words.

Tar & Roses

www.tarandroses.com.au

Tar & Roses is a series of wines made using fruit grown in Heathcote, Strathbogie Ranges and King Valley. The Rose Shiraz is a classically framed Heathcote example with rich, dark fruit, plush tannins and that iron-like Heathcote signature. The Tempranillo is lovely, capturing the ripe fruit and earthy spice character of the variety. The Sangiovese shows a charming earthy, dusty cherry fruit. Really good wines.

BENDIGO
(Djadjawurung and Taungurong Country)

Vines were originally planted in this area around 1855. The Gold Rush brought prosperity to the regions and wine production profited. By 1880, there were 215 hectares of vineyards and around 100 producers making wine. Phylloxera was discovered in 1893 and that signalled the start of the decline. This was also the year that the banks crashed, which was no doubt a contributing factor, as was a change in consumer tastes. Fortified wines were becoming more popular. The upshot was that wine production essentially stopped for almost 60 years.

In 1969, Stuart Anderson planted vines at Balgonie and a revival of grape growing and winemaking followed. The classic continental climate in Bendigo favours medium to full-bodied red wine production. Shiraz dominates plantings, with Cabernet Sauvignon playing a supporting role. There is some success with Sangiovese and Nebbiolo.

Area under vine

610 hectares[50]

Climate

This is distinctly continental, with warm to hot days and cool to cold nights.

Soils

The majority of soils in the Bendigo region are composed of sandy gravel, volcanic basalt or clay loams over clay subsoils.

50 Source: Wine Australia

> ## Varieties
>
> Shiraz and Cabernet Sauvignon are the predominant varieties. Sangiovese, Nebbiolo and Roussanne have a presence.

Producers

Balgownie Estate

www.balgownie.com

Stuart Anderson planted the first vines at Balgownie Estate, Bendigo, in 1969. It had been more than 80 years since a vineyard had been planted in the district. Cabernet Sauvignon and Shiraz were the focus and 1972 was the first vintage. Balgownie was the pioneer producer in the region, influencing a rapid expansion of viticulture in Victoria's central goldfields region. Anderson sold the estate in 1999.

Balgownie now produces wines from several regions and has established a vineyard-based resort and conference centre in the Yarra Valley. The estate has grown over the years and may have lost a little of its original historic benchmark sheen. The Bendigo-produced wines are still delicious and worth seeking out, especially the Estate Cabernet Sauvignon, Estate Shiraz and Black Label Sangiovese.

Sutton Grange

www.suttongrange.com.au

Established in 1998, this is a small producer whose wines are worth seeking out. The Estate Syrah is a lovely, mid-weight style wine with an accent on red fruit, spice and minerality.

STRATHBOGIE RANGES
(Taungurong Country)

There are no strong records of early viticulture in this region other than the Tubbs family vineyard, planted in 1900. The region's original hardwood forests were cleared, reputedly for use in the building of the Sydney to Melbourne railway line. These cleared areas became prime grazing land and there is a strong sheep farming tradition in the region. As is the pattern in Victoria, the modern era started in the late 1960s. However, Strathbogie is quite different from other central Victorian GIs. Vineyards are planted at between 160 and 600 metres above sea level so altitude plays a significant role in site selection and wine styles. The landscape is quite breathtaking, prime grazing land mixed with dramatic, granite strewn ridges. There are several vineyard sites that supply fruit to producers in other regions. Domain Chandon in the Yarra Valley sources Chardonnay and Pinot Noir for their sparkling wines in this region.

Area under vine

530 hectares[51]

Climate

This is a cool climate region overall, but the lower elevation sites are significantly warmer and suited to more full-flavoured red wines. Weather is consistently clear, dry and warm, with crisp, cool nights in the final ripening months. There is substantial site variation due to altitude differences. A constant wind and cool air drainage mitigates frost issues.

Soils

These are predominantly alluvial sands and sandy loam made up of decomposed granite. The broad range of elevations means that there are distinct differences from site to site.

Varieties

Chardonnay, Riesling, Shiraz, Sauvignon Blanc, Pinot Noir and some Cabernet Sauvignon.

51   Source: Wine Australia

Producers

Fowles Wines

www.fowleswine.com

Run by the energetic and charismatic Matt Fowles this is, by Strathbogie standards, a larger producer. Their top wines are under the Ladies Who Shoot Their Lunch label and while they opt to use the Victoria GI for labelling purposes, most of the fruit comes from Strathbogie Ranges. The Shiraz is a beauty and not to be missed and a fantastic example of cooler climate grown fruit. The same goes for the Chardonnay under the same label. Some fun, accessible and affordable wines are produced under the Farm to Table line, which is a lovely way to experience easy-drinking, lighter styled Australian wines. An excellent producer that is always tinkering with new ideas and refining their wines.

Elgo Estate

www.elgoestate.com.au

Family owned and operated with a strong focus on sustainability, this is the first winery in Australia to be powered by renewable wind energy. All wines are made from estate fruit, the Allira Chardonnay has a deserved reputation, and the Estate Riesling is delicious.

Maygars Hill Winery

www.maygarshill.com.au

The first plantings were in 1994 at this small, family run estate. Red wines are the stars here especially the Reserve Shiraz and Reserve Cabernet Sauvignon.

UPPER GOULBURN
(Taungurong Country)

The Upper Goulburn region butts up against the south-south-east of the Strathbogie Ranges. The original proposal was for both regions to be lumped together as the Central Victorian High Country but they are distinctly different, hence the separate GIs. There is no record of early viticultural endeavour in this region. The Goulburn River runs east to west through the centre of the region and this, along with Lake Eildon, is an important water source not just for viticulture but for the region in general. This is the start of the foothills to the Australian Alps and the landscape is picturesque – trout streams, grazing pastures, vineyards and ski slopes.

This is cool climate Victoria with vineyards planted as high as 800 metres above sea level. The Yarra Valley to the south and King and Alpine Valleys to the north have more well-known wines and producers so this region tends to fall under the radar.

Some local producers refer to parts of this area as the Yea Valley. Luke Lambert (see p. 221) says that Upper Goulburn doesn't have any meaning for him, his new site is in the Yea Valley.

Area under vine

290 hectares[52]

Climate

The climate is strongly influenced by the altitude which ranges from 300–800 metres above sea level. As is the case in all high-country regions, site selection is of paramount importance. North and north-east facing slopes offer the best chance of fully ripening the grapes.

Soils

There is a wide range of soils – granite, siltstone, clay, limestone and dolomite – and tremendous variation from site to site.

Varieties

Chardonnay, Riesling, Pinot Noir, Cabernet Sauvignon.

52   Source: Wine Australia

Producers

Mount Terrible Wines

www.mountterriblewines.com.au

Mount Terrible Vineyard is a stunning 2-hectare property tucked into the foothills of the Victorian Alps, just east of the township of Jamieson. The vineyard sits at about 300 metres above sea level. Jamieson falls just outside the Upper Goulburn GI so the appellation designation on the label is Victoria. They do make Chardonnay and rosé (from Pinot Noir), but I have not tried either of them. Pinot Noir is the speciality here and the wines were very good right out of the gates with their first vintage in 2006. Now they are excellent – detailed, focused, classically structured Pinot Noir. The wine is full of pure cherry and strawberry fruit, with some delicate earth and spice and a lovely savoury quality. Small production, superb wines.

Philip Lobley Wines

www.philiplobleywines.com

The Lobley family has owned this Glenburn property since 1992 and began planting in 1995. This small production, boutique producer makes around 1,000 cases of wine per year. The property is just outside the Upper Goulburn boundary but they, like many nearby producers, refer to the area as the Yea Valley. They do make a few Yarra Valley wines but of the estate wines, Pinot Noir is the shining star. The Phillip Lobley Pinot Noir is a fragrant, medium-bodied style wine with lovely strawberry-scented fruit and a savoury, gently earthy note. A very high quality producer.

Sparkletown

www.lukelambertwines.com.au

Small production superstar Luke Lambert has planted 1.6 hectares of Nebbiolo just near Glenburn. The property is called Sparkletown and that will be the name of the brand when the vineyards start producing. Keep an eye on his current website for future details. As noted in the Yarra Valley producers' entry (see p. 189), he has, in my opinion, consistently produced the best Nebbiolo in Australia. This is most definitely a space to watch.

NORTH EAST VICTORIA ZONE

The creation of zonal GIs in Australia does appear at times to be based on convenience for grouping of regions rather than anything congruous regarding landscape, climate, viticulture or wine styles. North East Victoria is a good example. Rutherglen, Glenrowan, Beechworth, Alpine Valley and King Valley are all part of this zone and could not be more different. Zonal GIs do benefit producers that fall outside the boundaries of specific regions but it is a reminder that a zonal GI is broad and not necessarily indicative of varieties grown or wine styles made.

RUTHERGLEN
(Waywurru Country)

Rutherglen is one of Australia's most historic and fascinating regions. Vineyards were first planted in 1839, which was prior to the Gold Rush. It thrived through the boom years between 1860 and 1893, becoming one of Victoria's most important regions. Unlike many other regions at the time, Rutherglen had the resilience to survive the ravages of phylloxera and the bank collapse and continued to make wine through the early decades of the 1900s. The taste for heavier red table wines and an increased demand for fortified wines domestically and in the UK seems to be at the heart of this survival. The warm climate is ideally suited to the production of heavier red wines and while this is significant economically, it was the fortified wines that floated this region and ultimately gave it global recognition.

Liqueur Muscat and Tokay (Topaque) are some of the most rich, luscious and unique dessert wines in the world. To sip a Rutherglen Muscat or Topaque is truly to taste the flavours of history. Explosively rich and sweet, these luscious wines offer unbelievable layers of complexity as they age in cask.

Area under vine

780 hectares[53]

Climate

The region has a classic continental climate – long, warm summer days and cool nights. Autumns are typically long and dry. Rain at harvest is sometimes a threat. Spring frosts are relatively common.

Soils

Soils are quite variable, though there are three main types. In the north, closest to the Murray River there is fine sandy loam. This well-draining soil typically produces floral wines with lower acidity and less tannin. On the lower slopes of the gentle hills, there is red loam over clay, with good moisture-holding capacity. This is the best-known soil of the region. The other soil type contains bands of shale and quartz. This is best suited to full-bodied red wine production.

Varieties

Durif (Petite Sirah), Shiraz, Muscat à Petits Grains Rouges (Brown Muscat), Muscadelle.

53 Source: National Vineyard Scan 2020 and ABS

Main wine styles

Red table wine production far outstrips fortified wine production and has done so for quite some time.

Shiraz has a long tradition in the region and while the style is rich, full-bodied and intense, the best examples are balanced and have the capacity to age gracefully.

Durif, a southern French variety, has been grown in Rutherglen for more than 100 years and is the sneaky superstar. It is a late ripening variety that is particularly well-suited to the climate in Rutherglen. Wines are full-bodied and inky but never cloying or over-extracted. The best age beautifully and can be more interesting than Shiraz in this region.

Plantings of the red clone of Muscat have been in the region for 140 years. It is the variety that is responsible for the production of the most famous wine of the region – Rutherglen Muscat.

Muscadelle is the variety used to produce Rutherglen Topaque. This is the newer name for what was historically called Rutherglen Tokay. Confusion with the Hungarian wine forced the change.

Rutherglen Muscat and Rutherglen Topaque are produced using classic fortification methods but the twist is in the maturation and blending. They are always non-vintage wines. The key to the style is the blending of developed, complex and layered flavours of older wines with the vibrant, fruity freshness of younger wine. A sort of modified version of solera ageing. Both Muscat and Topaque have four levels to the classification of the wines: Rutherglen, Classic, Grand and Rare.

Wines higher up the classification contain a greater quantity of older wines in the blend. The classification system is self-monitored by the winemakers who hold regular benchmarking classification tastings.

The Muscat styles are concentrated, with explosively rich, raisiny fruit that always shows the fragrant fruitiness of the variety. This is the most famous wine of Rutherglen. Rare Rutherglen Muscat is something that must be experienced at some point in one's wine-drinking journeys. There are many styles of sweet Muscat-based wines produced around the world but nothing compares to this.

Topaque production is smaller than Muscat and the style is lighter, with definite light toffee, malt and butterscotch aromas and flavours. Some tasters refer to a cold tea note. I always get a whiff of chamomile. Production has decreased dramatically over the years due to changing tastes. Thankfully, all the historic producers view themselves as custodians of an important part of Australian wine history and continue the tradition despite the diminished economic importance of these wines. We should all be grateful. These are uniquely Australian expressions that belong on the table with the greatest fortified wines in the world.

Producers

Chambers Rosewood

www.chambersrosewood.com.au

Chambers is a sixth-generation, family owned and operated business that was established in 1858. Muscat and Muscadelle are the cornerstone varieties, some of which are over 100 years old. They grow many other varieties, including Palomino, Roussanne, Riesling, Gewurztraminer, Tempranillo, Durif, Mondeuse, Cinsault and Shiraz. Chambers also grows the rare Gouais grape, a parent of Chardonnay and Riesling. This is one of the very best producers in the region. Their Rare Muscat is a wine of incredible depth, concentration and complexity. It repeatedly garners perfect scores from wine critics across the globe. This is possibly the best example in the region, which is saying something given the overall quality from other producers. Another must-try wine. Their table wines are very high quality too. The Gouais is really delicious and has the capacity to age very well for 10–15 years. Chambers Durif is one of the better examples of this commonly planted variety, full flavoured with generous fruit and soft, ripe tannins.

Morris Wines

www.morriswines.com

This family-run estate has been around for over 160 years. In 1859 George Francis Morris planted the first vines on the original family property. By 1885 they had 200 acres (80 hectares) under vine, making Morris the largest producer in the Southern Hemisphere at the time. This is one of the great Rutherglen producers. A full range of fortifieds is produced here, as you'd expect. The Rare Topaque and Muscat are superb, but you can't go wrong with anything from this producer.

All Saints

www.allsaintswine.com.au

This historic estate is run by fourth generation Brown family members Eliza, Angela and Nicholas Brown. The are many old vines in Rutherglen and All Saints are custodians of several old vine sites – Shiraz planted in 1920, Muscat planted in 1930, Cabernet Sauvignon planted in 1950 and Marsanne planted in 1958. The fortifieds are brilliant as you would imagine and they have the full range of Muscat and Muscadelle, from Rutherglen through to Rare. The fantastic fortified Tawny is well worth seeking out. There is an excellent range of table wines here too. Look for the structured, fleshy mulberry-accented Durif, a lemony and savoury Marsanne and their fantastic 1920 Old Vine Shiraz. A top flight producer.

Campbells

www.campbellswines.com.au

Campbells is a fifth-generation Rutherglen family. Their history here dates to 1868 when John Campbell first purchased 79 acres (32 hectares) of land and planted some vines. Campbells was established in 1870 with their first vintage of wine. We lost Colin Campbell in 2019. I think we toss the word legend around a little too freely in Australia, but Colin Campbell was indeed a proper legend. I had many conversations with him, and he never lost his passion and enthusiasm for the region. Campbells is my favourite producer in Rutherglen and I will openly admit that it is simply due to my fondness for Colin. I offer no apologies for putting my complete bias on display. Colin's enthusiasm was instilled in the family and the brilliance that is Campbell's continues. There is a top range of Muscat and Topaque. The Merchant Prince Rare Muscat has, like the top Chambers Muscat, been given perfect scores on several occasions. It is a masterpiece in the complex and varied world of fortified wines.

Stanton & Killeen

www.stantonandkilleen.com.au

Another story of generational Rutherglen history, with 145 years of family winemaking and seven generations of involvement, this is currently run by Wendy and Natasha Killeen. The focus is on Portuguese varieties, classic Rutherglen red wines and maintaining the tradition of Muscat, Topaque, Tawnys and Vintage fortifieds. A full range of excellent fortified wines and a really compelling line-up of table wines are made from Portuguese varieties. Natasha Killeen researched Portuguese varieties extensively before choosing three to plant in Rutherglen; Arinto, Alvarinho and Antão Vaz. The first two were planted successfully in 2015 and are yielding excellent results. Antão Vaz was planted recently, in 2020. The Arinto is crisp, lemony and delicious and the Alvarinho is fresh and lively with characteristic light peachy flavours and crisp acidity. A great producer that is maintaining the legacy of the Rutherglen traditions while keeping an eye on the future.

Pfeiffer Wines

www.pfeifferwinesrutherglen.com.au

In 1984, Chris and Robyn Pfeiffer purchased what was then the Old Distillery. It was owned at the time by Seppelts but the building has a history dating back to 1895. It took a tremendous amount of time and effort to get the facility back to working order, but the Pfeiffers had it fully operational by 1986. As with most top Rutherglen producers, they have a full range of fortified wines, including a few fun Apera (Sherry) styles. The range of table wines is solid.

BEECHWORTH
(Waywurru Country)

Gold found around the town of Beechworth in 1852 brought prosperity to this relatively small, altitude-influenced region. The first reference to vineyards being planted was in 1856 by a gentleman called Rochlitz. In 1863 he is credited with supplying the region with the initial vine propagation material. It is believed that he obtained the cuttings from the Adelaide Botanic Garden which in turn came from the Busby collection of 1832. By 1891, 70 hectares of vines had been planted but this had dwindled to virtually nothing by 1916. Some vines were planted in 1978 but the fruit was sold to Brown Brothers in Glenrowan. Rick Kinzbrunner purchased a small block of land near the town in 1980 and in 1982 started planting vines. In 1985 he established Giaconda, now one of Australia's cult wines. This was effectively the start of the modern era for Beechworth. Many new producers followed, but planting has generally remained small in scale. This region is home to a multitude of exciting, high-quality, small production wines. Chardonnay, Shiraz and Pinot Noir are the stars of the region.

Main wine styles

Shiraz here is typically in a medium-weight, cool climate style, with red fruit, spice and savoury character. Giaconda established this region's reputation for Chardonnay, which is intense and concentrated with weight and texture. There are stone fruit flavours with fresh acidity and wines have a capacity for ageing gracefully. Pinot Noir is medium bodied and finely structured but wines range in character depending on site. Typically, they are fragrant, scented with cherry and raspberry.

Area under vine

134 hectares[54]

Climate

The climate in general is continental, with warm, sunny days and cool nights. Altitude is the primary informant of the climate, but it varies depending on site – generalizations are difficult. Vineyards sit between 300 and 650 metres above sea level with some sites at 800 metres. The best vineyards are on the slopes for better air drainage to avoid the issues of frost.

Soils

There are two major groups of soils in the region: old sandstone, mudstone and shale, and granitic top-soils over clay derived from volcanic deposits.

Varieties

Shiraz, Pinot Noir and Chardonnay.

54 Source: National Vineyard Scan 2020 and ABS

Producers

Giaconda

www.giaconda.com.au

Rick Kinzbrunner founded Giaconda in 1981. The estate vineyard is 4 hectares planted at 400 metres altitude on granitic loam over decomposed gravel and clay. So much has been said about this iconic Beechworth producer but Giaconda's US importers Jane Lopes and Jonathan Ross sum it up succinctly: 'Giaconda is one of the great estate wineries of Australia. Having these expectations going into tasting these wines for the first time, we were *still* blown away by the impact they had on us: the expressiveness, power, precision, and pure deliciousness of Giaconda's wines make them not just one of the greats of Australia, but truly one of the great estates of the world.' The Giaconda Estate Chardonnay is expensive and hard to find. As it should be. Complex, layered and textured, it is an absolute delight. Giaconda Warner Shiraz is savoury, peppery, smoky and floral, a medium-weight, red fruited beauty. He also makes excellent Pinot Noir and Roussanne and lovely, floral Nebbiolo.

Castagna

www.castagna.com.au

Julian Castagna started this estate in 1995. The vineyard was planted in 1997 on what was previously grazing land. Five different clones of Syrah are grown, all of which are progeny of the original 1850s stock imported into Australia from the Rhône. The land has been farmed bio-dynamically from the very beginning. A cheeky, fresh-scented Chenin is worth finding. Un Segreto is a Sangiovese–Syrah blend. La Chiave is 100 per cent Sangiovese and it is a beautifully structured, savoury version, with classic dried-cherry fruit and a whiff of cinnamon spice. The Genesis Syrah is a fantastic wine and has always been a favourite. This medium-weight wine is more about red berry than dark berry fruit, peppery, savoury and very northern Rhône like. I hate making the comparison but it was what immediately came to mind when I first tried this wine. Castagna is one of the region's very best producers.

Sorrenberg

www.sorrenberg.com

This is a 2.5 hectare biodynamically certified vineyard owned by Barry and Jan Morey. The first vines were planted in 1985 and the first vintage was 1989. Their main varieties are Chardonnay, Sauvignon Blanc, Cabernet Sauvignon and Gamay, with smaller quantities of Cabernet Franc, Merlot, Semillon and Pinot Noir, which typically get used in blends. The Gamay is a drop-dead gorgeous example of the variety and probably the best Gamay in Australia. The Sauvignon Blanc–Semillon blend is also super delicious. The Chardonnay is layered, complex and savoury. A delightful boutique producer making fantastic wines.

Vignerons Schmölzer & Brown

www.vsandb.com.au

This is a partnership between Tessa Brown and Jeremy Schmölzer. They planted their Thorley vineyard in one of the highest elevation sites in the Beechworth region. They also make wines from fruit sourced in the King Valley and make a few blends using fruit from both regions. The selection of wines is exciting and diverse. The new Beechworth Pinot Noir is medium weight, fragrant and full of strawberry fruit and spice. The Beechworth Riesling is crisp and lively, with tart apple and lemon flavours bristling through the firm acid structure. The Prêt-à-Rouge is a delightful, juicy, red-fruited blend of Shiraz and Pinot Noir. Excellent wines from the King Valley are made too. There is a very cool Sylvaner and the Obstgarten Riesling Selection is deliciously complex, with a touch of botrytis broadening out the structure and palate weight. An excellent producer.

Golden Ball Wines

www.goldenball.com.au

This is a great producer making a lovely line-up of estate-grown and estate-bottled wines. All the fruit comes from either the Original Vineyard, planted in 1996 or the Lineage Vineyard, planted in 2005. Golden Ball Là-Bas Chardonnay is top-notch and one of the better examples of the variety in the region. I also like the textural and savoury nature of the Bona Fide Savagnin.

Traviarti

www.traviarti.com

This is a small producer making Chardonnay and Nebbiolo, of which I have only had the Nebbiolo. The Mezzo bottling is the more approachable style with the regular bottling being more classically structured and age-worthy.

Fighting Gully Road

www.fightinggullyroad.com.au

Top-notch viticulturist Mark Walpole is the man behind this venture. He has a cross-section of classic varieties planted: Cabernet Sauvignon, Merlot and Chardonnay alongside some Sangiovese, Tempranillo, Aglianico and Petit Manseng. The price:quality ratio is fantastic at Fighting Gully. You can try an excellent range of wines at very reasonable prices. The Tempranillo and Sangiovese are standouts for me, but you can experiment up and down the line-up and will not be disappointed.

KING VALLEY
(Waywurru Country)

The King Valley wine region is relatively large compared to the neighbouring regions of Alpine Valleys and Beechworth. The valley follows the King River, flowing from its upper reaches in the Alpine National Park, due north to the Rural City of Wangaratta. The valley ranges from a broad river basin in the north to the ranges in the extreme south, peaking at over 800 metres. The southern parts of the region sit in the foothills of the Alpine National Park. This was originally a tobacco-growing region, farmed by predominantly Italian immigrants, but as this became less profitable other crops became more important. Vineyard plantings started in the 1970s and many of the producers have Italian roots. The charm and natural beauty of this region is hard to deny, and the Italian influence gives it an additionally compelling reason to visit.

Area under vine

1,535 hectares[55]

Climate

The climate changes progressively and significantly from lower northern to higher southern elevations, with a progressive increase in rainfall and a de-crease in heat summations. Grape ripening is correspondingly delayed and the wine styles change. At the higher altitude sites, only the earlier ripening white varieties are suited to table wines.

Soils

The soil types vary significantly throughout the valley, changing with altitude, slope and site characteristics. Deep red clay loams are common, with some grey or brown loam.

Varieties

Prosecco, Pinot Gris, Sangiovese and Merlot are the main varieties but Nebbiolo and other Mediterranean varieties are also planted.

55   Source: National Vineyard Scan 2020 and ABS

Main wine styles

King Valley Prosecco is a thing in Australia and a *lot* is produced in the region. Frothy, delicious and ludicrously easy to drink, it is the first thing in your glass when you visit most producers. As you might imag-ine, the use of the name Prosecco has caused some controversy in Italy (see the Prosecco drama box, opposite).

Sangiovese is produced in a range of styles, from light, juicy and fresh through to more structured, savoury and age-worthy wines.

Different styles of Pinot Gris also exist. The lightweight, fresh and juicy versions are labelled Pinot Grigio, while medium-weight wines with more structure are labelled Pinot Gris.

Merlot is generally medium bodied and fragrant with a herbal lift.

There is not as much Nebbiolo planted as Sangiovese but some excellent examples exist and the producers who have hung their hats on this variety are dedicated and passionate.

The Prosecco drama

The Dal Zotto family initiated the importation of the Prosecco grape to Australia in the late 1990s. They planted the first vines in 1999 in the King Valley. Prosecco now grows in 20 regions across Australia and is of significant economic importance to many producers. Domestic consumption and export value have consistently increased for the last 8–10 years. At the end of 2021, sales value reached more than A$200 million (US$130 million).

The Italian disagreement with Australia goes back to 2009, when the Italian Prosecco producers moved to secure an expanded protected geographic designation under Italy's recognized DOC system. The new DOC was designed to protect Prosecco's brand and keep a grip on the ever-growing global market for Prosecco. The issue is one of nomenclature. Wine appellations are geographically designated areas tied to place names not grape varieties. Italian Prosecco had long been made with what was called the Prosecco grape, meaning you couldn't protect it. So, the Italians simply changed the name. In 2009 they removed Prosecco as a grape and began calling it Glera, an obscure synonym for the same variety. Effectively, in the minds of the Italians, Prosecco was no longer a grape variety and now described a style of sparkling wine and a region named for the tiny Italian-Slovenian border town of Prosecco. A full decade after Australian producers planted their first Prosecco grapes, Italy declared Prosecco a protected geographic area. It is not difficult to understand why Australian producers feel that Italy's rebranding of Prosecco as a region rather than a grape is disingenuous. Also, there is genuine concern that codifying Italy's manipulation of the Prosecco term in a major international trade deal could produce additional concerns for other varieties being used not just in Australia. As at writing (May 2023) the disagreement had not been resolved, but Australia is currently in discussions with the EU on wine and free trade agreements and the Prosecco issue is on the table, among other things.

Producers

Pizzini Wines

www.pizzini.com.au

This established King Valley producer has been working with Italian varieties from the start. The Nebbiolo is fantastic. Where can you try a vertical tasting of Nebbiolo back to the early 1990s outside Italy? Here at Pizzini. The Sangiovese Nonna Gizella is the epitome of a Monday to Thursday red wine. They also have a Verduzzo, Arneis and Brachetto.

Dal Zotto

www.dalzotto.com.au

This is the Pioneer Australian Prosecco producer (see box, p. 231). Their Col Fondo Prosecco is delicious and you will find all manner of lovely Italian varietal wines here, including Arneis, Garganega, Barbera and Sangiovese.

Brown Brothers

www.brownbrothers.com.au

Although not based in King Valley, this large, historic, family owned and operated wine company has property in the region. Their Prosecco fruit is sourced from King Valley.

Konpira Maru Wine Company

www.konpiramaruwinecompany.com

Friends Sam Cook and Alastair Reed got together to create this venture. The Konpira Maru mission statement is: 'to make mid-week wines great again'. I love it. Their goal is to make wines that are full of character and highly drinkable but also affordable. They have been working with growers in Queensland and other parts of Victoria and, in 2016, purchased their own site near Whitlands in the King Valley. Not only are they true to their mission statement, they do it with fantastic labels and more than a modicum of humour. Pan Opticon is a Riesling-based blend with some Pinot Gris and a splash of Gewurztraminer. It is super juicy and delicious and comes in a vibrant blue bottle – think Blue Nun bright blue. Over and Over Pinot Noir is a light-bodied, easy-drinking, red-fruited beauty. I need to meet these guys.

Eminence Wines

www.eminencewines.com.au

This was a new producer for me which is a tad embarrassing given that they are not that new. You can't be across everything, I guess. They are based in the Whitlands High Plateau which is technically part of the King Valley but is decidedly different. Clare Burder and partner Pete Allen are the people behind the wines today. The vineyards were first planted by Clare's parents, David and Sharon Burder in 1998. More vines were planted in 2003. Situated at over 870 metres above sea level, these are some of the highest vineyard sites in Victoria. As of 2022 they had around 12 hectares of Chardonnay, Pinot Noir, Pinot Meunier, Pinot Gris and some Pinot Blanc. I have tried five of their wines to date. A deliciously, juicy and frothy Pinot Meunier Pet Nat, a Skinsy Pinot Gris and a deep, dark, ripe fruited rosé, appropriately called Baritone. The Pinot Noir–Meunier blend is bright, lively and pure fruited and super appealing. I look forward to many more wines from this producer, and a visit is in order next time I am in the area.

ALPINE VALLEYS
(Waywurru and Jaitmatang Country)

Located in the northern foothills of the Victorian Alps, this region consists of five basins created by the Ovens, Buffalo, Buckland and Kiewa rivers. The name of the region is evocative and the landscape does not disappoint. This is a beautiful part of the state to visit. Altitude is the main element in shaping the climate. This area is a popular winter destination due to nearby ski resorts. There are a few very appealing wineries but a lot of fuit is sold to bigger companies outside the region and the smaller production Alpine Valley labelled wines are hard to find outside the state of Victoria as most is sold locally.

Area under vine

260 hectares[56]

Climate

The region has a strongly continental climate, with spring frost the major

56 Source: National Vineyard Scan 2020 and ABS

viticultural hazard, followed by autumn frost prior to harvest. Site selection on hillsides with good airflow minimizes the level of frost risk.

Soils

The soils in the major valleys are all formed on river deposits from similar rocks – mostly granite. Many different soil subtypes exist in the region, from sandy loams to red-brown duplex soils.

Varieties

Merlot, Chardonnay, Pinot Gris, Pinot Noir and several Mediterranean varieties.

Producers

Given that many growers sell fruit to wineries outside the region and some producers bring in fruit from neighbouring regions I am sticking to just one recommendation.

Mayford Wines

www.mayfordwines.com

This is my favourite producer in the region. The Tempranillo is delicious and one of the better examples you will try of this variety. The Shiraz is savoury and spicy but with surprising richness, and their signature Ovens Crossing is a predominantly Cabernet–Tempranillo blend (with other varieties).

GLENROWAN
(Waywurru and Taungurong Country)

Glenrowan sits in the north-west area of the North East Victoria zone and like so many regions in this part of Australia, its history and development is connected to gold. This is one of Victoria's most historic wine regions, with production dating back to 1870. Richard Bailey and his family established the Bundarra property in the 1860s and his son Varley Bailey planted vines in 1866. Phylloxera devastated the region in the late 1890s and early 1900s. Some vineyards were replanted on rootstocks, and winemaking resumed. Much like Rutherglen, the fortified wine production is where the history lies.

Area under vine

250 hectares[57]

Climate

The climate in Glenrowan is warm and quite like neighbouring Rutherglen. Rainfall during the ripening period is low and night temperatures are cool.

Soils

The Warby Ranges are the predominant geological formation in the region. Soils on these slopes are well-drained, fertile, deep red clay and loamy clay soils.

Varieties

Shiraz and Muscat à Petits Grains Rouges are the main varieties. Some Mediterranean varieties have been planted and are quite successful.

57 Source: Wine Australia

Main wine styles

Shiraz is the top variety for table wine production. Wines are rich, ripe and full-bodied, with concentrated dark berry fruit flavours. Fortified Muscat is the best wine of the region and while they tend to be overshadowed by the Rutherglen versions, they are every bit as good.

Producers

Baileys of Glenrowan

www.baileysofglenrowan.com

Established in 1870, this historic estate has gone through all manner of ownership changes. They produce a range of table wines and are organically certified in all their estate vineyards. The Fiano and Nero d'Avola would be my picks of the table wines. Their flagship wine is fortified and The Founders Series Muscat is a beauty.

Taminick Cellars

www.taminickcellars.com.au

Established in 1904, this is now a fourth-generation family-run estate. They have a lot of old vine Shiraz, Trebbiano and Alicante Bouschet.

Most vines were planted in 1919. The Trebbiano Dolce is delicious, and it is worth seeking out. The dry Trebbiano is made from the old vines planted in 1919.

WESTERN VICTORIA ZONE

This zone encompasses the GIs of Grampians, Pyrenees and Henty.

GRAMPIANS
(Jardwadjali and Djabwurung Country)

Grampians was originally called Great Western, a name which is now used for a subregion. This is a region that was established with the help of French winemaking expertise in the early years. Grampians also has a long history of sparkling wine production and is a place where three famous Australian winemakers honed their skills from the 1930s through the 1960s – Colin Preece (Seppelts), Maurice O'Shea (McWilliams) and Max Shubert (Penfolds).

The historically famous sparkling wine brand Great Western gave the impression that this was sparkling wine territory, but the reality is that most of the grapes for that wine were sourced in other regions. This is red wine country and Shiraz is the shining star.

Area under vine
650 hectares[58]

Climate
This is a cooler climate region with a continental climate – warm to hot days and cool to cold nights. There is some influence from the Southern Ocean even though it is over 100 kilometres away. Autumn weather is reliably stable – ideal for the later part of the ripening cycle.

Soils
There are two main soil types in the region. The first is acidic grey and grey-brown loamy sands with clay loam soils. The other soil is composed of hard yellow soil with structured clay subsoils, which is also quite acidic and requires lime adjustment.

58   Source: National Vineyard Scan 2020 and ABS

Varieties

Shiraz, Cabernet Sauvignon and Pinot Noir are the main varieties but there are many other varieties grown in the region. Best's Nursery (see p.57 and below) contains an impressive collection of old vines that includes Pinot Noir, Pinot Meunier and Dolcetto.

Main wine styles

This region is home to some brilliant Shiraz. Wines are medium to full-bodied and complex, with dark cherry, blackberry, liquorice and black pepper spice characters. Some very serious and age-worthy versions of sparkling Shiraz, a classic Australian style, are made in the region.

Producers

Mount Langi Ghiran

www.langi.com.au

Established in 1969, this is one of the region's top Shiraz producers. The Cliff Edge Shiraz is a great wine to show the character of this variety in the Grampians region. It also sits at a very affordable price point. The Langi Shiraz is the flagship wine. It is rich and structured without being heavy. There's always a backbone of firm tannins to harmonize the plush fruit. With mineral and savoury notes and a very distinct black pepper aromatic component, it is a wine that definitely benefits from 8–10 years of cellaring. One of Australia's iconic red wines.

Best's Wines

www.bestswines.com

Best's Great Western was established in 1866 by Henry and Joseph Best. The first vines were planted in 1868 and some of those original plantings are still being produced today. This is one of Australia's most historic estates. The property changed hands in 1920 when the Thomson family agreed to buy the Concongella Vineyard. Viv Thomson started working at the winery in 1961. He handed the reins to his son Ben in 2008 but remains the patriarch. A visit to Best's is a must! Walking through the cellars is like stepping back in time. I was lucky enough to do just that with Viv Thomson in 2022 and a better lens through which to view Australia's wine history you'd be hard pressed to find. The Nursery Block is so full of different old varieties that recent work

Over forty different old vine varieties grow in the Best's Nursery Block, some of which are still unidentified.

had to be done to identify exactly what was in there. Forty different varieties are planted but eight are yet to be identified. The old block of Pinot Noir, planted in 1868, might be the oldest Pinot Noir vines in the world. Best's has old-vine Dolcetto, old-vine Pinot Meunier, old vine Shiraz … the list goes on. There is a dizzying array of fantastic wines to try at Best's. The Foudre Ferment Riesling is a treat; lively and lemony, with additional texture from extended skin contact. The Concongella Blanc is a treat and aside from being a delicious mineral delight, it is a study of Australian grape vine history in a glass. It is a field blend of white varieties from the Nursery Block. If you can find the Thomson Family Shiraz it is the top Shiraz made here but Bin No. 0 is fantastic too. The Old Vine Pinot Meunier, only made in exceptional years, is a treat that should not be turned down. Ever.

The Story Wines

www.thestory.com.au

Rory Lane is behind this label, and while the wines are made in Melbourne, he sources a lot of fruit from Grampians. His Westgate

Vineyard Syrah is fantastic: spicy, savoury, detailed and complex, it really displays the cooler climate spectrum of flavours and weights of which Shiraz is capable. His Super G is a blend of Shiraz, Grenache and Mourvèdre and is a juicy, fresh, crunchy version of a classic blend.

PYRENEES
(Jardwadjali and Djabwurung Country)

Major Thomas Mitchell gave this region its name in 1836. The rugged hills reminded him of the European Pyrenees, which divide France from Spain. The first vineyards were planted in 1887, which was 30 years after gold was discovered in the region, so a slightly different development trajectory from many regions in Victoria. Vineyard and winery expansion continued well into the twentieth century. The original plantings were all but abandoned and by the late 1940s there were virtually no vineyards left. In the 1960s the modern Pyrenees wine industry saw a resurgence.

This is the south-west end of the Great Dividing Range and altitude ranges from 200–800 metres above sea level. Most of the vineyard sites sit at between 220 and 350 metres, although a few, most notably Dalwhinnie, sit above 500 metres. There is a diverse range of microclimates, which allows for many different varieties to grow successfully. The most noted wines to date are Shiraz and Cabernet Sauvignon based.

Area under vine
870 hectares[59]

Climate
The region has a continental climate, with warm, sunny days and substantial diurnal temperature ranges in spring and early summer. Growing season rainfall is limited, making irrigation almost essential. The southern end of the region is a bit cooler.

Soils
These are quite variable, ranging from grey-brown and brown loam to red sandstone and red clay quartz.

59 Source: Wine Australia

> ## Varieties
>
> Shiraz and Cabernet Sauvignon are the classic and most planted varieties in the region. Chardonnay and Pinot Noir are grown in the cooler sites and mostly used for sparkling wine production.

Main wine styles

Shiraz produces full-flavoured styles, with ripe black fruit characters and firm tannins. An iron-like minerality is common in many wines. Cabernet Sauvignon is medium to full bodied with classic blackcurrant and mint notes.

Producers

Dalwhinnie

www.dalwhinnie.wine

This iconic Australian winery was started by David Jones. Chardonnay and Cabernet Sauvignon are grown here but it is the Shiraz from this stunningly situated property that established the reputation. The site is 595 metres above sea level making it the highest in the region. It is also the most remote. Surrounded on three sides by hills, the 16-hectare vineyard is in a naturally undulating amphitheatre. When you see this vineyard, you know you are in a special site. Although a brilliant property, it has lost its sheen over the last decade. A tasting of random vintages back to 2013 showed why this winery has its reputation but there

Dalwhinnie vineyard is one of the highest and most perfectly situated sites in the Pyrenees region.

was unevenness in several wines, and I am being polite. The property is now in the hands of the Fogarty Wine Group, and when I visited I had a tasting of the 2021 Eagle Shiraz and 2021 Dry Block Shiraz from barrel. They were both fantastic. I think a march back to glory is well on its way. I am excited to watch this evolve.

Blue Pyrenees Estate

www.bluepyrenees.com.au

Originally established as a brandy-making facility by Remy Martin and named Château Remy, this was renamed Blue Pyrenees Estate in 1982 and the focus shifted to varieties such as Shiraz. It was purchased by an Australian group in 2002. The Richardson Shiraz and Richardson Cabernet Sauvignon are the two flagship red wines.

M. Chapoutier Australia

www.mchapoutier.com.au

Michel Chapoutier has partnered with several winemaking families in Australia but his Pyrenees venture, Domaine Tournon, is fully owned by him. The range of wines is excellent, and the Shays Flat Shiraz is a beauty worth seeking out.

Taltarni Vineyards

www.taltarni.com.au

Established in 1969, this is one of the pioneering wineries in the region. Owner John Goelet, a direct descendant of the Guestier wine merchant family of Bordeaux, discovered and purchased Taltarni Vineyard after an extensive search for a site comparable to the great vineyards of Bordeaux. Initial plantings were of Bordeaux varieties, including Cabernet Sauvignon, Cabernet Franc and Merlot. The plantings have expanded to include Sauvignon Blanc, Chardonnay and Shiraz, as well as Pinot Noir and Pinot Meunier. Dominique Portet (see Yarra Valley entry, p. 189) was the winemaker here for many years and helped establish its reputation.

Pyren Vineyard

www.pyrenvineyard.com

Planted in 1999, by brothers Brian and Kevyn Joy, the vineyard comprises Shiraz, Cabernet Sauvignon, Sauvignon Blanc, Cabernet Franc, Malbec and Petit Verdot. The Shiraz and Sparkling Shiraz are both delicious. The Little Ra Ra range of wines features their experimental,

edgier selections. The Little Ra Ra Roopa is a skin contact, spicy iteration of an orange wine. A really solid producer.

HENTY
(Jardwadjali and Gunditjmara Country)

Located in the far south-west corner of Victoria, this region was named
after Edward Henty, who came over from Tasmania and was the first
permanent settler in the area. He recorded that he brought sheep and
vines with him but it appears the sheep grazing was more successful
as there was no trace of the vines, if indeed he did plant them. Karl
Seppelt recognized the viticultural potential here and planted vines
in the 1960s. The Henty wine region covers a large area of Victoria
and extends from the Hopkins River across to the South Australian
border. Wine production is concentrated in two parts of the region,
Hamilton and Tarrington in the north-east and Heywood, Condah and
Drumborg in the south-west. It is a region that is sparsely planted but is
home to many brilliant wines.

Area under vine
139 hectares[60]

Climate
This is one of the cooler wine growing regions on the Australian mainland. The
cool temperatures are accompanied by long sunshine hours.

Soils
These are quite complex and depend on where you are in the region. There
is some older weathered basalt with gravelly loam topsoil overlying red clay,
as well as rich, black volcanic clays, maritime sandy loam over limestone, and
patches of *terra rossa* over limestone.

Varieties
Riesling, Chardonnay and Cabernet Sauvignon, with small amounts of Pinot
Noir, Sauvignon Blanc and Pinot Gris.

60 Source: Wine Australia

Main wine styles

Stunning Riesling is produced in Henty. The flavour profile is different from Clare and Eden Valley Riesling. Similar citrus elements are common but there is a nectarine or slightly underripe peach character and more fruit weight. Chardonnays are in a leaner, more mineral driven style and are elegant and age-worthy. The Cabernet Sauvignon is medium-bodied, fragrant, herbal and lifted but can tend towards greenness in cooler vintages.

Producers

Crawford River

www.crawfordriverwines.com

Established in 1975 by the Thompson family, not only is Crawford River one of the best producers in the region, it is also making one of the best Rieslings in Australia. It is all about attention to detail. Picking, pruning and canopy management is all done by hand and the detail is transparent in the wines. I have yet to have a bad wine from Crawford River. Fragrant, mid-weight Cabernet Sauvignon is a lovely reminder that this variety can be gentle. The first time I tried their Riesling it stopped me mid-sentence. I had not tasted a Riesling from Australia with such intensity and power that was delicate and layered at the same time. Lime zest character is there, as you find in many top Rieslings in Australia, but it is overlayed with nectarine and peach. Wines are hard to find, but do the work and get a bottle or three.

Seppelt Drumborg

www.seppelt.com.au

The Drumborg site was planted in 1964 by Karl Seppelt. The winery is actually in the Grampians region but the Drumborg range is sourced from this site in Henty. The vineyard produces excellent Chardonnay, Pinot Noir and Pinot Gris, but the Seppelt Drumborg Riesling is the wine that always stands out for me. In the same vein as the Crawford River, it can age gracefully for decades. If you were to pull together a list of the best Rieslings produced in Australia, Crawford River and Seppelt Drumborg would have to be on it.

GIPPSLAND
(Woiworung, Boonwurrung and Kurnai Country)

Gippsland is a zone but most in the area refer to it as a region. It is too large and too diverse to be a single region but it exists only as a zonal GI. I presume that this is because it wouldn't be possible to create any sub-regional GIs that would meet the current criteria. Phillip Jones, past owner of the iconic Bass Phillip asserts that there are six climatic areas within Gippsland. James Halliday suggests that it should, at the very least be subdivided into three areas: South Gippsland, West Gippsland and East Gippsland. Be that as it may, it is one large, zonal GI for now. The region has 400 kilometres of cool-climate coastline, wedged between the mountains and the sea and it is important to note that climate and soils vary greatly within such a large area. With fewer than 200 hectares of vineyards spread across the region, generalizations are difficult. This is an area dominated by small, family-owned vineyards and wineries.

Area under vine
190 hectares[61]

Climate
East Gippsland is under a strong cooling influence from the Southern Ocean. West Gippsland is still influenced by ocean breezes, but being further inland it is a little warmer in this section than in East Gippsland. South Gippsland is the coolest section of the region with more direct influence of the cooling ocean breezes.

Soils
These are extremely varied, as noted above. A couple of broad generalizations are: the deep, sandy clay loams of volcanic origin, in South Gippsland, and gravelly, sandy loams in East Gippsland.

Varieties
Pinot Noir and Chardonnay.

61 Source: Wine Australia

Main wine styles

Gippsland is home to one of Australia's most famous, and expensive, Pinot Noirs, Bass Phillip. This has inspired others and given Gippsland a reputation as a Pinot Noir region. Chardonnay is grown across the entire region so styles vary from richer and more structured in the warmer sites, to elegant and detailed in cooler sites.

Producers

Bass Phillip

www.bassphillip.com

Phillip Jones established Bass Phillip in South Gippsland in 1979. Pinot Noir is all that is made here. The property has very close planted vineyards in cool sites. All the wines are fantastic but the Bass Phillip Premium and Reserve are the top wines and, while expensive, should be tried at some point if you are a Pinot lover. Jones sold to a group of investors that included Jean-Marie Fourrier from Domaine Fourrier in Burgundy. I have not tried the wines made under Fourrier's guidance but I can't imagine he would let quality slide. The Estate Pinot Noir is fantastic and if you feel like splashing out A$800 or more try the Reserve Pinot Noir. It really is a fantastic wine. The Reserve Chardonnay is right up there in terms of quality but very hard to find. An iconic, top-class Australia estate.

William Downie Wines

www.williamdownie.com.au

Bill Downie has been making quality Pinot Noir in Australia for many years. It is getting hard to call him a young gun but that is how I still feel about him. Bill is gentle and sensitive and always interesting to talk to. He is quite philosophical and a strong proponent of low intervention. A two-year stint with Phillip Jones at Bass Phillip in his formative years established his Pinot passion and credentials. He has made Pinots from various regions across Victoria but now has a property near the town of Yarragon in West Gippsland and focuses solely on Pinot sourced in the Gippsland GI.

Patrick Sullivan Wines

www.patricksullivan.com.au

Patrick worked with Bill Downie on previous projects in the Yarra and moved to Gippsland around the same time. His property is near

Ellinbank and he is making a variety of low-intervention wines. His Baw Baw Shire Chardonnay is textural and delicious.

Momento Mori Wines

www.momentomoriwines.com.au

This small-scale natural producer works with small ferments, wild yeast, no new oak or mechanical pumps, no fining or filtering and no additions, including no sulphur dioxide at any stage. This producer is garnering a lot of interest. I have only tried a couple of wines, but like the Amphora Ribolla–Fiano.

Nicholson River Winery

www.nicholsonriverwinery.com.au

Established by Ken Echersley in 1978, Nicholson River is crafting delicious Chardonnays that are well worth seeking out. Try the Montview Chardonnay.

NORTH WEST VICTORIA ZONE

This zone includes the GIs Murray Darling and Swan Hill. Both are mostly about broadacre farming and volume production but there is tremendous history and character to the regions. Both straddle the Murray River and the GI exists in Victoria and New South Wales. For simplicity they are combined in discussion below

MURRAY DARLING AND SWAN HILL
(Njeri Njeri Country)

Straddling the Murray River in north-west Victoria and western New South Wales, the Murray Darling is a vast region. Combined with Swan Hill immediately to the south-east, it is the third-largest winegrowing region in Australia after the Riverland (South Australia) and Riverina (New South Wales). Agriculture in this region was made possible by the vision of Prime Minister Alfred Deakin. He saw the possibilities of large-scale irrigation here after he visited California in the 1880s and witnessed the incredible work done by irrigation engineers George and William Chaffey. He convinced them to come to Australia. Their work in realizing Deakin's vision has left an indelible mark on the viticultural history in many of Australia's large inland regions.

It is hot here, with long sunshine hours, low humidity and negligible growing season rainfall. The two GIs combined cover over 28,000 square kilometres. Although known for the production of easy-drinking, affordable wines made from the classic varieties, the emergence of alternative varieties has given added interest to the area.

Area under vine

Murray Darling – 16,100 hectares[62]
Swan Hill – 2,010 hectares[63]

Climate

Even though this is a large expanse, the climate throughout is very consistent. It is hot, with long sunshine hours, low humidity, and negligible growing season rainfall, making irrigation essential. The continental influence is strong, with high shifts in diurnal temperature ranges. Disease pressure is low. Swan Hill is marginally cooler than Murray Darling.

Soils

Soils of the Murray River system range from brown to red-brown loamy sand, sandy loam or loam.

Varieties

Cabernet Sauvignon, Shiraz, Sauvignon Blanc, Merlot, Petit Verdot and Pinot Gris are the main varieties. Alternative varieties are also doing well in this area; see Chalmers entry, page 249.

62 Source: Wine Australia
63 Source: Wine Australia

Main wine styles

Besides the other Mediterranean varieties, viticulture in these regions is generally established with the purpose of achieving the price points suited to large volume, mass-market wines. Mechanization is critical. This does nothing to undermine the fresh, easy-drinking character of all the classic varieties.

Producers

Deakin Estate

www.deakinestate.com.au

The Deakin facility is located on the Victorian side of the border, but they grow and source a lot of their fruit from the Big Rivers zone in New South Wales. The estate was established in 1967 and was purchased by the Calabria family in 2020. A full range of solid, affordable, and easy-drinking varietal wines is made under both the Deakin Estate label and the Deakin Estate Artisan's Blend label.

Lindeman's Wines

www.lindemans.com

Dr Henry Lindeman established Lindeman's in 1843 in the Hunter Valley. The history of this winery is long and storied. Wines used to range from fun and affordable through to fine and rare. But not today. It is hard not to be hit with a twinge of nostalgia for what once was. Lindeman's made magnificent wine from the Hunter Valley in the early years. Their Hunter River Burgundies are still regarded as some of the Hunter Valley's great red wines. In 2010 I was lucky enough to try the 1970 Lindeman's Hunter River White Burgundy (100 per cent Semillon) – it was extraordinary. The St George's red wine was a classic. And I think I had the Bin 65 Chardonnay on 'by the glass' in restaurants I worked in for close to ten years. Ultimately Lindeman's got swallowed up by corporate takeovers and the brand is not what it used to be. The Karadoc winery facility was built in 1973 and was the only place where anything bearing the Lindeman's name is made. Treasury just announced in June 2023 that they were closing this facility and I am not really sure where Lindemans wines are being made (and if I am being honest, I'm not sure I really care). These are easy-drinking varietal wines. Perhaps I will never get past my disappointment that a winery of this stature got relegated to the production of serviceable wines. It was not the first and, sadly, won't be the last.

Trentham Estate

www.trenthamestate.com.au

The winery was established in 1988 and is actually across the Murray River in New South Wales. Trentham is a very solid producer making a full range of varietal wines. The Estate range is great, especially the Pinot Gris and Sauvignon Blanc.

Zilzie Wines

www.zilziewines.com

This is a large property of about 685 hectares. They grow Prosecco, Sauvignon Blanc, Chardonnay, Pinot Grigio, Viognier, Shiraz, Cabernet Sauvignon, Merlot, Sangiovese, Muscat Gordo Blanco, Petit Verdot, Colombard and Semillon. They also source fruit from other regions. The winery has solid sustainability credentials and produces a very good range of wines.

Chalmers Wines

www.chalmers.com.au

Bruce and Jenni Chalmers started growing grapes here in the 1980s. Over the years the business became a well-regarded nursery and they were responsible for importing close to 70 new clones and varieties. These varieties were released to Australia in 2000 and have since been a major factor in the improvements in sustainability and quality. Daughters Kim and Tenille now run the business, which includes their Heathcote vineyards in Central Victoria. Their US importer, Jane Lopes, sums up their importance in the broader scheme of Australian varieties: 'Their success has been largely dependent on their ability to match Italian grapes to Australian climates, focusing on thick-skinned grapes that are drought tolerant, resistant to sunburn, and have plenty of natural acidity. Kim and Tennille have been instrumental in the amplification of the Australian Alternative Varieties Wine Show, and in 2015 they also spearheaded 21st Century Vino, an initiative to increase awareness and expertise in Italian varieties grown across Australia.' See notes on their Heathcote vineyard on page 214.

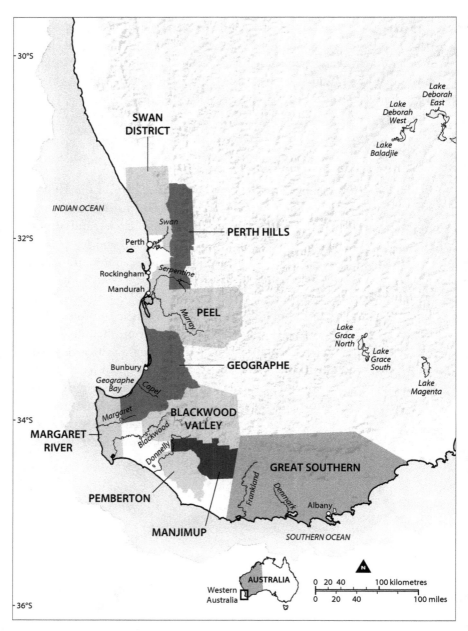

Map 5: The Geographic Indications of Western Australia

9

WESTERN AUSTRALIA

The history of wine production in Western Australia dates back to 1840 with the establishment of Sandalford Winery in the Swan Valley region. While this region is one of the hottest in Australia, it remained the centre of early wine production. A more focused investigation of cooler climate fine wine possibilities emerged in 1955. UC Davis viticulturist and Fulbright Research scholar Harold Olmo was invited to do research work in Great Southern (see p. 265). In addition, Dr John Gladstones was commissioned to write a paper on the viticultural potential in Margaret River in 1965 (see p. 253). As a result of this research, vineyard plantings expanded in Great Southern and Margaret River rapidly from the late 1960s onwards. There are many compelling wine regions in Western Australia but Great Southern and Margaret River are the beacons of quality wine production. Western Australia is, by a large margin, Australia's biggest state. It extends across the entire western third of the continent. Most of the land is not at all suited to viticulture, so the wine regions are all clustered in the cooler climate of the south-western area.

Western Australia produces less than 5 per cent of Australia's annual production but the state receives an outsized percentage of attention, accolades, and press coverage. It must be noted that this is largely due to the global reputation of Margaret River.

The GIs of Western Australia

There are five GI Zones but only two of these zones contain regional GIs: Greater Perth and South West Australia. If you are looking for a head-scratching

251

moment regarding the awarding of zonal GIs, it exists here. In his 2014 *Wine Atlas of Australia* James Halliday notes: 'The Eastern Plains, Inland and North of Western Australia Zone is a massive blank page, roughly comparable to the land mass of New South Wales, Victoria and South Australia combined. To date, only two wineries have ventured into this vast area.'

It is bewildering. If for example your winery and vineyard happened to fall outside the boundaries of either Greater Perth or South West Australia zones and was technically able to use the clumsy, nonspecific zonal GI of Eastern Plains, Inland and North of Western Australia would it not make sense to just put Western Australia on the label? Perhaps I am missing something.

South West Australia zone

The most important zone, containing the regions of Margaret River, Blackwood Valley, Geographe, Manjimup, Pemberton, Great Southern and its five subregions – Albany, Denmark, Frankland River, Mount Barker and Porongorup

Greater Perth zone

The regions of Swan Valley, Peel and Perth Hills sit within this zone.

Additional Western Australia zones

Given the dearth of wineries actually using these as labelling terms, the zones of Eastern Plains, Inland and North of Western Australia, Central Western Australia and West Australian South East Coastal are simply mentioned here and not covered in detail. Due apologies to any wineries located within these boundaries.

SOUTH WEST AUSTRALIA

This is the most significant GI zone in Western Australia. It encompasses the important regional GIs of Margaret River and Great Southern and its five subregions of Frankland River, Albany, Denmark, Mount Barker and Porongurup. The GIs of Geographe, Blackwood Valley, Manjimup and Pemberton make up the balance. While not all regions are in direct contact with the coast, they are all, to a greater or lesser degree, affected by the influence of either the Indian or Southern Ocean.

MARGARET RIVER
(Wardandi Country)

Margaret River is a late arrival on the Australian fine wine scene. In the 1960s Dr John Gladstones was commissioned to undertake a study on the viticultural potential of the area. He published a paper in 1965 stating that, 'being virtually frost free and having a much lower ripening period, cloudiness, rainfall and hail risk than Manjimup and Mount Barker, it has distinct advantages over both those areas and indeed over all other areas in Australia with comparable temperature summations'. He also made comparisons to Bordeaux and noted the suitability of Cabernet Sauvignon. This inspired planting, and expansion of wine production. The first producer was Vasse Felix in 1967 and many followed in quick succession. It did not take long for Margaret River to establish itself as a world-class producer of Cabernet Sauvignon based wines. On the strength of a hunch by legendary Napa producer Robert Mondavi (see Leeuwin Estate, p. 257), Chardonnay was planted, and Margaret River now produces some of the best examples of the variety in Australia. From the beginning, this region has maintained a primary focus on quality rather than quantity. Margaret River is not a place to find cheap and cheerful, mass-market wines, which has played a strong part in its international recognition and success. Paying attention to vine material being planted in the earlier years has contributed to that success and the subsequent high quality of the wines. For more on this see pages 255 and 256 on Chardonnay and Cabernet Sauvignon clones.

The region is 120 kilometres long and about 25 kilometres wide and has ocean influence on three sides. Cape Naturaliste is the northern tip of the region and has a more Mediterranean climate. Cape Leeuwin, the southernmost tip of the region, has more of classic maritime climate and is distinctly cooler. Given the climate and soil differences, there is a strong feeling that there need to be subregions within Margaret River. In 1999 John Gladstones suggested there should be six subregions based on these climate and soil differences: Yallingup, Carbunup, Wilyabrup, Treeton, Wallcliffe and Karridale. This has yet to materialize but some sort of subdivision will no doubt happen in the future.

Area under vine

5,725 hectares[64]

Climate

The regional boundary only extends about 25 kilometres inland, which makes this is the most obvious maritime climate of any region in Australia but the variable influence of two quite different oceans makes it necessary to qualify the maritime nature of the Margaret River climate. Although generally accepted as having a Mediterranean climate, given the milder Indian Ocean influence, the significantly cooler influence of the Southern Ocean means that the southern sections of the region are cooler than the north. Most of the rainfall occurs in the winter months. Summers are typically warm and dry, and the risk of frost or hail is quite low. The low diurnal temperature range leads to very even heat accumulation.

Soils

Soils are quite varied given the size of the region but deep, well-drained, red gravelly loams exist in several parts. Running through the middle of the region is the Leeuwin-Naturaliste ridge, which connects Cape Naturaliste to the north and Cape Leeuwin to the south. The granite bedrock of this ridge is 150–600 million years old, layered in places with two-million-year-old limestone. Over time, the ridge has created a complex network of gneiss, schist and granite-based soils, the oldest in the world. These soils are low in nutrients, resulting in low vigour in the vineyard making them ideal viticultural soils.

Varieties

Cabernet Sauvignon, Chardonnay, Shiraz, Sauvignon Blanc and Semillon.

64   Source: National Vineyard Scan 2020 and ABS

Main wine styles

Although Margaret River doesn't have the history of Coonawarra, its reputation for Cabernet Sauvignon is on a par. Classic maritime influences and gravelly soils in the best sections of the region make it ideally suited. The style differs from Coonawarra, with similar richness and intensity of fruit, but wines are more elegant and aromatic. Blackcurrant, violets and mint, with velvety tannins, are typical signature characteristics.

Chardonnay is typically rich, with ripe, complex flavours but never cloying due to a consistent backbone of lime-like acidity.

Semillon and Sauvignon Blanc are often blended together in varying proportions. Two main versions exist, unoaked, crisp, fresh and lively and the slightly more serious and age-worthy version that sees some oak fermentation and/or maturation. Classic Dry White is an additional version that often includes a little Chenin Blanc and would qualify as the everyday drinking wine of Margaret River.

Shiraz is medium bodied in style, with spice and raspberry aromas and flavours. Underrated, it often sits in the shadow of the more famous and sought-after Cabernet blends. It is worth seeking out. Margaret River Shiraz can be charming and delicious.

Chardonnay clones in Margaret River

Chardonnay clones have been experimented with since Margaret River was established as a grape-growing region in 1967. Specific clones are believed to be a key factor in the distinctive style of the region. The most significant, and most widely planted clone is known locally as the Gingin clone. It is typified by low yields, loose and small bunches, and a feature called hen and chicken – a phenomenon where grape bunches contain berries varying greatly in size and maturity. It is known for producing powerful yet elegant wines with concentration and complexity. The origins of the Gingin clone have been a bit murky but the Western Australian Government's Department of Primary Industries and Regional Development has been researching its origins. It is now thought that the Gingin clone, previously known as 'FPS 1', was brought to Western Australia from California in 1957 thanks to Professor Harold Olmo, professor of viticulture at the University of California. The clone was recognized in Western Australia as the Old Farm (OF) selection of Chardonnay, and later became known as the Gingin selection, named after the vineyard site where it was planted.

Another common Chardonnay clone in Margaret River is the Mendoza. The Gingin clone was often believed to be the same as the Mendoza clone, just with a different name, but recent research shows that they are not the same. A number of more recently imported French clones are also commonly used, with some producers favouring them for their finer, more restrained wine styles with lower alcohol levels than Gingin.

Cabernet Sauvignon clones in Margaret River – the Houghton Clones

From 1968 to 1970, the Department of Agriculture conducted a survey of the Houghton Vineyard in Swan Valley, with the objective of sourcing high-quality vines for Margaret River. The team sought vines of good health and fruit flavour, and wanted them to deliver solid yield improvement. The mission was a success, with 21 vines selected – which were initially planted as cuttings from 1930s vines. These high-performing vines would become known as the 'Houghton clones'. Houghton Clones were used to establish the first vineyards of Cabernet Sauvignon in Margaret River.

Producers

Vasse Felix

www.vassefelix.com.au

This pioneer producer is still at the top of its game. Virginia Willcock has been the winemaker since 2006 and while the wines were fantastic prior to her arrival, they are exceptional now. A full span of Margaret River classics is made here but the Chardonnays and Cabernet Sauvignons shine. There are three levels to both varieties. For Cabernet Sauvignon Filius is the entry level with the middle range being Premier. These two are great examples of the Vasse Felix style and also great wines to give you an understanding of Margaret River Cabernet. The flagship wine is Tom Cullity, named after the founder. This is Cabernet Sauvignon dominant but blended with Malbec – typically around 20 per cent. It is one of Australia's very best Cabernet-based wines. Filius and Premier exist in the Chardonnay range too with the flagship white being the Heytesbury Chardonnay. This is a selection of the best fruit from their estate vineyards, all Gingin clone. It is textbook Margaret River Chardonnay with power and richness tempered by a vibrant backbone of limey acidity.

Cullen Wines

www.cullenwines.com.au

Cullen is another pioneer of the region. Vanya Cullen, who runs the estate, is a force of nature. She was an early adopter of biodynamic practices and is fiercely committed to minimizing Cullen's impact on the environment. Cullen is certified biodynamic and has been since 2008. They are also carbon neutral. If you are a jaded, long-time industry professional, make a trip to Cullen. It is a visit that will restore your faith and remind you why you became involved in wine in the first place. Vanya is an important figure, not just in Margaret River but in the Australian wine business as a whole. In early 2023 Vanya was awarded the Order of Australia (OAM) for her services to viticulture and oenology. I doubt there is anyone in the Australian wine business surprised by this richly deserved accolade. It doesn't matter what wines you select from Cullen. They are all brilliant, but the following are a must.

Diana Madeline is a top-flight Cabernet based blend. Elegant, structured and perfumed, it is a wine that reminds you of Cabernet Sauvignon's gentle, medium bodied, fragrant nature. Kevin John Chardonnay is quite different from many other top Margaret River Chardonnays but in the very best way. It is textured, layered and complex with a distinct savoury quality. I am also a fan of her Mangan Vineyard Sauvignon Blanc–Semillon. Recent vintages have contained a small percentage of Verdelho, but this is a vibrant, citrus-blossom scented classic.

Moss Wood

www.mosswood.com.au

The first vine plantings at Moss Wood were made in 1969 by Bill Pannell and his wife Sandra, qualifying this estate as one of the early pioneers. Since 1985 the property has been run by Keith and Clare Mugford. This is one of the top-class producers in the region, with a bevy of classic wines. Ribbonvale Cabernet Sauvignon is a great introduction to the Moss Wood style as well as being a pinpoint example of the fragrant, elegant Margaret River style of Cabernet Sauvignon. Moss Wood Semillon is a beauty and a single varietal wine that has been made since the early 1980s. Rich, ripe, concentrated and packed with waxy lemon-scented fruit, it ages beautifully. Their Cabernet Sauvignon, which typically contains small amounts of Petit Verdot and Cabernet Franc, is a classic, long-lived wine that repays patient cellaring.

Leeuwin Estate

www.leeuwinestate.com.au

Tricia and Denis Horgan did not start out as wine producers. The story, as told to me by Tricia, was that they had purchased the land in Margaret River because she thought Denis needed an excuse to visit the area for the beaches and surfing. Apparently, a group of people showed up in

1972 to enquire about buying the property. Robert Mondavi was part of the group. He felt that the land was ideally suited to Chardonnay and wanted to start a project. The Horgans were not interested in selling but were very interested in his idea. To cut a long story short, they developed the property with the guidance of Mondavi, who became a great friend. Mondavi was spot on: Leeuwin Estate Art Series Chardonnay is absolutely stunning and probably the most awarded Chardonnay in the history of Australia. It is textbook Margaret River, with an overlay of the Leeuwin style. The last decade or so has seen most Chardonnay producers dial back on oak and make more restrained wines. Not Leeuwin. It is one of the few Chardonnays I can think of that still ferments and ages in 100 per cent new oak. And one of the few where it works! It is a wine of power and richness, balanced with structure, elegance and finesse. It is a remarkable wine.

The Art Series Cabernet tends to sit in the shadow of the Art Series Chardonnay, but the recent vintages are the very best they have produced. The Art Series Riesling is annoyingly good, and I say that because it leaves people thinking Margaret River is a strong region for Riesling. It really isn't, but this is a beauty. Both the Prelude Vineyard Chardonnay and Cabernet Sauvignon are a great way to acquaint yourself with the Leeuwin Estate style. They are both sub A$40.00 wines and frankly outshine a few considerably more expensive wines from the region.

Pierro

www.pierro.com.au

In 1985 Dr Michael Peterkin started this venture with the intention of becoming a serious Riesling producer. 'I had initially intended to specialize in Riesling,' he says. 'It was a tad fortuitous that Chardonnay became Pierro's most famous wine. My vine supplier had been let down on a large order of Chardonnay rootstock, approximately 5,000 cuttings, and offered them to me. In order to help him out I agreed to take them.' Lucky for all of us! Pierro has an enduring reputation for Chardonnay, and this is still their best wine. This is classic Margaret River Chardonnay, with power, intensity, concentration and length. They make lovely red wines too; look for the Cabernet Merlot L.T.C.F (little touch of Cabernet Franc), which is lifted, pure fruited and aromatic.

Burch Family Wines

www.burchfamilywines.com.au

The Burch Family has three established brands under its umbrella. Madfish, Howard Park and Marchand & Burch. The focus is Margaret River and Great Southern. Madfish Wines (www.madfishwines.com. au) serves as the entry point, with a range of delicious, accessible varietal wines. Howard Park Wines (www.howardparkwines.com.au) is the most established of the three, with an excellent range of wines from both Margaret River and Great Southern. The flagship Cabernet Sauvignon is the cellar-worthy Abercrombie. It is a blend of their best fruit from the Leston Vineyard in Margaret River and the prized Abercrombie Vineyard in Mount Barker. Riesling was one of the original varieties they planted, and they have two beauties, one from vineyards in Porungurup and the other from Mount Barker. The Howard Park Flint Rock Shiraz is a mid-weight charmer with spicy raspberry fruit. Marchand & Burch Wines (www.marchandburchwines.com.au) is a joint venture from Jeff Burch and Pascal Marchand. They are playing with a range of wines from the Côte d'Or and Great Southern. The Mount Barrow vineyard Pinot Noir is from Mount Barker and definitely worth seeking out.

Flametree Wines

www.flametreewines.com

The cellar door and winery is located in the very north of the region, right on Geographe Bay near the town of Dunsborough. Formed in 2007 by the Towner family, they quickly established themselves as a topflight producer. The very talented Cliff Royle took up head winemaking duties in 2013 after twelve years as chief winemaker at Voyager Estate. Flametree is a strong producer of classic Chardonnay and Cabernet Sauvignon. The Sub Regional Series (SRS) aims to amplify the characteristics of the various 'unofficial' subregions as recommended by Gladstones. SRS Karridale Sauvignon Blanc is a tropical, herb-tinged classic. SRS Wallcliffe Chardonnay and SRS Wilyabrup Cabernet Sauvignon are both textbook examples.

Cloudburst

www.cloudburstwine.com

Started by New York transplant Will Berliner, Cloudburst is a small, boutique estate selling expensive wines. This is very much a non-interventional producer. All vineyard tasks are done by hand and, while farming practices are biodynamic, Berliner isn't interested in certification. The wines are really good. The Chardonnay is the only Cloudburst wine I have tried, and it is layered, complex and textured with incredible length and persistence. His Cabernet Sauvignon and Malbec receive high praise from people I trust, and I look forward to trying them at some point in the future. The attention to detail from top to bottom is obvious but you do hear criticism of the high prices. While I see that the prices will prevent some from trying the wines, I like the approach. We are too conservative in Australia when it comes to valuing our best wines. For sure, the quality needs to be there to justify a high price but at Cloudburst it is. We could use a little more of this attitude ... within reason.

Stella Bella

www.stellabella.com.au

In 1996, Stuart Pym and Janice McDonald took over the Suckfizzle Vineyard, the most southern vineyard in the Margaret River Region. The first vintage of the Suckfizzle Sauvignon Blanc–Semillon was made in 1997, a white Bordeaux style wine inspired by Domaine de Chevalier. The name was inspired by Lord Suckfizzle, a character in the sixteenth-century book *Gargantua and Pantagruel* by François Rabelais. They then established the Stella Bella in 1999, a superb estate making a full range of excellent wines. Winemaking is now under the guidance of Luke Jollife. The Suckfizzle Semillon–Sauvignon Blanc is one the best examples of this classic blend in the region. The Luminosa Cabernet Sauvignon is an absolute beauty and the lightly fizzy Stella Bella Moscato is super delicious. They were one of the first producers to make this style of Moscato in Australia, so it makes sense that this is fantastic.

Xanadu Wines

www.xanaduwines.com

A really strong producer in the stable of wineries owned by the Rathbone Wine Group, Xanadu was always a solid middle of the pack producer. Since 2005, under the guidance of Darren Rathbone and talented winemaker Glenn Goodall, this has become one of the premier properties in the region. The Reserve Chardonnay and Cabernet Sauvignon are perennial medal winners.

Thompson Estate

www.thompsonestate.com

It is hard to imagine a nicer couple than Jan and Peter Thompson. Established in 1997, Thompson Estate has a full range of the Margaret River classics. The Estate Range Chardonnay and Cabernet Sauvignon are good starting points, and I particularly like the small batch Cabernet Franc. The Specialist Cabernet Sauvignon and Chardonnay are their flagship bottlings.

Voyager Estate

www.voyagerestate.com.au

A visit to Voyager Estate feels like being transported to the Cape winelands in South Africa. It is a lovely family-owned, family-run estate, making an excellent range of wines. Broadvale Block 6 Chardonnay is fantastic, and the Modern Cabernet Sauvignon is vibrant and pure fruited.

Corymbia Wines

www.corymbiawine.com.au

This is a relatively new venture by Rob and Genevieve Mann. Rob Mann grew up in the Swan Valley hanging out on the property with legendary winemaker, Jack Mann (see p. 278) who happens to be his grandfather. The Mann family has six generations of winemaking history in Western Australia so there is some serious pedigree here. I first met Rob when he was the winemaker at Cape Mentelle. He has had a busy career working in many different countries. The winery is located in Margaret River but they produce two wines from Swan Valley fruit. Their Margaret River wine is Cabernet Sauvignon from the Calgardup Vineyard. I have not tried it yet but given the history and pedigree here, I am confident that it is fantastic.

See also entry in Swan Valley, page 279.

Woodlands

www.woodlandswines.com

Established in 1973 by David and Heather Watson, this was one of the first five vineyards to be planted in the Margaret River. There is a great line-up of wines. I particularly like Woodlands Brook Chardonnay and the Woodlands Vineyard Margaret, a blend of mostly Cabernet Sauvignon with a small proportion of Merlot and Malbec.

Deep Woods Estate

www.deepwoods.wine

Deep Woods Estate was established in 1987 and acquired by the Fogarty family in 2005, making it part of the Fogarty Wine Group. This is a top-notch winery, with a full compliment of classic Margaret River wines. I am a fan of the Single Vineyard range especially the Single Vineyard Cabernet–Malbec. The Reserve Chardonnay is excellent too.

Wines of Merritt

www.winesofmerritt.com.au

Merritt is a newer producer in the region, making small-batch, low-intervention wines. Nick James-Martin and his wife Sarah are the dynamic duo behind this label. Nick has a solid wine background having worked at Rosemount, Vasse Felix and Stella Bella, plus overseas vintages in Hawke's Bay, New Zealand and Languedoc, France. They are playing with the Margaret River classics but not solely focused on Cabernet Sauvignon and Chardonnay. There is a lovely Vermentino and fantastic Chenin Blanc; the Rouge is a Shiraz–Cabernet blend and the Cabernet Franc (if you can find it) is a fragrant beauty.

Ashbrook Estate

www.ashbrookwines.com.au

Established in 1975, Ashbrook Estate is one of the classic early producers in the region. Still family owned and operated, it offers a full range of Margaret River classics that are extremely well priced given the quality and pedigree. Aside from the excellent Estate and Reserve Cabernet Sauvignon they have always made fantastic varietal Semillon, vibrant Sauvignon Blanc and a stupidly delicious Verdelho. This is a really solid producer making a great range of wines.

Si Vintners

www.sivintners.com

Started by Sarah Morris and Iwo Jakimowicz in 2006, this estate works with the region's classic varieties of Chardonnay, Cabernet Sauvignon, Semillon, Sauvignon Blanc and some of the region's oldest Pinot Noir. Although firm proponents of biodynamic farming practices and distinctly low intervention, the wines actually range from quite 'natural' to borderline classic. The ADA Chardonnay leans towards classic but has a real savoury character and The Pekoe Pinot Noir is worth a try – there is not a whole lot of Pinot in Margaret River. Baba Yaga is a skin-contact Sauvignon Blanc co-fermented with a small amount of Cabernet Sauvignon. It is wild and aromatic, textural and fresh, a really fun wine. Lello is a skin-contact Sauvignon Blanc, fermented in eggs, cask and stainless steel. Delicious and textural with fruit and savoury characters, the wine is made with 'no intervention at all, save a little sulphur at bottling'.

Blind Corner

www.blindcorner.com.au

After many years of tinkering with fruit from various sites and then owning a small vineyard in Wilyabrup, Ben and Naomi Gould sold up and bought a larger site further north in the region. They didn't think that organic farming went far enough so now farm biodynamically. There is a lot to like about Blind Corner. They are thoughtful and honest and approach everything with an unpretentious authenticity. I tend to be cautious with recommendations of low intervention wines but not here. Knock yourself out – there are so many good wines. The Governo is a Sauvignon Blanc wine where a portion of grapes are hand-picked early and air-dried, before being wild fermented on skins. The remaining grapes are basket pressed and wild-fermented in old French oak, stainless steel and a concrete egg. Wild, savoury and textural, this is a delicious departure from what you may expect from Sauvignon Blanc. The Chardonnay–Aligote is really good as is their orange wine, called Orange* in Colour, a textural blend of skin-contact Pinot Gris, Chenin Blanc and Sauvignon Blanc.

L.A.S. Vino

www.lasvino.com

Started as a side project in 2013, L.A.S. Vino is now a solidly established brand. Nic Peterkin is the son of Pierro founder Dr Mike Peterkin and Shelly Cullen of Cullen wines fame, so you just know that if he had a crack at something, it would be interesting. He did and it is. I have loved the wines from L.A.S. Vino from the first time I tried them in a wine bar in Sydney.

Wines are staunchly Margaret River-focused, with a couple of delicious Grenaches made from fruit sourced in the Ferguson Valley in Geographe. Two drop-dead delicious Chenin Blancs, the CBDB (Chenin Blanc Dynamic Blend) and the regular Chenin Blanc, are both sourced from a certified organic and biodynamic site in the northern section of the region.

The Pet Nat is a Chenin–Pinot Noir blend and is a frothy, tart cherry, mineral delight. The Cabernet Sauvignon is dense and concentrated but with layers of complex fruit and a distinct graphite mineral edge.

Side note: I rarely want to try something solely based on the label and accompanying statements, but I really want to get a bottle from a series made to show support for the people of Ukraine in their fight. PUTIN, in the 'Fuck Him' range is a red wine, the proceeds from which go to the Red Cross Ukraine Appeal. The Fuck Him Chardonnay is Trump focused and the back label reads:

'Our wine is made in Margaret River, Australia, with vines imported from France, watered by Israeli irrigation and tended to by an American tractor. It's made with grapes picked by a group of Irish, German, Estonian and Korean travellers under the supervision of a South African. Those grapes are pressed with a Swiss press, and using an Italian pump the juice is transferred into French oak by a Hungarian Canarian and then bottled with the help of a lesbian. The wine is sealed with a cork from Portugal and wax from the Czech Republic and placed into boxes made in China. This was written with a program downloaded from India with a label designed by a legend in the USA, proofread by an Eurasian Australian woman in New York. Our wine is exported to Singapore, Sweden, Tokyo, Shanghai, Dubai and the U.K., and drunk by those wanting to bring friends together from all countries, ethnicities, sexes, sexualities and religions! The flavour inside this bottle attests: we are more than where we come from. We are what we contribute.'

Dormilona

www.dormilona.com.au

Small-batch winery Dormilona is run by Jo Perry and husband Jim Crespin. The name Dormilona means lazybones in Spanish and is reflective of their minimalist winemaking approach. They only work with certified organic and biodynamic sites. Work in the winery is minimal intervention with no additions except a small amount of sulphur dioxide at bottling. Orenji is a lovely partial skin contact blend of Semillon and Sauvignon Blanc. Pinku is rosé made from Shiraz. There is delicious Chenin Blanc and a classically structured Cabernet Sauvignon. The Clayface wines are all made in terracotta amphorae and the Chenin Blanc bottling is a stunner.

Nocturne Wines

www.nocturnewines.com.au

This is a project by Julian Langworthy, with tight focus on single vineyard wines. His Cabernet Sauvignon is particularly good, but you can't go wrong with anything Julian makes. The Sangiovese–Nebbiolo Rosé is a beauty. It sits in the more serious camp of rosés, showing lovely strawberry fruit but with texture and grip that make it all the more interesting.

McHenry Hohnen

www.mchenryhohnen.com.au

Murray McHenry has a strong grape-growing history in Margaret River. In 1984 he planted his first vines in Margaret River at the Burnside Vineyard, selling grapes for many years to Cape Mentelle, which was then owned by David Hohnen. Their southernmost vineyard, Hazel's Vineyard is certified biodynamic. Located near Witchcliffe in the south of the Margaret River region, it is planted to Chardonnay, Cabernet Sauvignon, Zinfandel, Merlot, Grenache, Petit Verdot and Mataro. This site forms the backbone of their wine range. Under the McHenry Hohnen range the Grenache is terrific as is the GSM. The Tempranillo is from a small block in Hazel's vineyard and is classically structured with lovely dark cherry fruit. As you might imagine, the Sauvignon Blanc is excellent too.

GREAT SOUTHERN
(Minang Country)

The Great Southern is a very large, expansive region located in the southwestern corner of Australia. The geology is ancient, and it is one of the most isolated wine regions in the world. The first grape vines were planted in 1859 but interest in the region didn't really take off until much later. In 1955, the state Government invited Californian viticulture professor Harold Olmo to assess the region. His conclusions were that Mount Barker and Frankland River had excellent potential for viticulture. In 1969 the first commercial plantings took place at Forest Hill in Mount Barker. Slow expansion and development followed. Although only planted to about half the vineyard area of Margaret River, Great Southern contains five significant subregional GIs: Albany, Denmark, Frankland River, Mount Barker and Porongurup. Due to the size of the region and distinctly different climate influences, many varieties do well in Great Southern. The wines of Great Southern are not as widely known or distributed as Margaret River, which is a shame since there are so many exciting and diverse styles emanating from this stunningly beautiful region.

Area under vine

2,545 hectares[65]

Climate

Denmark and Albany's climates are heavily influenced by the Southern Ocean. Summers are warm and dry, while winters are cool and wet. Frankland River is the most northerly GI in Great Southern but its climate is still Mediterranean in nature. Afternoon breezes make their way north, up the river valley. Mount Barker has the most continental climate in Great Southern. Porongurup's climate is mostly continental in nature. Spring frost can be an issue in both Porongurup and Mount Barker.

Soils

These are quite varied given the size of region. Albany and Denmark have similar gravelly, sandy loams in the best sites. Frankland River is predominantly open, rolling hill countryside. Soils tend to be richer, with granite and gneiss outcrops. Mount Barker has relatively poor soils with gravelly sandy loam being dominant. Porongurup soils are mostly weathered granite.

Varieties

Several varieties excel in the varied soils and climate of Great Southern. Chardonnay, Riesling, Sauvignon Blanc, Pinot Noir, Cabernet Sauvignon, and Shiraz are the mainstays. Malbec and Cabernet Franc have a presence in a few areas.

65 Source: National Vineyard Scan 2020 and ABS

Albany

Established in 1826, Albany was the first European settlement in Western Australia. The surrounding area is known not only for outstanding produce, but also for its spectacular scenery, shaped by coastal inlets and craggy granite outcrops. The low-lying subregion has a maritime climate, mediated by the Southern Ocean, which allows both red and white varieties to flourish, including Sauvignon Blanc, Chardonnay, Pinot Noir and Shiraz.

Producers to look for include Chardonnay and Pinot Noir specialists **Wignalls Wines** (www.wignallswines.com.au). **Parish Lane Wines** (www.parishlanewines.com.au) make sparkling *blanc de blancs* and a delicious Pinot Noir. **Bunn Wine** (www.bunnwine.com.au) is a small production, biodynamically farmed estate. Part of the natural wine movement in the region, they produce small amounts of Cabernet Sauvignon and Shiraz

Denmark

Denmark is a coastal town located just west of Albany. The subregion has a similar, slightly cooler, maritime climate, as well as steep hills and valleys that create a number of microclimates. Chardonnay, Riesling and Pinot Noir are the main varieties that thrive here. Both Chardonnay and Pinot Noir are also used for sparkling wine production.

Singlefile Wines

www.singlefilewines.com

This estate was co-founded in 2007 by geologists Phil and Viv Snowden. The brilliant Reserve Chardonnay uses fruit exclusively from the best blocks on the property. They also make wines with fruit sourced from various Great Southern subregions.

Brave New Wine

www.bravenewwine.com.au

Run by husband and wife duo Andries and Yoko Lüscher-Mostert, this producer makes small-batch minimal intervention wines. It is a really cool, interesting producer and worth seeking out. The frothy, delicious Pinot Gris based Pet-Nat and the Ambergris, a ramato-styled Pinot Gris are particular favourites.

La Violetta

www.laviolettawines.com.au

Here's another really exciting producer to look for. Fruit is sourced from several of the subregions but the property is based in Denmark. La Ciornia Shiraz is fantastic and the delicious Das Sakrileg is a Riesling sourced from Denmark and Mount Barker. Up! Shiraz is from Mount Barker fruit and is juicy, fragrant and fun to drink.

Castelli Estate

www.castelliestate.com.au

This beautiful family-run estate was established in 2007. Strong Italian roots inform the production ethos. The Estate range includes a medium-weight, finely detailed Pinot Noir. The Il Liris Chardonnay is their flagship wine and worth seeking out.

Willoughby Park

www.willoughbypark.com.au

This estate makes solid Pinot Noir and Chardonnay from the Kalgan River vineyards site, which is technically in Albany.

Frankland River

The first vineyard in the Frankland River region was planted in 1968. Originally called Westfield, it is now owned by Houghton. In 1971 Alkoomi Vineyard and Winery was established. This is the largest, warmest and most northerly subregion in Great Southern, and the furthest inland. With long sunlight hours, cool nights and rich, gravelly loam soils, the subregion has developed a reputation for Riesling and Shiraz. Cabernet Sauvignon also does well in certain sites.

Alkoomi Wines

www.alkoomiwines.com.au

The is one of the original Frankland River estates. They make lovely Riesling, especially the Melaleuca bottling from 1971 planted vines. Top range Blackbutt Cabernet Sauvignon is blended with a little Malbec and Cabernet Franc and is a fragrant, medium- to full-bodied charmer. The varietal wines in the Collection Series are all fantastic and represent excellent value for money given the quality.

Frankland Estate

www.franklandestate.com.au

Frankland Estate is a second-generation winery run by brother and sister Hunter and Elizabeth Smith. The vineyards were first planted on the estate in 1988 by their parents Judy Cullam and Barrie Smith. The Isolation Ridge vineyard, planted with Shiraz and Riesling is the beating heart of the wines at this fantastic property. Isolation Ridge Riesling is a wine with surprising concentration and weight but with laser-sharp precision and purity of fruit. It is one of the best Rieslings in the country, never mind the region. They label the Shiraz as Syrah, and it is the archetype of the cooler climate Shiraz style; medium weight with spice and savoury characters wrapped in a blanket of dark raspberry fruit. This region gets accolades for Riesling and Cabernet Sauvignon but ignore Shiraz at your peril. It is a strong suit. They single out certain blocks of Riesling and Syrah from the Isolation Ridge vineyard in good vintages and bottle them under the SmithCullam label, a dedication to their parents. They also make a Cabernet-based blend called Olmo's Reward, a tribute to Harold Olmo, the scholar who first noted the region's wine potential.

Plan B! Wines

www.planbwines.com

Terry Chellappah established Plan B! in 2003. It is a medium-sized operation with a solid portfolio of classic and contemporary wines, self-described as a minimal pretension winery, which perfectly describes Terry too. They make several wines from fruit sourced in other regions in Western Australia but of the Frankland River sourced wines look for the Dr Riesling. A citrus-laden beauty. Juicy, fresh and very easy to drink. The Frespañol Shiraz is a lively version of the variety with 5 per cent Tempranillo blended in for interest. All the wines are solid and well made.

Mount Barker

Mount Barker is the coolest of Great Southern's subregions, with a higher average elevation. It sees consistent sunny days and cool nights, with a distinct diurnal variation. Riesling and Shiraz are the strong varieties here.

Forest Hill

www.foresthillwines.com.au

Forest Hill Vineyard was the first cool climate vineyard planted in the state, in 1965. It is family owned and operated. The winery is actually in Denmark, but grapes are sourced from old, dry-grown vines at Forest Hill Vineyard in Mount Barker. They are an all-round top producer. Highlights include the fantastic Riesling, especially the Block 1 and a savoury, raspberry-scented Shiraz. The Block 8 Chardonnay is dynamite – one of the best I tried on my last visit to the area.

Plantagenet

www.plantagenetwines.com

In 1968 Tony Smith planted trial vineyards of Shiraz and Cabernet Sauvignon on his Bouverie property in Denbarker. 1974 saw the first vintage under the Plantagenet label. Since 2000 it has been owned by the Lionel Samson Sadleirs Group (LSSG). Plantagenet remains a Mount Barker stalwart. The entire range is rock-solid. Riesling is a strength, but the peppery, raspberry-scented Shiraz is fantastic.

Howard Park wines

See Burch Family Wines (p. 259).

Porongurup

This is the smallest subregion, situated just east of Mount Barker. The range of ancient granite peaks has a strong influence on the soils. A nocturnal thermal zone, created by rising warm air, reduces the risk of frost and generates ideal ripening conditions for cool-climate varieties, especially Riesling, Chardonnay and Pinot Noir.

Castle Rock Estate

www.castlerockestate.com.au

Riesling is the star here. Different bottlings of fantastic examples make it hard to choose but I particularly like the flagship Estate Riesling and the RS21 (made leaving some residual sugar).

Duke's Vineyard

www.dukesvineyard.com

Duke Ranson planted the vines in 1999, starting on his sixtieth birthday. Winemaker Ben Cane and his partner, Sarah Date, took over this award-winning property and brand in April 2022 after Duke retired at the age of 82. The Magpie Hill Reserve Riesling is world class and the Whole Bunch Shiraz is a lovely expression of cooler climate Shiraz character. Ben is a very experienced and talented winemaker so it will be interesting to watch the evolution of this first-class estate.

BLACKWOOD VALLEY
(Kaniyang Country)

The first vineyards in the region were established in 1976. This has slowly expanded and there are now just over 50 vineyards scattered across the region. This is a small but stunningly beautiful region that remains an area of mixed farming and grazing land. The vineyards in the region developed around suitable locations carved out by the Blackwood River. The river winds its way down through some of the most elevated areas in this part of Western Australia. The best sites are planted on the free-draining sandy gravels or on the alluvial soils deposited on the floors of steep-sided valleys. This is a little slice of paradise sitting in the shadows of the better known regions of Western Australia. A detour worth making for the small, mostly boutique production wines.

Area under vine

450 hectares[66]

Climate

The region sees wet and relatively cool winters with warm, dry summers – sort of Mediterranean but with a more continental climate influence than Margaret River. Winter frosts can extend into spring. There is a slightly higher temperature range in the summer months.

Soils

The soils are part of the Darling Plateau system. Overall, soils are well-drained sandy gravel. Gravel and sandy gravel soils are found on the divides, with yellow clay loam and red earths on valley slopes.

Varieties

Cabernet Sauvignon, Shiraz, Sauvignon Blanc and Chardonnay.

66 Source: Blackwood Valley Wine www.blackwoodvalleywine.com.au

Producers

It is hard to find wines from this region in Australia let alone in export markets but two estates are worth hunting down. **Curlew Estate** (www.curlewestate.com.au) is a boutique winery making high-quality Shiraz from its estate vineyards. There is a full flavoured, delicious *saignée* style rosé too; really lovely wines. **Hillbillé Estate** (www.blackwoodvalleyestate.com) is a gorgeous property nestled in a small valley.

Established in 1998, they make excellent Chardonnay and Shiraz and a delicious Semillon–Sauvignon Blanc.

GEOGRAPHE
(Wardandi and Kaniyang Country)

This region is situated on the coast with its southern boundaries meeting the northern section of Margaret River. Most people drive through the area along the South Western Highway, then the Bussell Highway, on their way to Margaret River, not even realizing they are driving through an established wine region. While this is a coastal region it is where the Whicher and Darling Ranges meet and there are several river valleys creating varied climates. It is a single GI but there are three distinctly different areas. The coastal section, which is clearly maritime, the Donnybrook area – inland and more continental – and Ferguson Valley, which sits in the foothills of the Darling Ranges. While known for quality Chardonnay and Cabernet Sauvignon there are now all manner of varieties planted (36 according to the regional association) and it has quietly become one of the more exciting regions in Western Australia.

Area under vine
790 hectares[67]

Climate
Warm temperatures are moderated by the prevailing south-west sea breezes coming off the Indian Ocean. Summers are dry but rainfall is generous during winter and relative humidity is quite high. Conditions change as you move inland and over the ranges, where the climate influence is more continental.

Soils
The coastal sands sit over a limestone base. The soils of Donnybrook are richer, with gravelly sandy loam and richer loam soils in certain sites.

Varieties
Cabernet Sauvignon, Chardonnay, Sauvignon Blanc and Shiraz are the main varieties but Tempranillo, Viognier, Chenin Blanc are also grown.

67   Source: National Vineyard Scan 2020 and ABS

Producers

Capel Vale

www.capelvale.com.au

This is the most established and well-known producer in the region and the one you are most likely to find in export markets. The caveat is that they own vineyards in Margaret River and Mount Barker and those are now the primary focus of their production, rather than the Geographe GI. Look, however, for the Regional Series Malbec Rosé which is sourced in Geographe. The wines sourced in Margaret River and Mount Barker are all solid and worth experimenting with. A very good Western Australian producer.

Willow Bridge Estate

www.willowbridge.com.au

Jeff Dewar purchased land situated in Ferguson Valley in 1997 and now has 60 hectares under vine. This is one of the more significant Geographe producers. Solano Tempranillo and Gravel Pit Shiraz are both fantastic as is the dark berry fruited, fragrant Coat of Arms Cabernet Sauvignon.

Aylesbury Estate

www.aylesburyestate.com.au

Aylesbury Estate has a history dating back to 1883. Originally producing citrus, stone-fruit, potatoes, dairy and beef, in 1998 viticulture became part of the mix. Of the 80 hectares of farmland, 3.5 are planted to vines. Fifth generation son, Ryan Gibbs, and his wife, Narelle, run the property now. Initially known for Cabernet Sauvignon, Merlot and Sauvignon Blanc, they recently decided to focus on experimentation with other varieties. Vermentino, Grenache and Touriga are all coming in the near future. Their Sauvignon Blanc is zippy and fresh and in the Waterfall Gully range both the Merlot and Cabernet Sauvignon excellent. I will be keeping an eye on this producer.

Talisman Wines

www.talismanwines.com.au

Vineyards were planted in 1999 by Kim and Jenny Robinson and this is now a really solid producer. Initially they sold fruit to several wineries but created the Talisman brand in 2009. They work with all the classic varieties: Chardonnay, Riesling, Merlot, Shiraz, Cabernet Sauvignon,

Malbec and Sauvignon Blanc. The Riesling is top class, as is the Merlot, and they also have a sneaky Zinfandel which is superb.

Windfall Estate

www.windfallwine.com.au

This is a well-run, small family estate that adheres to biodynamic practices. They are Merlot specialists, so that should be your starting point. Try either the Single Handed Merlot or the Ivor Reserve Merlot.

MANJIMUP
(Bibbulman and Kaniyang Country)

This is a small region encircling the town of Manjimup. There were no vineyards here until 1988. It has a moderate climate where, to date, Bordeaux varieties seem to do best. Most producers are small production boutique wineries and wines are hard to find outside the region.

Area under vine

155 hectares[68]

Climate

The climate is influenced by the Indian and Southern oceans. It has some similarities to Margaret River, but with higher altitude, so is more continental. Winters are cold and there is decent rainfall in the spring. Summer and autumn are relatively dry.

Soils

The best soils are sandy, red, gravelly loams.

Varieties

Cabernet Sauvignon, Merlot, Sauvignon Blanc, Semillon and Chardonnay with some Pinot Noir and Verdelho.

68 Source: National Vineyard Scan 2020 and ABS

Producers

Peos Estate

www.peosestate.com.au

The Peos family were originally from Macedonia and have been in the region for over 90 years. They planted the first vineyards in 1996. They make a full range of classic varietal wines. The Four Aces range of wines is particularly good, especially the Chardonnay and the Pinot Noir.

PEMBERTON
(Bibbulman Country)

The region was first planted experimentally in 1977, with commercial vineyards following in 1982. This is a region noted for karri forests. In fact, the area is so densely forested that there is only a small percentage of land available for agriculture and viticulture. A relatively small region, this has similarities to Manjimup but with more producers and correspondingly more area under vine.

Area under vine

455 hectares[69]

Climate

Pemberton is cooler than neighbouring Manjimup, with fewer sunshine hours, more rainfall and relative humidity.

Soils

There are two major soil types: gravelly sands found on many of the higher slopes around Pemberton and the more fertile karri loam – deep, fertile, red loam soil.

Varieties

Chardonnay, Riesling, Pinot Noir, Merlot and Shiraz.

69   Source: National Vineyard Scan 2020 and ABS

Producers

Picardy

www.picardy.com.au

Picardy is one of Australia's top boutique producers. Established in 1993, it is owned and operated by Bill, Sandra and Dan Pannell. Bill and Sandra were pioneers of the Margaret River region, establishing Moss Wood vineyard and winery in 1969. They adhere to sustainable management practices. All Picardy fruit is estate grown and their fantastic Chardonnay and Pinot Noir set the standard for the region – these are must try wines.

Bellarmine

www.bellarmine.com.au

Established in 2000, the first vintage of Bellarmine wines was 2004. The estate specializes in Riesling and all are excellent. Wines are made in dry, off dry and sweeter styles. There is very good fine-boned, strawberry-scented Pinot Noir too. A really good producer.

Marri and Karri Trees

The south-western area of Australia is known for its impressive and unique hardwood forests. Karri trees (*Eucalyptus diversicolor*) are part of the Eucalyptus genus of trees and one of the tallest hardwoods in the world. Karri forests are only found in the south-west corner of Western Australia.

The Marri tree (*Corymbia calophylla*) is an impressive forest tree also only found in the south-western part of Australia. It was previously classified as a Eucalyptus species but in 1995 was reclassified as Corymbia. However, some organizations do not recognize this and still classify it as a eucalypt. It is a large tree which can grow to over 30 metres. It belongs to the bloodwood genus, so named because of the dark red gum it bleeds. The fruits are large and urn-shaped and known colloquially as honkey nuts. Flowers are produced from mid-summer to late autumn and Marri nectar makes excellent honey. A late blossom can be beneficial for grape growers. Bird pressure is a significant issue in many regions in south-western Australia, especially Margaret River. The flowering of the Marri has a strong influence on food supply for the various bird species, most notably the Silver Eye. If the flowering coincides with the time in the vineyards when fruit is ripe and appealing, birds prefer the nectar from the Marri flowers. As a result, they are drawn away from vineyards and deeper into native forest.

GREATER PERTH ZONE

This zone encompasses the three regional GIs of Swan Valley, Peel and Perth Hills.

SWAN DISTRICT AND SWAN VALLEY
(Nyoongar Whadjuk Boodja Country)

The first vines went in the ground in Swan Valley in 1830, making it the oldest wine region in Western Australia and one of the oldest in the entire country. Although those vines were planted by an Englishman, Thomas Walters, most of the original immigrants to the region were from what was then Yugoslavia. This eastern European influence is at the heart of the traditional wine culture that developed in the region. Swan Valley is technically a subregion of Swan District but is the beating heart of wine in this area. The region is still renowned for very good fortifieds, as well as warm-climate Shiraz, Petit Verdot, Chenin Blanc and Verdelho. In recent years, several natural, low intervention producers have taken advantage of the old vines and lesser-known varieties and are making a raft of really exciting, vibrant wines. It has given this region, one known for traditional warm climate wines, an injection of enthusiasm and attention. This is definitely a region that needs to be on any Australian wine enthusiast's radar.

Area under vine

890 hectares[70]

Climate

The Swan District has a warm to hot Mediterranean climate. It is very dry during the key ripening and harvest months. Most rainfall occurs during winter and spring. The area is afforded some relief from the heat by the famous Fremantle Doctor, a cooling, south-westerly sea breeze. The Gingin/Moondah Brook area is somewhat cooler.

Soils

These are quite varied. Typically, young alluvial soils; very deep, with excellent moisture retention capacity. Deep sand over limestone along the coastal strip around Wanneroo. Well-drained gravelly loam along the fringes of the Darling Scarp. Deep, rich, red loam around the Swan River. Grey sand over clay in the Herne Hill flats of the Swan Valley subregion. The lower slopes of the Darling Range are gravelly sand to gravelly sandy loam overlying brown clay.

70 Source: National Vineyard Scan 2020 and ABS

> ## Varieties
> Chardonnay, Chenin and Verdelho with some Grenache, Shiraz and Petit Verdot.

Producers

Houghton

www.houghton-wines.com.au

This historic winery was established in 1836 and has a fond history in Australia largely due to one specific wine. I grew up drinking Houghton White Burgundy – a name that was permitted back in the day. It was a blend of Chenin Blanc, Chardonnay, Verdelho, Muscadelle, Semillon and Riesling. It was developed by Western Australian legend Jack Mann (see below) and was affordable, delicious, easy to drink and had the sneaky capacity to age beautifully for 10 or more years. The wine is now called Houghton Classic White.

> ## Jack Mann 1908–1989
> Jack Mann was a pioneer in the Western Australian wine industry. He was head winemaker at Houghton from 1930 to 1972 and developed Houghton's famous White Burgundy, which became a flag bearer for Western Australian wines and remained popular for decades. His wines in general received dozens of awards and accolades and he is known for adopting and developing many innovative techniques. In 1932 he introduced a butcher's mincing machine which fragmented grape skins, but not the seeds, after the stalks had been separated from the bunches. In 1936 he acquired a Seitz germ-proof filter, the first to be imported into Australia, which allowed sterile filtration.

Garbin Estate Wines

www.garbinestatewines.com.au

Established in 1956, this is one of the family-run properties in the region. The full gamut of Swan Valley styles exists here. Excellent fortified wines, frothy traditional method sparkling and a well-regarded basket-pressed Shiraz.

Bella Ridge

bellaridge.com.au

Small, boutique, family-run winery making lovely wines from vines mostly planted in the 1960s. Delicious Chenin Blanc and a fun, easy drinking Trebbiano. The old-vine Grenache is not to be missed.

Vino Volta

www.vinovolta.com.au

The owners of this super exciting, relatively new producer have history in the region. Garth Cliff worked for 10 years at Houghton before he and partner Kristen McGann started Vino Volta in 2018. Old-vine Chenin and Grenache are at the heart of what they do, but they do it a little differently. Funky & Fearless Chenin is textural, savoury and a delight to drink. Post Modern Seriousism Grenache is super delicious; vibrant, bright and aromatic and follows the lead of modern Grenache producers in McLaren Vale and Barossa, but with its own region stamp. The two Method Ancestrale wines – one made with Chenin Blanc and the other with Grenache – are fun, frothy and very easy to drink. This is one of Australia's exciting new producers. Look for them and experiment.

Corymbia Wines

www.corymbiawine.com.au

This Margaret River based estate (see p. 261) has two Swan Valley wines. The Rocket's Vineyard Tempranillo–Malbec field blend is a juicy, intense mouthful of berries and spice, while the Rocket's Vineyard Chenin Blanc is a fragrant, textural beauty.

Sitella

www.sittella.com.au

Established in 1993, Sitella has been a solid and innovative producer from the start. I have not tried many of their wines, but the Avante-Garde El Vivero Blanco is delicious. It is a field blend of bush vine Pedro Ximenez, Albarino, Arinto, Verdejo and Glera.

John Kosovich Wines

www.johnkosovichwines.com.au

The first of the Kosovich family came to Australia in 1911 from Croatia (part of Yugoslavia at the time). The winemaking operation was started in 1922 but up until 2003 it was known as Westfield Wines. This was changed to John Kosovich Wines to honour John's fiftieth vintage. This is one of the historic estates in Swan Valley. They do have interests in Pemberton but Swan Valley Chenin Blanc is their strong suit. The Mara Chenin Blanc is from vines planted in 1962 and is tight, mineral and complex. The do a late-release, bottle-aged Chenin too, and if you are lucky enough to find one, just buy it. The Verdelho is also juicy and delicious. Not quite in the same league as the Chenin Blanc but super easy to drink.

PEEL
(Pinjarup and Wiilman Country)

The European settlement of Peel dates back to 1829. Peel lies between the Swan District and Perth Hills to the north and Geographe to the south. The first vines were planted in the region in 1857 but not much happened viticulturally until the 1970s. The first commercial vineyard was established with a planting of Shiraz by Will Nairn at the Peel Estate in 1974. While most other varieties have also now been established, Shiraz remains the flagship variety for the region.

Area under vine
60 hectares[71]

Climate
This is a coastal region and has a Mediterranean climate with cool, wet winters and hot, dry summers. Sections of the region located inland and those at higher altitudes have stronger land breezes, higher rainfall and slightly lower temperatures. The Indian Ocean and the region's lakes and dams supply cooling summer sea breezes.

Soils
Generally these are limestone based sands along the coastal section with more granitic soils in the eastern sections of the GI.

Varieties
Shiraz, Cabernet Sauvignon, Chardonnay, Chenin Blanc and Verdelho.

71 Source: Wine Australia

Producers

It is difficult to find Peel region wines outside the region. But **Peel Estate** (www.peelwine.com.au) is a very high-quality producer that is worth seeking out. Established in 1974, it produces top-notch Shiraz and Chenin Blanc.

PERTH HILLS
(Wadjuk Country)

Viticulture has been part of Perth Hills for more than a century. The first vineyard was planted in Darlington in the 1880s, followed by Glen Forrest in 1896. However, the earliest of the present-day wineries in the region date back to the mid-1970s.

Area under vine

120 hectares[72]

Climate

The tempering influences in the region are the altitude exposure to afternoon sea breezes. The climate varies significantly with altitude.

Soils

The valley slopes have ironstone and gravel sandy loams as well as gravelly loams which overlay clay.

Varieties

Chenin Blanc, Verdelho, Shiraz and Cabernet with some Tempranillo, Vermentino and a few other Mediterranean varieties.

72 Source: Wine Australia

Producers

Myattsfield Wines

www.myattsfield.com.au

The pick of the whites are the excellent Vermentino and delicious Chenin Blanc. There is an interesting Tempranillo and a solid Shiraz.

Millbrook Estate

www.millbrook.wine

This estate is owned by the Fogarty Wine Group and is worth a visit. They source fruit from other regions, but the restaurant is fantastic and the surroundings are exquisite. The Estate Viognier is really good, as is the intense and age-worthy Petit Verdot.

Aldersyde Estate

www.aldersyde.com.au

Established in 1974, this is one of the region's pioneer producers and they are still making handcrafted, estate-grown wines. Wines are made in tiny quantities and pretty much sold through the winery. It is worth visiting if you are in the area as it is hard to find the wines outside the region.

10

TASMANIA (*LUTRUWITA COUNTRY*)

The pristine island state of Tasmania is situated off the southern coast of Australia in the cool waters of the Southern Ocean. Bartholomew Broughton is credited with planting Tasmania's first commercial vineyards in 1823. Planting and production continued until the 1860s but the gold rush on the mainland led to an exodus of sorts and labour shortages became an issue. Interestingly, wine was being made in Tasmania before vines were planted in either South Australia or Victoria, and Tasmania had a hand in establishing the viticulture in those states. William Henty sailed from Tasmania to a coastal port in Victoria with vine cuttings in 1834 and both John Reynell and John Hack, pioneer grape growers in South Australia, are said to have sourced their original vines from Port Arthur in Tasmania.

Frenchman Jean Miguet arrived from Provence in the 1950s to work on the Hydro Electric Commission, and while there decided to buy land and plant vineyards north-east of Launceston. Development of vineyards was slow in the subsequent years. By the mid-1980s Piper's Brook area had just six vineyards and Tamar Valley only eleven. Climate change has inspired many noted mainland producers to venture across the Bass Strait to purchase land or existing vineyards and the viticultural landscape is now a mix of larger companies and boutique family-run estates, with a smattering of smaller producers making small batch wines.

The next stop south of Tasmania is Antarctica, with nothing but cold ocean separating the two. Being so far south and being an island with a range of mountains running north–south, presents both challenges

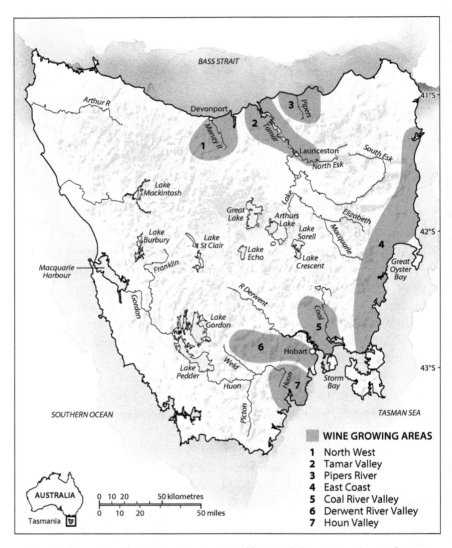

Map 6: Tasmania. The entire state is covered by one GI but it is made up of seven noted unofficial sub-regions.

and opportunities. In weather terms these can be rain, lack of rain, hail, snow, wind (lots of wind) and lots of sunshine. The range of mountains creates a distinct rain shadow. The western side of the island is dense, temperate rainforest and not at all suited to viticulture. All grape growing is east of the mountains in the northern, southern and eastern parts of the island. While the general narrative is about the overall cool climate of Tasmania, there are distinctly different regions with varied sites, climates, and soils.

There has been much written and debated about the Aboriginal clans of Tasmania. What we do know for sure is that the history has been lost or rewritten, such was the devastation of these indigenous clans. The Tasmanian Aboriginal Centre helped recreate an Aboriginal language, now called palawan, from the few words that did remain. Lutruwita is the name used to describe Tasmania, the Big Island, but there are other named places. Peerapper, Tommeginne, Tyerrernotepanner and Pyremmairrener countries run across the northern sections of the island. Lairmairrener Country is in the centre, Paredarerme Country occupies the lower section of the East Coast, Nuenonne Country is the southern tip and Toogee Country runs up the west coast and butts up to the southern section of Peerapper Country.

THE REGIONS AND WINES

Tasmania is the only GI at present. Clearly this won't suffice for the future and further GIs will need to be granted to fully express the sub-regional differences. However, the word Tasmania resonates in the global marketplace. Keeping it front and centre makes a lot of sense. Currently, most producers do list the region of origin as a means of differentiation and if new GIs are granted, the Tasmania name may indeed still be something producers will wish to keep on their labels.

There is no official way of breaking down the regions but separating the island into northern and southern areas helps to set the stage. The regions below are separate and recognized as distinct locally. If additional GIs are awarded in the future, this may well be how it breaks down. I was interested to note that Wine Australia's Climate Atlas[73] breaks Tasmania into eight regions based on distinct climates: King Island, Furneaux Islands, North West Coast, Central North, North East, East

---

73 www.wineaustralia.com/growing-making/environment-and-climate/climate-atlas

Coast, South East and Upper Derwent Valley. I am sure this will also be a consideration when determining future GIs.

Area under vine
2,084 hectares[74]

Northern Tasmania

Regions: Northwest, Tamar River Valley, Pipers River, and the upper section of the East Coast – *Tommeginne, Tyerrernotepanner and Pyremmairrener Country*

Climate: Overall, it is quite cool and generally wetter than parts of the south as many areas do not see the same protection from the western mountain range. Forty per cent of the annual rainfall comes during the growing season. Spring frosts are an issue in many sites, as is humidity. The Pipers River climate is typically cooler than that of Tamar Valley and harvest times are about two weeks later. The East Coast is the warmest section in Tasmania.

Soil: Pipers River has deep, free-draining, friable soils. Tamar Valley is gravelly basalt on a clay and limestone base. Many vineyard sites are situated on north, north-east and east-facing slopes.

Southern Tasmania

Regions: lower section of East Coast, Coal River Valley, Derwent Valley and Huon Valley/d'Entrecasteaux Channel – *Paredarerme and Nuenonne Country*

Climate: There is nothing but cold ocean between southern Tasmania and Antarctica so the obvious assumption is that southern Tasmania is colder than the north. That is true of the south-western corner of the island, but the southern vineyard areas are east of the mountains, generally tucked into various river valleys. As a result they are more protected and see drier and sunnier conditions.

The Coal River Valley is the driest region in Tasmania. Derwent Valley gets more rainfall than Coal River Valley. Huon Valley is the coolest and wettest of the southern Tasmanian regions. The lower section of the East Coast is similar to the upper section (see northern Tasmania, above).

Soils: Extremely varied. Sandstone and schist predominate in Derwent Valley. Peaty alluvial and sandy low humus soils are common in Coal River Valley.

74 Source: National Vineyard Scan 2020 and ABS

> ## Varieties
>
> Pinot Noir and Chardonnay are the most planted varieties in Tasmania. Other varieties include Riesling, Sauvignon Blanc, Pinot Gris, Grüner Veltliner, Gewurztraminer and Gamay. Note, however, that there are small, warmer pockets on the island where Shiraz and Cabernet Sauvignon are grown and do very well (see notes on Domaine A and Glaetzer-Dixon, below). At present, Tasmania is not ideal for later ripening varieties.

Main wine styles

Traditional method sparkling wine represents 40 per cent of wine production. It is a Tasmanian speciality, and the quality is world-class. Pinot Noir is used as the base in many traditional method sparkling wines but still-wine production of this variety has also increased, and it is now second to sparkling wine in terms of overall production. Various styles exist, depending on the regional fruit sourcing but delicacy, fragrance and purity of fruit are the hallmarks of Tasmanian Pinot Noir.

Chardonnay has always been important but has really hit its stride in the last decade and many top Tasmanian examples belong in the discussion with the very best regional examples of this variety in Australia.

Tasmanian Riesling is not as well-known globally as Clare Valley or Eden Valley but there are brilliant examples to be found. Typical wines are vibrant and aromatic, with apple and citrus accents.

Sauvignon Blanc is well suited to the cool and sunny conditions of Tasmania. Wines are vibrant and lively with guava and passion fruit notes.

TASMANIA'S PRODUCERS BY VARIETY AND STYLE

It is a challenge to single out producers as there are so many high-quality wines being crafted in Tasmania at present. Given that Tasmania is one GI and many producers are working with fruit sourced in multiple regions, I have grouped producers of note under varieties and styles rather than separating them into the regions of production. Specific regional commentary is given on certain wines.

Sparkling wine

House of Arras

www.houseofarras.com.au

This is possibly the best sparkling wine producer in Australia. Ed Carr is a national treasure and the only winemaker I know of in Australia who has dedicated his entire career to sparkling wine production. You can't go wrong with anything he makes but the Vintage Collection wines are superb. E.J Carr Late Disgorged, Grand Vintage and Blanc de Blancs are the very top wines in this stable of beauties.

Clover Hill

www.cloverhillwines.com.au

Founded by the Goelet family in Pipers River in 1986, this is another exceptional producer making a range of very fine wines. There are many to choose from but my go-to favourites are the Vintage Brut and the Exceptionnelle Blanc de Blancs. Their Prestige Late Disgorged is brilliant and priced accordingly.

Jansz Tasmania

www.jansz.com.au

A well-known and highly regarded producer. The wine used to be made on the mainland, but they now have their own facility in the Pipers Brook region where their cellar door is. The Premium Cuvée NV is delicious and affordable and is consumed so frequently by the Davidson family that it qualifies as our house wine. The Vintage Brut and Vintage Rosé are a distinct step up in length, depth, and complexity.

Delamere Vineyards

www.delamerevineyards.com.au

This is joint venture between Fran Austin and Shane Holloway, making top-notch traditional method wines. All fruit is estate grown and all production elements are done on the estate. I recommend you find a way to try their entire line of sparkling wines: Non-Vintage Cuvée, NV Rosé, Vintage Cuvee, Vintage Rose, Vintage Blanc de Blancs and the stunningly complex Late Disgorged Blanc de Blancs.

Heskens Rankin

www.henskensrankin.com

This small scale, artisanal producer is focused on high quality, making a Vintage Brut, a Blanc de Blancs and a Brut Rosé. Owners Frieda Heskens and David Rankin say, 'Henskens Rankin of Tasmania is founded on the principle that luxury is ethical. It guides our winemaking and how we choose our partners. It extends to every aspect of the business, particularly our supply chain: wherever possible our materials are ethically-sourced and our packaging re-useable, compostable and/or recyclable. From 2020 all our wines are completely vegan friendly. It's a journey in progress.' Production is deliberately small and wines are purposefully expensive. They were not on my radar until recently but are now, and are well worth checking out.

Bream Creek Vineyard

www.breamcreekvineyard.com.au

The vineyards at Bream Creek were planted in the early 1970s, making it among the earliest commercial vineyards planted in Tasmania. The Bream Creek brand was established by Fred Peacock in 1990, at a time when there were fewer than 10 commercial wineries in the entire state. This pioneer East Coast producer is now making a range of wines that includes excellent sparkling wines.

Chardonnay

Tolpuddle Vineyard

www.tolpuddlevineyard.com

This vineyard, situated in Coal River, was purchased in 2011 by Michael Hill-Smith MW and Martin Shaw of Shaw and Smith in the Adelaide Hills (see p. 122). Prior to this it was a source of fruit for some very good wines. Since they acquired the vineyard, the wine has been bottled as a single vineyard wine. Attention to detail is at the core of everything Michael Hill Smith does. With this ethos and the skill of head winemaker Adam Wadewitz, Tolpuddle Chardonnay has quickly worked its way up the ranks and is known as one of Australia's best Chardonnays.

Tolpuddle Vineyard, in the Coal River Valley, is the source for one of Tasmania's and Australia's best Chardonnays.

Stoney Rise Wine Company and Holyman Wines

www.stoneyrise.com

Joe Holyman is crafting excellent wines on his Tamar River Valley property. There are many different wines to play with here, under both the Stony Rise and Holyman labels (for Pinot Noir recommendations see p. 292). His Chardonnays are precise, focused and pure fruited. Stony Rise serves as the entry point and is vibrant, fresh and layered. The Holyman is more complex, textured and layered. One of my favourite producers on the island. Really lovely wines.

Dr Edge

www.dr-edge.com

Peter Dredge is a character. To expand on that would require unpublishable commentary. He is very talented and makes the wines for the stunning Meadowbank property as well as his own wines under the Dr Edge label. His Tasmania Chardonnay (a blend of Tamar Valley and Derwent Valley fruit) is drop-dead delicious; textured, layered and complex.

Ossa

www.ossa.wine

The Chardonnay from this small production, new venture is made with fruit from the East Coast and Coal River Valley. With stone fruit and salted lime notes, it is lovely stuff. A producer to pay attention to.

Pinot Noir

Chatto Wines

www.chattowines.com

Jim Chatto is a very accomplished winemaker with a strong history in the Hunter Valley. He purchased his Huon Valley property in 2006 and planted in 2007 – all Pinot Noir. Everything he makes is fantastic. Bird is Pinot Noir from Pipers River and is a fine-boned, delicate and fragrant charmer. Isle is his top estate wine and he is quick to point out that this is not a barrel selection. The intent with this cuvée is to select the best fruit from the vineyard. Textured, layered, fragrant and seductive, everything I want from Pinot Noir lives in this wine. Here is a top producer at the top of his game.

Chatto's vineyard in the cool environs of Houn Valley.
A special place for Pinot Noir.

Stefano Lubiana Wines

www.slw.com.au

Steve Lubiana is a charming, quietly spoken man with a family history of farming six generations deep, mostly in South Australia. He moved to Tasmania and started his venture in 1990 in the Derwent Valley. Specializing in Chardonnay and Pinot Noir from the start, he and now his son are tinkering with all manner of different varieties and styles. This was Tasmania's first biodynamically farmed estate. His Pinot Noirs have always grabbed my attention. The Primavera bottling is always lighter and more delicate, La Roccia is more compact, dense and structured, without losing the perfume and charm.

Pooley Wines

www.pooleywines.com.au

Established in 1985 in the Coal River valley, this is one of Tasmania's iconic producers. The Butcher's Hill Pinot Noir is lifted and fragrant with dark cherry and spice characters. The Cooinda Vale is more compact and dense with a long savoury finish. Both are superb examples and worth seeking out.

bubb + pooley

www.bubbandpooley.com.au

Keep an eye out for this relatively new venture from Anna Pooley and husband Justin Bubb. The first releases were from the 2021 vintage. The Pinot Noir is excellent, with bright cherry fruit, savoury characters and a whiff of herbs. This and a savoury, spicy, peppery Syrah are the only two wines I have had to date. The pedigree is there. This is a space to watch.

Tolpuddle Vineyard

www.tolpuddlevineyard.com

A few years ago, I may not have included the Tolpuddle Pinot on my list of must-try Tasmanian Pinot Noirs but a recent tasting of the 2021 changed my opinion. This wine has hit its stride and while the Chardonnay tends to get all the accolades, the Pinot Noir now belongs in the discussion too.

Stoney Rise Wine Company and Holyman Wines

www.stoneyrise.com

Joe Holyman is also making delicious Pinot Noir. His Holyman Pinot Noir 2020 showed beautiful soft, fragrant, red fruit character. Compact, layered and very charming.

Meadowbank vineyard, a picture-perfect place to get a sense of the Derwent Valley in southern Tasmania.

Stargazer Wines

www.stargazerwine.com.au

There is not a bad wine here, which makes sense given that Sam Connew is the woman behind the wines. Her Pinots are consistently delicious, fragrant and beautifully balanced.

Meadowbank Tasmania

www.meadowbank.com.au

This stunning property situated above the Derwent River has a total of 2,500 hectares, with 52 of them under vine. Several producers source fruit from this vineyard, most notably Stargazer, Glaetzer-Dixon, Dawson & James and House of Arras. The Meadowbank wines are made by Peter Dredge and the Pinot Noir is fantastic; vibrant and pure fruited with a savoury finish.

Glaetzer-Dixon Family Winemakers

www.gdfwinemakers.com

Nick Glaetzer moved from the Barossa to Tasmania in 2007 and carved out a reputation quickly, especially with Shiraz and Riesling (see below). His Pinots are lovely; the Avancé Pinot Noir is a great entry into his style and his new, limited release Rêveur Pinot Noir is fantastic. La Judith is the top cuvée and priced accordingly.

Tasmanian Vintners

www.tasvintners.wine

This is a venture under the Fogarty Wine Group umbrella. This group owns many top Australian estates on the mainland – Deep Woods, Evans and Tate, Dalwhinnie, Mill Brook, Smithbrook, Lakes Folly, and Lowestoft Wines in Tasmania. This is quite a large winery facility by Tasmanian standards but small-batch production remains the focus. It also serves as a custom crush facility for some really small producers. Liam McElhinney has been the chief winemaker since 2020 and he runs a tight ship. I tasted many lovely Pinot Noirs on a 2022 visit.

Lowestoft Wines

www.lowestoft.wine

Another winery under the Fogarty Group umbrella, Lowestoft wines is its own brand but made at Tasmanian Vintners. The regular bottling of Pinot Noir is from fruit sourced in several regions and is a beautifully structured, fragrant and medium-weight expression of the variety. The Lowestoft La Maison is a single vineyard wine from the close-planted estate site in Derwent Valley. It has a bit more concentrated fruit with firmer tannins. These are excellent wines.

Dawson James

www.dawsonjames.com.au

This venture was started by two friends, Tim James and Peter Dawson. They have a connection to the family which owns Meadowbank in the Derwent Valley and fruit for their Pinot is from the older blocks planted on the estate. It is a delightful, medium-weight Pinot Noir, with classic cherry and strawberry characters.

Sailor Seeks Horse

sailorseekshorse.com.au

Paul and Gilli Liscombe purchased an abandoned vineyard in the Huon Valley in 2005 and set about restoring it to health, ripping out some of the vines and replanting Chardonnay and Pinot Noir. Production is small but their Pinot Noir is full of energy and character. The vines are getting some age now so it will be interesting to see what the future brings.

Home Hill

www.homehillwines.com.au

Owners Rosemary and Tony Bennett have been crafting excellent Pinot Noir from their small estate for 25 years. The first vines were planted in 1992 and their first vintage was 1998. They started with just six rows of vines but gradually added an additional hectare of vines every few years. The estate now has 6 hectares planted to vines. Look for the Home Hill Landslide Pinot Noir and the Home Hill Estate Pinot Noir.

Domaine Simha

www.domainesimha.com

The expensive, micro-production wines made here are hard to find but are very good. The wines are made at the Meadowbank facility and some fruit is sourced from their estate vineyards. Three excellent Pinot Noirs are made under the Domaine Simha label – Rama, Raja and Rana. All grapes come from the Derwent Valley.

Freycinet Vineyard

www.freycinetvineyard.com.au

This was established by Susan and Geoff Bull, who planted the first vines in 1978, making Freycinet the pioneer producer on the East Coast. Their daughter Lindy and her partner Claudio Radenti are now running the estate. A very fine producer making classic, elegantly structured Pinot Noir.

Tamar Ridge

www.tamarridge.com.au

One of the original high-quality estates in Tamar Valley, set up initially by industry legend Andrew Pirie but now owned by Brown Brothers Wines. There is a range of Pinot Noir bottlings, all solid.

Devil's Corner

www.devilscorner.com.au

Based on the east coast, this producer is also owned by Brown Brothers. The regular bottlings of Pinot Noir are some of the easiest drinking and most accessibly priced wines on the island. A great place to start.

Riesling

Tasmania is a fabulous place for Riesling and there are several producers making delicious wines.

Stargazer Wines

www.stargazerwine.com.au

Stargazer's regular Riesling is laser focused and pure fruited, while the concrete egg fermented Palisander Riesling is more textured and weighty with a firm spine of lime-like acidity. Both are fantastic.

Pressing Matters

pressingmatters.com.au

Pressing Matters is a Riesling-focused producer making lovely wines in the Coal River Valley. They have four specialized Rieslings that are labelled according to the approximate residual sugar levels in the bottlings: R0, R9, R69 and R139.

Meadowbank and Dr Edge

www.meadowbank.com.au; www.dr-edge.com

Peter Dredge cut his teeth making Riesling at Petaluma and did a couple of vintages in Germany with Ernie Loosen. He loves the variety and it shows in the wines he makes at both Meadowbank and Dr Edge. The Meadowbank Riesling is more classically styled – taut, focused and razor-sharp. Dr Edge Riesling is fermented in old oak casks with a small proportion of whole clusters, offering a more textured, savoury look at the variety.

Pooley Wines

www.pooleywines.com.au

While best known for the quality of their Pinot Noir, Pooley Wines have a brilliant line-up of Riesling too. Butcher's Hill and Cooinda Vale Riesling are excellent, as is the Butcher's Hill Cane Cut Riesling, a sweet wine in the mould of Mount Horrocks Cordon Cut Riesling from the Clare Valley.

Other top Riesling producers to look for

Freycinet Vineyard (www.freycinetvineyard.com.au) makes tight, taut wines with lime and floral character. The Old Vine Reserve Riesling from **Bream Creek Vineyard** (www.breamcreekvineyard.com.au) is from the original 1974 plantings. It is only made in good years and if you can find a bottle, buy it. **Holm Oak** (www.holmoakvineyards. com.au) has a very fine, mineral, lime-scented style. At **Glaetzer-Dixon Family Winemakers** (www.gdfwinemakers.com) look for the delicious Überblanc Riesling. It is uber delicious. **Mewstone** (www.mewstone-wines.com.au) makes excellent Riesling under the Hughes and Hughes label.

Other varieties

Gamay

Meadowbank's (www.meadowbank.com.au) Gamay is a delight. Juicy and fresh, it is one of my favourite examples of the variety in Australia.

Trousseau

This is a variety that is slowly making waves in Australia. **Stoney Rise** (www.stoneyrise.com) winemaker Joe Holyman's super-vibrant iteration is delicious: light, lifted, tight and full of juicy rhubarb and raspberry flavours.

Pinot Gris

It may seem weird to single out Pinot Gris from **Holm Oak** (www.holmoakvineyards.com.au) when they make a lot of really good wine but the Pinot Gris is a consistent shining star.

Shiraz

Yes – Shiraz from Tasmania. There are pockets on the island where later ripening red varieties do well and **Glaetzer-Dixon** (www.gdfwinemakers.com) is one of them. Their Mon Père is a classic cooler climate Shiraz.

Cabernet Sauvignon

The top-ranked Cabernet Sauvignon from iconic Moorilla Estate-owned producer **Domain A** (www.domaine-a.com.au) *must* be tried. It is a perfumed, herb-tinged, medium-weight wine that rewards a little cellaring patience.

Sauvignon Blanc

Domain A also makes a Sauvignon Blanc, called Lady A, which is a revelation. It has weight, texture, aromatics and length. While very much crafted to emulate top-notch Pessac-Leognan it has its own unique character. This is one of Australia's truly great white wines.

11

QUEENSLAND

Queensland has a long history of wine production. Vines were first planted at Roma and in the Granite Belt region in the 1860s. Queensland has two GIs: Granite Belt and South Burnett. There are a few other regions making wine but, to date, they don't meet the criteria for GI status. An interest in wine tourism has encouraged more ventures, which increased the number of wineries dramatically in the early 2000s. The climate in Queensland is, for the most part, a challenge for quality grape growing. Factors that mitigate the warm, wet tropical conditions are critical to success in this state.

In recent times vignerons have gone beyond the traditional varieties of Chardonnay, Semillon, Shiraz, Cabernet Sauvignon and Merlot and have passionately embraced alternative varieties such as Tempranillo and Viognier, among many others.

The GIs of Queensland

This a small wine producing state that has one Zonal GI, Queensland, and four regions, Granite Belt, South Burnett, Darling Downs and Coastal and Hinterlands.

GRANITE BELT

(Ngarabal Country)

The Granite Belt is located south-west of Brisbane in Queensland on the border of New South Wales. This region is at the northern end of the New England Tablelands. The underlying geology is all granite, and this protrusion has given rise to the unique landscape and climate of the region. The first grapes were planted in 1965 and expansion has slowly continued. Elevation is a critical piece of the puzzle for a region positioned as it is, in a subtropical climate. The region's elevation is between 600 and 1,500 metres above sea level overall. Most of the vineyard plantings are in the 700–1,000 metres range. Since many of the wines are made by small, boutique producers it is hard to find them outside the region.

Area under vine

315 hectares[75]

Climate

Altitude is the single most important factor that allows the Granite Belt to even contemplate being a quality wine producing region. Subzero winter nights are common and spring frosts are an annual concern. The typical pattern is for cold nights at the beginning and end of the season. Relatively low humidity and the peak summer temperatures are moderated by sub-tropical monsoon influences and intermittent heavy late season rainfall.

Soils

The main geological influences are Permian sedimentary rocks, intrusive granites and extensive basalts.

Varieties and styles

Classic varieties established the region's initial reputation: Chardonnay, Semillon, Verdelho, Viognier, Shiraz and Cabernet Sauvignon and all do well here. But it is the alternative varieties and styles that have cemented this region as a place worthy of attention. Strange Bird is the local term that producers have given to wines made from alternative varieties. The Strange Bird Wine Guide (www.granitebeltwinecountry.com.au/strangebird) was developed to help visitors navigate the wines. It is quite an extensive list and makes this region even more exciting to visit.

75   Source: National Vineyard Scan 2020 and ABS

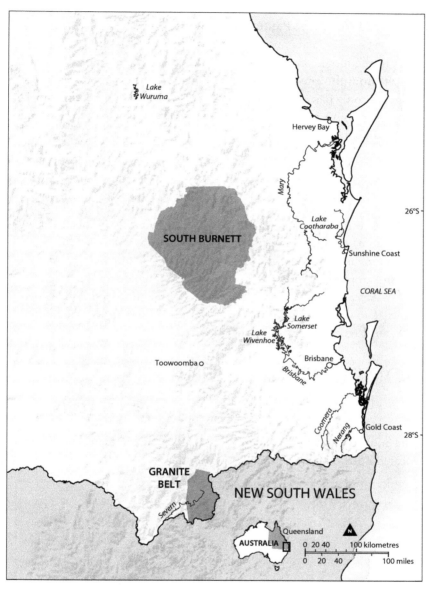

Map 7: The Geograpic Indications of Queensland

Producers

Bent Road Wines & La Petite Mort

www.bentroadwine.com.au; www.winecult.org

One of the more compelling wines I have had recently was the Gentil Qvevri from this producer. Based in Ballandean they are, to my knowledge, the only place in Australia with a qvevri 'farm'. This consists of 14 clay vessels buried underground in the same fashion as the traditional Georgian approach. The wine is a Gewurztraminer and Muscat blend, qvevri-aged on skins for 150 days.

Other producers

There are several excellent producers creating wines using alternative varieties in interesting styles. At **Ballandean Estates** (www.ballandean-estate.com) try the Malvasia and the Saparavi. **Symphony Hill** (www.symphonyhill.com.au) has a Reserve Graciano, Fiano and Tempranillo worth sampling. **Golden Grove Estate** (www.goldengroveestate.com.au) makes a fun SPV Reserve Sparkling Vermentino and a juicy, delicious Nero d'Avola. And from **Witches Falls Winery** (www.witchesfalls.com.au) I recommend trying the Verdelho.

SOUTH BURNETT

(Waka Waka Country)

The South Burnett wine region is is 8,274 square kilometres in size and located north-west of Brisbane in Queensland.

> ## Area under vine
> 204 hectares
>
> ## Climate
> The region has a very warm, subtropical climate, but its elevation, maritime influence and crisp nights keep things mild enough to produce good-quality grapes.

> ## Soils
> Soils vary from light sands to red, brown and black clays, and all have a pH level well suited to grape growing.
>
> ## Varieties
> Verdelho, Viognier and Semillon are the three major white grape varieties. Red varieties have been evolving and excitement rests with Tempranillo, Sangiovese, Saperavi and Nebbiolo.

Producers

It is virtually impossible to find the wines outside Australia, but the following producers are worth seeking out. **Clovely Estate** (www.clovely.com.au) makes a lovely Semillon and a light, easy drinking Sangiovese. At **Kingsley Grove Estate** (www.kingsleygrove.com) try the Verdelho and, if you get a chance, the lightly effervescent Semillon called Tingle. It may not necessarily be a wine to be paraded around at a wine show but it is one I want to chill, pour in a tumbler and gulp down with carefree abandon. **Moffatdale Ridge** (moffatdaleridge.com.au) has a Semillon and a Verdelho that are both lovely, easy drinking whites.

DARLING DOWNS

(Barunggam Country)

This region is centered around the town of Toowoomba, a farming and grazing area for over 150 years. Wines are locally made and sold. I have not had any wines made from grapes grown in this region.

QUEENSLAND COASTAL AND HINTERLANDS

(Bundjalung, Yuggera Waka Waka & Gubi Gubi Country)

This is an area of unofficial region that largely focuses on a tourist trade. The most noted and significant producer is Sirromet Wines which is located just south-east of Brisbane. They actually have most of their vineyards in Granite Belt.

APPENDIX I: 101 WINES THAT ILLUMINATE AUSTRALIAN WINE TODAY

The purpose of this book is to illuminate the broad, diverse and complex range of wines available from Australia. Australian wine today covers the full spectrum of wine styles. This remains an under-appreciated fact. It is not possible to have the time and opportunity to go to every region and taste the wares of every producer in Australia. I have been immersed in Australian wine for over 20 years and have not seen and tasted everything. In an effort to simplify a complex subject, I have compiled a list of specific wines to try. If you worked your way through this list, you would have a much clearer understanding of the complexities of Australian wine. There are lists within the list which serve to highlight the diversity of particular varieties, Shiraz being the most obvious. Some are stand-alone selections based on their singular brilliance.

Sparkling wines

1. Delinquente Wine Co Tuff Nut Bianco Pet Nat – Riverland/Meru Country, South Australia

This is not only a delicious, easy-drinking froth ball with a fun label, it is made with grapes from the only Bianco d'Alessano vineyard in Australia, in the Riverland.

2. Dal Zotto l'Immigrante Vintage Prosecco – King Valley/Waywurru Country, Victoria

Nomenclature drama aside, this is a delightful, frothy mouthful of deliciousness. It speaks to the suitability of the variety in the cool environs of King Valley and to the charming Italian heritage that defines the regional ethos and character.

3. Jansz Vintage Rosé Brut – Tasmania/Lutruwita Country

Delicate strawberry and red apple character with lovely yeasty complexity. An affordable introduction to the excitement of traditional method wines from Tasmania.

4. Deviation Road Vintage Beltana Blanc de Blancs – Adelaide Hills/ Peramagnk Country, South Australia

Kate Laurie's training in the Champagne town of Avize shines through in her impeccably made range of Traditional Method wines. This is a laser beam of taut, tightly focused, lemon scented and brioche flavoured brilliance.

5. House of Arras Museum Release Vintage Late Disgorged Blanc de Blancs – Tasmania/Lutruwita Country

Ed Carr is a true legend in the Australian wine business, a man whose entire career has been dedicated to making sparkling wine. This is his pinnacle wine and shows why Tasmanian fruit is so sought after for sparkling wine in Australia. It also demonstrates clearly and articulately that Australia has a seat at the table with all the great traditional method wines of the world.

6. Ashton Hills Sparkling Shiraz – Clare Valley/Ndadjuri and Kaurna Country, South Australia

Sparkling Shiraz is a classic, historic and uniquely Australian wine style; rich, textural and full of concentrated fruit, yet balanced and light on its feet. This wine is made by Stephen George and if you are a lover of this style, it doesn't get much better than this. A good proportion of the fruit comes from 100-year-old vines at Wendouree.

White wines

Riesling

Clare and Eden Valley Rieslings have a global reputation for good reason. The best examples are rippling with energy, packed with lively fruit and good acidity, and can develop beautifully for decades. But to fully appreciate the history and character of Riesling in this country you must try a broader range and there are a few absolute stunners from other regions.

7. Grosset Polish Hill Riesling – Clare Valley/Ndadjuri and Kaurna Country, South Australia

By history and reputation, this is a Riesling that must be tried. It shows why people have been raving about Clare Valley Riesling for decades and is a touchstone wine. Try to get one with 10 or more years of age.

8. Pewsey Vale The Contours Riesling – Eden Valley/Peramagnk Country, South Australia

This is an aged release wine and is, year in, year out, one of the very best Rieslings in Eden Valley. See entry under Yalumba, page 105.

9. Crawford River Riesling Old Vines – Henty/Jardwadjali and Gunditjmara Country, Victoria

This is a different expression of the variety and one of my favourite Rieslings produced in Australia. Stony, floral and always showing a nectarine-like fruit character, it is textural and complex.

10. Helm Premium Riesling – Canberra District/Ngunawal Country New South Wales

With upwards of 45 vintages under his belt, and a passion for Riesling dating way beyond that, Ken Helm is a Riesling wizard. This is a focused and pure-fruited wine with texture, length and complexity.

11. Frankland Estate Isolation Ridge Riesling – Frankland River/ Minang Country, Western Australia

For decades this has been a benchmark example of Riesling in Great Southern. It can age beautifully but in its youth it shows more of the mandarin/orange fruit notes I tend to find in Rieslings from this part of the country.

12. Granite Hills 1971 Block Riesling – Macedon Ranges/Dja Dja Wurrung, Taungurung and Wurundjeri Woi Wurrung Country, Victoria

An apple–citrus fruit-laden beauty from one of the cooler regions in Victoria.

13. Best's Foudre Ferment Riesling – Grampians/Jardwadjali and Djabwurung Country, Victoria

This sees extended skin contact, wild fermentation and maturation on lees in foudre. It is light on its feet, yet textural and complex. An absolutely delicious example of Riesling made in a less conventional style, this provides a lovely contrast to the classic Clare and Eden styles with more texture, fruit weight and apple-scented character.

14. Stargazer Riesling – Coal River Valley/Lutruwita Country, Tasmania

A lovely combination of floral, citrus and apple elements. It is important to remember that Tasmania is a great place for Riesling and this is the perfect place to start.

15. Pressing Matters RS 69 Riesling – Coal River Valley/Lutruwita Country, Tasmania

A crystalline, pure fruited medium sweet style from a Riesling specialist in Tasmania. The producer is dedicated to illuminating different styles of Riesling with various residual sugar levels. A wine for lovers of Mosel Spätlese. See entry in Tasmania.

Chardonnay

As noted in several areas of the book, the evolution of Chardonnay is one of the more thrilling and dynamic developments in Australian wine at the moment. This list could be 50 wines long but those below will give you a solid grasp of the best regional expressions and contemporary styles.

16. Leeuwin Estate Art Series Chardonnay – Margaret River/Wardandi Country, Western Australia

A benchmark wine that has set a standard for decades. Very much the Leeuwin style, but it also screams Margaret River.

17. Cullen Kevin John Chardonnay – Margaret River/Wardandi Country, Western Australia

A perfect counterpoint to Leeuwin. A savoury, textural interpretation of the region.

18. Tolpuddle – Coal River Valley/Lutruwita Country, Tasmania

One of the truly great Tasmanian Chardonnays being produced at present and one of Australia's really exciting examples.

19. Bindi Quartz – Macedon Ranges/Dja Dja Wurrung, Taungurung and Wurundjeri Woi Wurrung Country, Victoria

A perennial beauty that shows the deft touch of Michael Dhillon and the electric spine of acidity I find in Macedon.

20. Oakridge Hazeldene Vineyard Chardonnay – Yarra Valley/ Woiworung Country, Victoria

Dave Bicknell set the standard for the modern Yarra Valley style of Chardonnay and continues to tinker and evolve. A top notch, peach-scented classic.

21. Murdoch Hill The Tilbury Chardonnay – Adelaide Hills/ Peramagnk Country, South Australia

A textural, compact and layered wine that is also light on its feet. I have liked this wine for many years.

22. Ten Minutes by Tractor Estate Chardonnay – Mornington Peninsula/Boon Wurrung Country, Victoria

Lemony, limey and textural with a hint of the cashew/almond notes that seem to appear in the best Chardonnays from this region.

23. Patrick Sullivan Baw Baw Shire Chardonnay – Gippsland/ Woiworung, Boonwurrung and Kurnai Country, Victoria

An interesting, nervy Chardonnay that is more about texture and savoury character than opulent fruit. This very much shows Patrick's style and may in the future be indicative of Chardonnay from this relatively new enclave tucked in the broader region of Gippsland.

24. Giaconda Chardonnay – Beechworth/Waywurru Country, Victoria

An Australian classic. Rich and textural, this has for many years been one of the top-ranked Chardonnays in the country. It's the perfect wine to remind us that there are sneaky pockets of quality Chardonnay all across Australia.

Other White Wines

25. Tyrrell's Vat 1 Semillon – Hunter Valley/Wonnarua Country, New South Wales

Hunter Semillon is unique. Vibrant and lemon scented when young, with 10 or more years of age it puts on weight and texture with layers of complexity. Year in, year out, this is the very best example in the country.

26. Peter Lehman Margaret Semillon – Barossa Valley/Peramagnk Country, South Australia

Made in an early picked, leaner style but still showing more weight than the Hunter style. Can age gracefully for 20 or more years.

27. Shaw & Smith Sauvignon Blanc – Adelaide Hills/Peramagnk Country, South Australia

As discussed in the regional chapter, this is the benchmark for Sauvignon Blanc in Australia. A quince and passion fruit scented beauty.

28. Domaine A Lady A Sauvignon Blanc – Coal River Valley/Lutruwita Country, Tasmania

Completely different to the Shaw & Smith expression, this barrique-aged wine is layered, complex and brilliant. One of Australia's truly great white wines.

29. Cullen Grace Madeline – Margaret River/Wardandi Country, Western Australia

There is no better wine to represent the classic Margaret River blend of Sauvignon Blanc and Semillon than this. Made from the old Sauvignon and Semillon vines planted on the estate. Made in the mould of classic Pessac-Leognan, the wine sees some oak maturation. It is vibrant and fresh but with lovely length, texture and complexity.

30. Sorrenberg Sauvignon Blanc Semillon – Beechworth/Waywurru Country, Victoria

A wonderfully precise wine with structure, texture, and complexity and an excellent counterpoint to the Cullen Grace Madeline.

31. Tahbilk Museum Release Marsanne – Nagambie Lakes/ Ngurraiillam Country, Victoria

This is a Tahbilk speciality. The wine comes from some of the oldest Marsanne vines on the planet and the largest single-site plantings.

32. Tscharke Gnadenfrei White – Barossa Valley/Peramagnk Country, South Australia

A Grenache Blanc that shows wonderful texture and savoury character and is a laser pointer to the suitability of this variety in the Barossa.

33. Yangarra Estate Ovitelli Blanc – McLaren Vale/Kaurna Country, South Australia

A blend of Grenache Blanc, Roussanne, Clairette, Picpoul and Bourboulenc. The future of white wines in warmer climate regions in Australia will include varietal blends like this. Textured, mineral and delicious.

34. Delinquente Screaming Betty Vermentino – Riverland/Meru Country, South Australia

I was trying not to repeat producers on this list, but this wine is brilliant in so many ways. Style, price point, label and the story of a region reimagined.

35. Coriole Picpoul – McLaren Vale/Kaurna Country, South Australia

The first example I tried of varietal Picpoul in Australia, it remains a favourite.

36. Oliver's Taranga Fiano – McLaren Vale/Kaurna Country, South Australia

Corinna Wright has been tinkering with this variety for over 15 years. It captures the weight that you expect from the variety but with a bristling spine of acidity.

37. Hahndorf Hill Gru Gruner Veltliner – Adelaide Hills/Peramagnk Country, South Australia

One of the pioneers of this variety in the Hills and one of the best.

38. Jauma Blewitt Springs Chenin Blanc – McLaren Vale/Kaurna Country, South Australia

One of the best all round natural producers for me. This is a delicious

Chenin. In addition, it is nice to be reminded that this variety has a long history in McLaren Vale.

39. La Petit Mort Gentil Qvevri – Granite Belt, Queensland

This is a fifty-fifty blend of Gewurztraminer and Muscat. The fruit actually comes from three different regions in three different states: Heathcote, New England and Granite Belt. The wine is aged in qvevri for 150 days. It's the only qvevri-aged wine I know of in Australia and that is the reason it is on the list. It is one of the best extended skin contact white wines I have had from Australia in the last five years!

40. Brash Higgins ZBO – Riverland/Meru Country, South Australia

The winery is based in McLaren Vale but the Zibbibo fruit for this wine is from Ricca Terra Farms in the Riverland. The wine is fermented in amphorae, on skins, for 150 days. A flor film develops adding extra complexity. Along with La Petit Mort, one of my favourite skin-contact whites in Australia.

41. Latta Vino Rattlesnake Blanc Contact – Victoria

Owen Latta's wines draw me in. Nothing is out of place in these balanced and complex, gentle wines … if that makes sense. This wine is made up of many different skin-contact ferments – Riesling, Viognier, Sauvignon Blanc, Pinot Gris, Gewurztraminer and Chardonnay.

42. Ravensworth Pinot Gris – Canberra District/Ngunawal Country, New South Wales

A delicious, brassy-hued, skin-contact version of the variety. This has a savoury, lightly tannic textural element that adds weight and complexity. A great way to handle a variety that can be terminally dull … if we are all being honest.

43. Lucy M La Sarriette Pinot Blanc – Adelaide Hills/Peramagnk Country, South Australia

A consistently strong wine from the original natural wine guru.

44. Gentle Folk Rainbow Juice – Adelaide Hills/Peramagnk Country, South Australia

Technically, this is a rosé but more importantly, it is textured, juicy and stupidly delicious.

Red wine

Pinot Noir

The evolution of this variety has been a revelation. There are so many fantastic examples available. The following gives a good cross-section of the best regional expressions.

45. Bindi Original Vineyard or Block 5 Pinot Noir – Macedon Ranges/ Dja Dja Wurrung, Taungurung and Wurundjeri Woi Wurrung Country, Victoria

I can't decide, so take your pick (or try both). Either way you'll be experiencing some of the best Pinot Noir in Australia.

46. Bass Phillip Reserve Pinot Noir – Gippsland/Woiworung, Boonwurrung and Kurnai Country, Victoria

For years this has been a Pinot Noir to aspire to. It is brilliant, and very expensive, but if you can afford the outlay, this is one of Australia's original, top shelf, terroir driven Pinot Noirs.

47. Main Ridge Half Acre Pinot Noir – Mornington Peninsula/Boon Wurrung Country, Victoria

Production is small but this is one of the very best from Mornington Peninsula.

48. Mac Forbes Woori Yallock Pinot Noir – Yarra Valley/Woiworung Country, Victoria

Mac shows his gentle touch with this fragrant beauty and it is a great example of the contemporary Yarra Valley style.

49. Ashton Hills Reserve Pinot Noir – Adelaide Hills/Peramagnk Country, South Australia

A riper, classic style that illuminates the suitability of Pinot Noir in the right sites in Adelaide Hills.

50. Sangreal By Farr – Geelong/Wathaurong Country, Victoria

You can't go wrong with any of the By Farr Pinot Noirs. Sangreal is from the oldest vines on the property. Along with Bass Phillip, By Farr Pinots have the most storied history with Pinot Noir in Australia and have, year in year out made some of the best examples in the country.

51. Chatto Isle Pinot Noir – Houn Valley/Lutruwita Country, Tasmania

Some of the best Pinot Noirs I tried in Tasmania on my last visit were at Chatto. A layered, detailed wine with all the elements I look for in great Pinot: floral aromatics, focused, seductive, cherry/strawberry fruit and a layered, complex finish.

52. Holyman Pinot Noir – Tamar Valley/Lutruwita Country, Tasmania

A textbook example of Tamar Valley Pinot Noir. A perfect counterpoint to the Chatto style, showing similar textural elements but with a really vibrant spine of fresh acidity.

53. Tappanapa Foggy Hill Pinot Noir – Fleurieu Peninsula Peramangk and Ngarrindjeri Country, South Australia

From a pioneering site on the Fleurieu Peninsula,this is a wine that seems to be getting better every vintage. This area was uncharted territory before Croser planted vines. As is the case with Pinot Noir almost everywhere, vine age and a fine tuning of winemaking start to show. The early versions, while still interesting, did not seem to show the complexity of the more recent vintages. I also think the wines are now a bit lighter and more fragrant.

Grenache and blends

54. Ochota Barrels Fugazi Grenache – McLaren Vale/Kaurna Country, South Australia

A wine that fundamentally changed how we looked at Grenache. Sourced from a rocky ironstone and gravelly clay vineyard located between Onkaparinga River Gorge and Blewitt Springs and planted in 1947. The wine is usually around 50 per cent whole cluster, it spends 10–30 days on skins and is aged on old, neutral barrels. It is savoury, seductive and as charming as Taras Ochota was.

55. SC Pannell Smart Grenache – McLaren Vale/Kaurna Country, South Australia

Steve Pannell is one of the most thoughtful and articulate winemakers in Australia. Any of his Grenache will tell a story but I particularly like this one. Fruit is sourced from the Smart vineyard, the highest altitude Grenache vineyard in McLaren Vale. The site is located in the Clarendon district and was planted in 1955. A modern example but made in a classic way: destemmed, some skin contact, aged in large-format old oak.

56. Yangarra Hickinbotham Grenache – McLaren Vale/Kaurna Country, South Australia

The fruit is from the Hickinbotham Clarendon Estate and is fermented in cocciopesto clay amphorae. The wine is aromatic, spicy and floral with seductive, raspberry scented fruit.

57. Jauma Like Raindrops Grenache – McLaren Vale/Kaurna Country, South Australia

The wines is made in the light, fragrant and ethereal style and comes from one of the best 'natural' producers.

58. Charles Melton Nine Popes – Barossa Valley/Peramagnk Country, South Australia

The wine that set the modern standard for the classic GSM blend.

59. Spinifex Papillon – Barossa Valley/Peramagnk Country, South Australia

Predominantly Grenache, the wine also contains around 20 per cent Cinsault, depending on the vintage (see p. 110). This is a style of Barossa Valley red that should be replicated and screamed about from the rooftops. So deliciously appropriate as a weekday Barossa red.

60. Cirillo 1848 Grenache – Barossa Valley/Peramagnk Country, South Australia

This is from the oldest Grenache vineyard anywhere on the planet. Rich and structured, its a classic wine with one foot in new- and one in old-school styling.

Cabernet Sauvignon and blends

61. Wynns Coonawarra Black Label Cabernet Sauvignon – Coonawarra/Boandig Country, South Australia

You can't talk about Coonawarra Cabernet Sauvignon without discussing Wynns. This should be your first Coonawarra Cabernet Sauvignon.

62. Balnaves The Talley Cabernet Sauvignon – Coonawarra/Boandig Country, South Australia

A top-notch, premium example of Coonawarra Cabernet Sauvignon.

63. Yarra Yering No1 Dry Red – Yarra Valley/Woiworung Country, Victoria

A historic and revered wine, now made under the guidance of wine-maker Sarah Crowe and better than ever. It is typically around 60 per cent Cabernet Sauvignon and 25–30 per cent Merlot, with the balance being Malbec and Petit Verdot.

64. Mount Mary Quintet – Yarra Valley/Woiworung Country, Victoria

Fragrant, mid-weight elegance. This might be my favourite Cabernet blend in Australia. Although it varies from year to year, the blend is typically around 50 per cent Cabernet Sauvignon, 25 per cent Merlot, 15 per cent Cabernet Franc, with splashes of Malbec and Petit Verdot making up the balance.

65. Vasse Felix Tom Cullity Cabernet–Malbec – Margaret River/ Wardandi Country, Western Australia

Classically structured, fragrant Margaret River Cabernet Sauvignon.

66. Cullen Diana Madeline – Margaret River/Wardandi Country, Western Australia

One of the very best in Margaret River, this is always predominantly Cabernet Sauvignon, with 90 per cent being fairly common. The balance is made up of small amounts each of Merlot, Cabernet Franc and Malbec. There is, additionally, something vibrant, focused and pure about this wine. An almost luminescent quality.

67. Henschke Cyril Henschke Cabernet Sauvignon – Eden Valley/ Peramagnk Country, South Australia

Yes, this is from Eden Valley but a reminder that Cabernet Sauvignon in the right sites in Barossa can be magnificent.

68. Hickinbotham Trueman Cabernet Sauvignon – McLaren Vale/ Kaurna Country, South Australia

A stylish and seamless example of McLaren Vale Cabernet Sauvignon from the historic Clarendon property.

69. Yalumba The Signature Cabernet–Shiraz – Barossa Valley/ Peramagnk Country, South Australia

Year in, year out, one of my favourite examples of this Australian blend.

70. Wendouree Cabernet Malbec – Clare Valley/Ndadjuri & Kaurna Country, South Australia

Any Wendouree will thrill the senses but I just happen to give the nod to this wine whenever I get a chance to try the wines.

Shiraz and blends

Further to my thoughts on Shiraz on page 41, this line-up will show clearly and unequivocally, the diversity and quality that this variety can achieve when grown in the right sites and handled with the care and attention a 'heritage' variety deserves.

71. Penfolds St Henri Shiraz – South Australia

I could have picked Grange but didn't. It is well known enough and prohibitively expensive. Plus, I have secretly adored this Shiraz from Penfolds for as long as I can remember. It is about Penfolds' style of impeccably selected fruit, but aged in large, older 2,000-litre casks so it is not about new-oak character. It has been made since the 1950s, and while I bristle at the term 'Australian Shiraz' this is a top-flight wine that shows the very best qualities of warmer region Shiraz: ripeness, purity of fruit and elegance.

72. Standish Wine Co. The Standish – Barossa Valley/Peramagnk Country, South Australia

From the Laycock vineyard in the Greenock area of Barossa Valley comes this small batch wine, made with serious attention to detail. It is rich, layered and complex.

73. Sami Odi Hoffmann Dallwitz Syrah – Barossa Valley/Peramagnk Country, South Australia

Assembled from the two oldest sections of the Hoffmann vineyard; the first planted on their own roots in 1927 and the oldest vines planted between 1888 and 1912. The wine also has welcome smidgens of fruit from the neighbouring blocks planted in 1994, 1995 and 1996.

74. Rockford Basket Pressed Shiraz – Barossa Valley/Peramagnk Country, South Australia

Rockford is one of the original small-batch producers in Barossa. This is a classic Shiraz that balances the earthy spice and warmth of the region with purity of fruit and layers of supple tannin.

75. Henschke Mount Edelstone – Eden Valley/Peramagnk Country, South Australia

I could have picked Hill of Grace but didn't. It is magnificent but very limited in production and very expensive. Mount Edelstone delivers elements of the Hill of Grace character but it has its own unique quality as mentioned on page 103. It is ripe and concentrated but textured and elegant, with blackcurrant fruit and sage, bay leaf and pepper. This is one of the great, single vineyard Shirazes on the planet, never mind in Australia.

76. Craiglee Shiraz – Sunbury/Woiworung Country, Victoria

A wine that has history and pedigree (see p. 203), made in a medium weight cooler climate, restrained style. This can age gracefully for decades.

77. Clonakilla Shiraz Viognier – Canberra District/Ngunawal Country, New South Wales

This is a must-try wine (see p. 79). There are layers of complexity, with power and perfumed elegance. This is one of the most seductive examples of Shiraz in Australia.

78. Best's Thompson Family Shiraz – Grampians/Jardwadjali and Djabwurung Country, Victoria

Grampians is such a great area for Shiraz with a multitude of brilliant wines. I am going with a classic: ripe black fruit but balanced and elegant.

79. Luke Lambert Syrah – Yarra Valley/Woiworung Country, Victoria

One of my go-to wines to show cool climate Shiraz character. It is medium-bodied and red fruited with savoury, smoky and pepper notes.

80. Tyrrell's 4 Acres Shiraz – Hunter Valley/Wonnarua Country, New South Wales

This medium-weight liquorice and spice-box delight comes from a vineyard planted in 1879. Savoury Hunter Shiraz to a tee: a classic.

81. Castagna Genesis Syrah – Beechworth/Waywurru Country, Victoria

The epitome of medium-weight Australian cooler climate Shiraz: peppery, savoury, layered and complex.

82. Koomilya GT Block Shiraz – McLaren Vale/Kaurna Country, South Australia

From relatively young vines, this is one of three single-block Shirazes under the Koomilya label. Grown on grey slatey siltstone and ironstone, it is a restrained style that is tight and structured but opens up to show the classic McLaren Vale blueberry scented fruit with layers of savoury spice.

Other red wines

83. Sorrenberg Gamay – Beechworth/Waywurru Country, Victoria

This wine set the standard for this variety in Australia.

84. Ochota Barrels The Mark of Cain Pinot Meunier – Adelaide Hills, South Australia

Ochota Barrels always has the touch, with light, fragrant and ethereal wines. This is a delicately framed delight.

85. Best's Old Vine Pinot Meunier – Great Western, Victoria

Only made in good years, this is a must-try wine if you can get your hands on it.

86. Ministry of Clouds Mencia – McLaren Vale/Kaurna Country, South Australia

One of the early Australian versions of this variety I tried. It is medium-to full-bodied but captures the density of fruit and lovely floral elements the variety can show.

87. Hither and Yon Nero d'Avola – McLaren Vale/Kaurna Country, South Australia

A variety that I am continually impressed with. This is a lovely mid-weight, fragrant version of Nero.

88. Luke Lambert Nebbiolo – Yarra Valley/Woiworung Country, Victoria

There are several very good examples of Nebbiolo in Australia. Year in year out, Luke is making the best.

89. Koerner Mammolo Sciacarello – Clare Valley/Ndadjuri and Kaurna Country, South Australia

A lightweight, violet-scented beauty.

90. Chalmers Aglianico – Heathcote, Victoria

Another one of the newer varieties that is a late ripener and seems ideally suited to the warmer zones in Australia. The variety can be a concentrated, structured beast but Chalmers have managed to tame it and produce a complex, layered wine with moderate alcohol.

91. La Linea Tempranillo – Adelaide Hills/Peramagnk Country, South Australia

A fragrant, middleweight, savoury beauty.

92. Gentle Folk Vin de Sofa – Adelaide Hills/Peramagnk Country, South Australia

This is Gamay with some Pinot Noir, Sangiovese, Syrah, Merlot, Grenache and Mataro but it really doesn't matter what it is made from. Light, fresh and juicy, the epitome of a smashable red.

93. Unico Zelo Fresh AF – Riverland/Meru Country, South Australia

This is mostly Nero d'Avola with about 15 per cent Zibibbo. It is a drop-dead delicious, fragrant red wine that is impossible not to be charmed by.

Sweet and fortified wines

94. Seppeltsfield DP 117 Dry Flor Apera – Barossa Valley/Peramagnk Country, South Australia

A classic style and a reminder that the complex history of fortified wines in Australia included 'sherry' styles

95. Mount Horrocks Cordon Cut Riesling – Clare Valley/Ndadjuri and Kaurna Country, South Australia

A unique and delicious, late harvest version of Riesling from the Clare Valley. The cutting of the cordons late in the season (see photo, p. 144) stops the ripening cycle and the Riesling berries slowly start to shrivel on the vine, giving intense, sweet juice which is fermented into a luscious delight.

96. DeBortoli Noble One – Riverina/Wiradjuri Country New South Wales

A textbook botrytis-affected Semillon that belongs on the same table as top-flight Sauternes and Barsac.

97. Campbells Rutherglen Muscat – Rutherglen/Waywurru Country, Victoria

A perfect entry into the world of Rutherglen Muscat. Shows some developing aged characteristics but is full of floral, fruity Muscat character.

98. Chambers Rare Muscat – Rutherglen/Waywurru Country, Victoria

This is as good as aged Rutherglen gets. Expensive but absolutely worth every penny.

99. All Saints Grand Muscadelle – Rutherglen/Waywurru Country, Victoria

A stunning example of the less well-known fortified from Rutherglen.

100. Penfolds Grandfather Tawny – South Australia

Australia has a storied history of fortified wine production. Tawny styles are some of my favourites and this complex beauty from Penfolds never disappoints.

101. Seppeltsfield Para – Barossa Valley/Peramagnk Country, South Australia

This is a large range of styles and a magic place to explore the style of fortified tawnies in Australia. If you get the chance to try the current release of the Centennial range, do it. This is a vintage dated tawny released at 100 years of age. The first barrel was laid down in 1878 and not bottled until 1978. The tradition has continued since (see p. 114).

APPENDIX II: IMPORTANT AUSTRALIAN WINE VOICES

There are many voices in Australian wine that the reader should pay attention to if wanting to learn more. The list below is not exhaustive but contains the details of a few people who have inspired me and helped illuminate my thoughts and ideas on Australian wine over the last 20 years. I have kept the detailed entries to writers and journalists simply because the reader can access these people readily. Not so easy to access are conversations with winemakers and viticulturalists. I have included a few whose ideas and practices have inspired me; if you ever get the opportunity to speak with any of them, take it!

Writers and journalists

James Halliday – author

www.winecompanion.com.au

Born in 1938, James Halliday is an Australian wine writer and critic, winemaker, and senior wine competition judge. Since 1979 he has written and co-authored more than 40 books on wine, including contributions to the *Larousse Encyclopedia of Wine* and *The Oxford Companion to Wine*. In 1986 he began publishing an annual overview of Australian Wine, which has been known as the *Halliday Wine Companion* since 2000. He is referred to as The Great Man by most in the industry. He has for decades been Australia's most prolific and respected wine writer.

Nick Ryan – journalist and presenter

Instagram: @nickryanwine

Thrown out of university in Adelaide, Nick Ryan moved to Sydney and used the knowledge he'd gained raiding his old man's cellar to land a job with one of Sydney's leading wine merchants. Realizing writing about it was easier than lifting cases of it has led him to where he is now. He's a columnist for *The Australian, The World of Fine Wine* and *Country Style*, and a regular contributor to *Halliday* magazine and *The Robb Report*. He is a highly sought after wine show judge, a graduate of the prestigious Len Evans Tutorial and a hugely engaging speaker and presenter. Nick is a large, bearded man with a mane of tousled hair and would not be out of place at the helm of Viking Longship. He is one of the more thoughtful, insightful and erudite writers we have in Australia.

Mike Bennie – freelance journalist, retailer, wine judge and speaker

Instagram: @mikebennie101

Mike is the wine and drinks editor for Australia's leading food magazine, *delicious*, and editor-at-large and contributing writer to Australia's most interactive wine commentary, *Wine Front* (www.winefront.com. au). He wrote for *Gourmet Traveller Wine Magazine*, and his work is found in the online version of Australian magazine *Broadsheet* and a variety of international publications. He is part of the team of critics behind the esteemed *Halliday Wine Companion*. Mike is also a co-founder and partner in the landmark P&V Wine + Liquor Merchants, a store and education space devoted to artisan fermented, brewed and distilled products. Mike is also drinks director of the highly-respected *WA Good Food Guide*. He was a co-founder and co-director of the now retired artisan and sustainability-focused Rootstock Sydney food and wine festival. Mike is currently the chair of the Australian Organic Wine Awards. He is a regular presenter at festivals, and corporate and industry events. He has been pigeonholed by some as the oracle for natural wine but that is a shortsighted view of this brilliant man. He understands the length and breadth of Australian wine today.

Andrew Caillard MW – author and presenter

Instagram: @andrewcaillardmw

Andrew Caillard MW, a former wine auctioneer and co-founder of auction house Langton's, is a well-known authority on Australian wine. He is the author of *Penfolds: The Rewards of Patience* (six editions). He also writes for *The Vintage Journal*, which specializes in Australia's fine wine agenda, and occasionally contributes to other Australian and international publications. Andrew Caillard was also the associate producer of acclaimed documentaries *Red Obsession* (2011) and *Blind Ambition* (2021). He is about to publish a three volume fully illustrated book called *The Australian Ark*, a history of Australian wine from 1788 to contemporary times (November 2023). There is nobody who knows the history of Australian wine better than Andrew.

Erin Larkin – author, wine judge and presenter

www.erinlarkin.com.au

Instagram: @erinllarkin

Erin is an independent wine writer, judge and presenter based in Perth, WA. She reviews Australian wines full time for *Robert Parker Wine Advocate*. Prior to this, Erin was part of the Halliday Tasting Team, at the *Halliday Wine Companion* (her areas include all of Western Australia, Clare Valley, Coonawarra, the Limestone Coast and others in South Australia), and was a regular contributor to the *Halliday* magazine. I really enjoy her writing style and wine reviews. She covers all of Australia for the *Advocate* but she knows Western Australia better than anyone.

Max Allen – writer, journalist and speaker

www.maxallen.com.au

Instagram: @maxallendrinks

Max Allen is an award-winning journalist and author, and honorary fellow in history at the University of Melbourne. Max has been writing about booze for almost 30 years: he is the wine and drinks columnist for the *Australian Financial Review*, and was a longtime contributor to *Gourmet Traveller Magazine*. He is the Australian correspondent for JancisRobinson.com and a regular presenter at masterclasses and festivals around the world. His latest book, *Alternative Reality* focuses on the alternative varieties in Australia and will be published in 2023. Max is a very thoughtful and sensitive writer and always seems to have his finger on the pulse of change in Australia.

Christina Pickard – US-based journalist and presenter

Instagram: @christinakpickard

www.christinakpickard.com

Christina Pickard has been telling wine stories for nearly 15 years, first from her former home in London, England, then from her second former home in Perth, Australia, and now in her current home in New York's Hudson Valley. She has written for publications around the globe, including *Decanter*, *Gourmet Traveller Wine*, the *Halliday Wine Companion* and *Food & Wine*. Christina is currently *Wine Enthusiast* magazine's writer at large, covering the wines of Australia, New Zealand, New York and Great Britain. She tastes and reviews over 1,500 wines per year from these regions, 1,000 of which are Australian. As a presenter and educator, Christina was the co-host of one of wine's first podcasts, The Crush. She was a regular television and live presenter in the UK, and founded the School of Wine in Western Australia. I often pick up the phone and ask Christina questions on various things. She has an easy writing style and a wealth of knowledge. She produces more annual coverage about Australian wine than any other journalist in the US.

Matthew Jukes – UK-based writer, journalist and presenter

www.matthewjukes.com

Instagram: @matthewjukes

Matthew Jukes has worked in the UK wine business for more than 35 years. With experience in all sectors of the industry, he has been writing about wine for over two decades and during this time has published 14 wine books. Each year he takes a selection of the 100 Best Australian Wines on a roadshow around the UK. He also runs an annual competition in Australia to find The Great Australian Red. Created with Brisbane-based wine writer Tyson Stelzer, this tasting sets out to determine the best Cabernet Sauvignon–Shiraz wines in the country, which Matthew describes as the blend that defines Australia. Matthew was made Honorary Australian of the Year in the UK at the 2012 Australia Day Foundation Gala dinner. He joins an eminent list of previously appointed Honorary Australians, including Lord Carrington, Sir Robert Wilson, Baroness Greenfield, and Sir David Attenborough.

Jane Lopes and Jonathan Ross – US-based importers and authors

www.legendaustralia.com

It may seem odd to add a couple of US wine importers to the list of important voices but they have just written an excellent book called *How to Drink Australian*. They are relatively new to Australia wine but spent time living and working in Australia. The expression 'convictions of a convert' aptly applies here. Both are passionate advocates of Australian wine and the more we have in the US the better off we are.

Winemakers and viticulturalists

Vanya Cullen – Cullen Wines, Margaret River

www.cullenwines.com.au

Instagram: @cullenwines

In June 2023, Vanya received the Medal of the Order of Australia (OAM) for her contribution to viticulture and oenology. It is a richly deserved honour. She is profoundly dedicated to the health of her vineyard sites and is a guiding light for what is possible, not only in Australia but also to the global community.

Louisa Rose – Yalumba, Barossa Valley

www.yalumba.com

Louisa is the Head of Winemaking at Yalumba. I can't begin to list the things I have learned from my many chats with her. She is brilliant, direct and does not suffer fools gladly. All the more reason to adore her.

Virginia Willcock – Vasse Felix Wines, Margaret River

www.vassefelix.com.au

A dynamic and talented winemaker who is at the top of her game. Always engaging and thought-provoking. I have quoted her way too many times when lecturing on various topics.

Michael Dhillon – Bindi Wines, Macedon Ranges

www.bindiwines.com.au

Instagram: @bindiwines

I think Michael is making the best Pinot Noirs of his life right now and for me, the best in the country. Like the best producers everywhere, he is always tinkering with his thoughts and practices. Erudite, articulate and sensitive, we are lucky to have him in Australia.

Dr Dylan Grigg (PhD) – viticulturalist and vineyard owner

www.vinyavella.com

Instagram: @gdylla

Dylan has been a viticulture consultant since 2008. His area of study for his PhD was old vines and there may be nobody more knowledgeable on this subject right now. He has been an incredible source of contemporary information and is very generous with his time. He is quoted several times in this book. His viticulture consulting company is Meristem Viticulture, and he has a small wine brand called Vinya Vella.

Mac Forbes – Mac Forbes Wines, Yarra Valley

www.macforbes.com

Instagram: @mac_forbes_wines

Thoughtful, open and honest, Mac Forbes is always looking to improve what he is doing and will likely never sit still in his quest to make expressive and individual wines. Many hours of thoughtful conversation with Mac have been invaluable in helping me understand the Yarra Valley.

Michael Hill-Smith MW – owner, Shaw and Smith Wines, Adelaide Hills

www.shaw&smith.com

Instagram: @mhsnotebook

Michael was the first non-European Master of Wine. His understanding of what makes Australian wine compelling and his ability to speak eloquently about any aspect of it have been an inspiration. He is Australia's best fine wine ambassador and has been a patient sounding board over the years.

Stephen and Prue Henschke – Henschke Wines, Eden Valley

www.henschke.com.au

Instagram: @henschke

Australian wine royalty. Prue is a mine of viticultural information and Stephen is a soft-spoken winemaker and historian. Given their status in the industry and reputation globally I am to this day always surprised and humble that they have time for me. Whether it is a visit, an email or a call, they respond generously with their knowledge and expertise. Prue will find something inaccurate in this book and she will let me know about it. Politely, but firmly.

Steve Pannell – SC Pannell Wines, McLaren Vale

www.pannell.com.au

Instagram: @scpannell

When I talk to Stephen Pannell, I have notebook handy to jot down gems of wisdom. He is one of Australia's most insightful winemakers. There are several inciteful quotes in this book attributed to Stephen Pannell.

Stu Proud – viticulturalist and winemaker

www.thousandcandles.com.au

Instagram: stuart01proud

Stu is now at the helm of Thousand Candles in the Yarra Valley. Super patient and throughtful, his background is in viticulture with a particular strength and speciality in soil health.

APPENDIX III: SCHOOL OF ROCKFORD BY NICK RYAN[76]

Robert O'Callaghan has long lauded the old methods of winemaking. His back-to-basics attitude and appreciation of the past has spawned a new generation of extraordinary winemakers, all with the same philosophical bent.

When sacred sites are subject to fire sales because the suits can't find the bottom line, where does the winemaker with modest dreams fit? What's real in the age of the deal?

These questions entered my mind during the opening stages of a masterclass held in Brisbane almost a year ago, and by the time the tasting was over they had made themselves at home and started unpacking their stuff.

The once reserved, reluctant superstar of the New Barossa movement, Chris Ringland, whose eponymous label was formerly called Three Rivers Shiraz, was presenting a line-up of wines from the next generation of the valley's winemakers. To show the subregional diversity, Ringland poured everything from tightrope-taut Eden Valley riesling to brooding Marananga reds. While the differences were illuminating, it was their commonality that really stood out. This was the work of a young generation of winemakers eschewing their youthful right to strike out in search of the new, choosing instead to follow an almost puritanical dedication to the old ways.

So just what is it that connects this group of youthful artisans? Although they are spread throughout the Barossa, there is a series of

76 Courtesy of Nick Ryan. Originally published in *Gourmet Traveller Wine*.

songlines threaded through the valley that leads them back to a spiritual home. Some are a direct line to the source, others intersect at multiple points. Eventually, they all link back to Robert O'Callaghan at Rockford Wines.

Established in 1984 on Krondorf Road, Rockford today exerts an influence that goes far further than its rough-hewn walls, stretching throughout the Barossa and beyond. In the early 1980s, O'Callaghan was struggling to scrape together A$6000 to buy the ramshackle property. Conventional wisdom said the market wanted cabernet, the more wispily elegant the better, and century-old shiraz vines lay scattered around the Barossa as forlornly as headstones in graveyards.

But O'Callaghan's winemaking instincts were driven by something more permanent than prevailing market trends. The offspring of two generations of growers, his childhood had been shaded by vine canopies and his working life spent learning the lessons of a trade more familiar with tough times than good.

Rockford was dream-built with old stone and salvaged equipment, its lifeline a network of old growers who, in O'Callaghan, had finally found someone who understood the true value of the vineyards into which they had poured their lives.

For the first few years, O'Callaghan ran Rockford virtually single-handedly, but as the wines began to capture attention, not only did the customers come, so did an army of young wine rookies wanting to learn the kinds of things that no winemaking school could teach them.

The list of graduates from "The Rockford Academy", as O'Callaghan fondly calls it, is as impressive as it is long, reading like a Who's Who of the Barossa and beyond.

Initially this was going to be a story about the graduates, but the more I spoke to them, the more I was drawn back to the source, and I came to realise that you can't tell the story of the Rockford academy without telling the story of the headmaster himself.

Everything that O'Callaghan, now 60, has done has been informed by his humble beginnings at Monash in South Australia's Riverland region. "I grew up in a very basic house, rainwater tap through the wall, dunny out the back ... surrounded by an orchard and grapevines and a dry block of mallee for firewood," he reminisces. "We're all the same in the way that how we spend our first 10 years has a huge influence on the rest of our lives.

"My grandparents, on both sides, were pioneering grape growers who cleared land around Monash after the war and they actually had adjoining blocks," he continues. "My mother's mother, Mrs Whitelaw, was an old-school Protestant wowser, and the O'Callaghans were full-blown ratbag Irish. Mrs Whitelaw's worst nightmare was that one of her four daughters would marry the neighbour's kids. My dad's brother married my mum's sister, so she actually got two!"

Life on the soldier settler blocks was pretty barren, but it forged a strong sense of community that still resonates with O'Callaghan. His father eventually took a job with Seppelt at Barooga further up the Murray River and, aged 17, O'Callaghan joined the company as a trainee winemaker at Rutherglen.

Those who have done stints at Rockford speak of the experience more as an education than as work, and that philosophy was forged among the bubbling ferments of Rutherglen.With a thirst for knowledge, O'Callaghan soaked up the stories of the old-time winemakers of the district. "When you're 17 you think you know everything because you actually know nothing. You haven't been dropped on your arse enough times to know what's going on," he says. "That's why the old boys of Rutherglen were so fascinating to me. This was back in the '60s, so these boys had come from a totally different time. I'd always make a point of hanging around and listening, and when you do that, they respond positively and tell you even more."

But it wasn't just winemaking lessons that O'Callaghan received in Rutherglen. He also learned that this was a business of booms and busts, and that understanding became fundamental to the way he has run Rockford over the past 23 years.

"Rutherglen had been an enormously wealthy place, booming at the end of the 19th century and declining ever since," he says. "There was this great sense of fading empire. The grand abandoned wineries of Rutherglen, like Mt Ophir and St Leonards, sent me a strong message at a young age that no matter how grand it all gets, it can all go arse up. That's why I've always had a very conservative approach to expansion at Rockford. This is a business for stayers, not for sprinters."

O'Callaghan was eventually transferred to the Barossa to manage Seppelt's Dorrien winery and act as a grower liaison. It was here that he discovered the valley's unique viticultural treasures.

"I got to see all of the Barossa on a very real, personal level, out in people's backyards," he recalls. "I was discovering the real Barossa at a very impressionable time for me.

"You'd walk through these people's sheds and everything they'd had since settlement was still in there. Then you'd walk through the cucumber patch, out through the orchard, through to the vines. They didn't call them vineyards, they'd call them 'gardens', and that's pretty much what it was: dry grown and tended by the family because there was no money to pay anyone else."

When the time came for O'Callaghan to start his own place, his philosophy about the wine business was fully formed. It still extends into every part of Rockford today and is what attracted so many of the people who went to work there – including Chris Ringland, who just wandered in one day in 1989, picked up a fork and started work.

"I immediately sensed the beginning of an opportunity," Ringland says. "Rockford was just starting to take off and Rob had been virtually doing everything himself, with a little bit of help here and there. He was getting to the point that he could no longer do everything himself and I was in the right place at right time."

Ringland's single-vineyard shiraz is one of Australia's most sought-after wines, with production as small as the price tag is big. O'Callaghan helped him buy the vineyard, and ever since, Ringland has sold half the fruit back to Rockford. With a wine selling for more than $500 a bottle, the chance to effectively double production by keeping all the fruit would be too much of a temptation for many, but not Ringland. And you can imagine marketers scratching their heads at O'Callaghan's refusal to promote such an illustrious fruit source.

O'Callaghan has never been one to worry about money, and he knows those who come to work for him are not motivated by the almighty dollar either. "Chris got shit money for years, barely cellar-hand rates," he admits before adding, "What he did get was knowledge, a network and the chance to make his own wine. And that's turned out pretty well for him."

"I didn't worry so much about the money because I knew I was learning so much and it would put me in good stead for the future," agrees Ringland. It's a sentiment echoed by Christian Canute of Rusden, who is also one of the new breed inspired by Rockford.

"You were basically getting paid for what turned out to be a really valuable education," he says. "And the wine allowance was bloody good. Robert always said the best way to learn was to drink the stuff, but I think the first year I worked there I drank my entire allocation before the year ended."

Canute is in the middle of vintage when I call in to see him, up to his elbows in fruit with his colleague, Ben Chipman, and Lunar Wines' Corey Chaplin, both graduates of the Rockford school.

These guys are prime examples of what O'Callaghan thinks may be a vital part of his legacy: "I think the most valuable thing, in practical terms, I've been able to show these guys is that you can create a real top-quality winery without a whole heap of money if you're prepared to get right back to basics."

And this is basic winemaking – the basket press is being cranked as I talk to the Rusden guys – but the results are highly impressive.

"Working at Rockford really motivates you," says Chipman. "You can almost imagine yourself somewhere in Europe 100 years ago doing the same thing, and that's just super special. I think it does [make you want] to go out there and see if you can do it for yourself."

Chaplin recalls one vintage in which he and Canute rescued an ancient basket press and had it working alongside the original Robertson press and a newer hydraulic one: "We had all three working together at one stage and you could just stand back and see this chronological representation of winemaking techniques in action all at once. Being able to do stuff like that really urges you on."

O'Callaghan is neither competitive nor proprietorial, and has always said that a region can never have too many good winemakers. He's quick to point out the enormous contribution of an earlier group who dirtied their hands and strained their backs in the Rockford cellar. "Look at what Chris Ringland has done, look at Torbreck [Dave Powell], Turkey Flat [Peter Schulz] and Greenock Creek [Mike Waugh]. They've lifted the profile of this region through the roof. They've all committed in their own ways to the principle of understanding the value of these old vineyards and making sure that value is acknowledged and realised, and by doing so they lift the profile of the region enormously."

Powell is arguably the highest profile of the Rockford alumni. He's certainly the most outspoken. There are many fundamental principles that Rockford and Torbreck share. Both make wines which reflect the unique character of old Barossa vineyards, and although the winery equipment at Torbreck may be more modern than Rockford's, the basic process is almost the same.

But it's the differences between the two that tell an interesting story. Powell has built a successful market for his wines overseas, while export has hardly registered on the Rockford radar. And Powell has attained prices for his wines in Australia and overseas that put Basket Press and Black Shiraz in the shade.

"My attitude is, if you can make world-class wines, why shouldn't you get world-class prices?" Powell says. It's hard to argue. Just because Rockford's wines may be under-priced, it doesn't mean that Powell's are too expensive. They ably justify the price tags.

Powell is unashamedly ambitious, and it's tempting to speculate what might have become of Rockford if O'Callaghan had a fraction of Powell's entrepreneurial zeal.

Powell admits that they are both too opinionated and headstrong to ever be close friends, but he is also quick to recognise the influence of O'Callaghan in his success. "If I hadn't worked six years at Rockford, Torbreck wouldn't exist," he says.

"We use a basket press, open fermenters [and] a crusher here that we don't even use the crushing rollers on. It's used really just as a de-stemming cage, like the old Bagshaw at Rockford. All that stuff I learned at Rockford; I'd never been exposed to that in the other places I'd worked."

With access to some of the best old vineyards in the Barossa, Powell is well placed to comment on the influence of O'Callaghan beyond the winery walls: "When Robert started out making Basket Press, a lot of people around here were trying to make their top wines cabernet. At the end of the day, Robert O'Callaghan is the one who I reckon saved the Barossa.

"Would someone else have done it? Maybe, maybe not. But Robert is a great orator, a great storyteller, a great person to inspire people. I don't think anyone could have done it quite as well. And it's not just winemaking. There's his involvement with the Barossa Residents Association and making sure the whole place wasn't turned into one bloody big housing estate. I think virtually all the successful wineries here could trace that success back to Robert in one way or another."

The most directly drawn line leads to O'Callaghan's eldest son, Tim, and the wines he produces for his Diggers Bluff label. Tim – bushy-bearded, a dead ringer for his old man – takes his father's fondness for the old ways to almost masochistic extremes. In a small shed towards Seppeltsfield, Tim produces wines that actually deserve the often misused term "hand-crafted".

The basket press rescued at Rockford by Chaplin and Canute now resides at Diggers Bluff. Each ferment takes two days of gradual hand cranking to be pressed, the gases in the must gently forcing the juice out through the press, resulting in a softer, finer extraction.

Tim uses a tiny crusher with a one tonne an hour output. It would make most winery accountants despair but means a lot of full berries in the fermenter. And he releases his old-fashioned shiraz cabernet blend, The Watchdog, at a financially perilous seven years of age. This approach will never make him a millionaire, but it does result in wines that capture the spirit and personality of the maker more than almost any I've seen. They perfectly encapsulate the philosophical bent that characterises so many of those who have spent time working at Rockford. Some may have transferred the skills they learned there down the road, and others taken them to the world, but their time at with O'Callaghan is something that links them all. There is a strong sense of giving something back to the wine communities that support them, nurturing venerable vineyards, preserving many of the old winemaking methods and sharing knowledge.

O'Callaghan sees it as a chance to remind ourselves what is real in a rapidly changing world. "There's always something from the past that has a greater value now than it did a century or two ago," he says. "As the world gets increasingly advanced and digital, there is a great opportunity for a group of winemakers to have something really simple, basic and close to the ground.

"A wine that has a real close connection to the ground, that is organic in the truest sense, is going to be so important. Wine can do that. Wine should do that."

"It's about the pleasure you get from [making wine] and sharing that pleasure with the people who drink it," O'Callaghan concludes. "Do that and we'll all make a quid, we'll pay our bills, and that's enough."

BIBLIOGRAPHY

Bests Great Western, *Celebrating 150 Years*, Bounce Books (2016)

Busby, James, *Journal of a tour through some of the vineyards of Spain and France*, Stephens and Stokes (1833), facsimile reprint David Ell Press (1979)

Gladstones, John, *Wine, terroir and climate change*, Wakefield Press (2011)

Halliday, James, *James Halliday's Wine Atlas of Australia*, Hardie Grant Books (2014)

Halliday, James, *A History of the Australian Wine Industry 1949–1994*, Australian Wine and Brandy Corporation in association with Winetitles (1994)

Helm, Ken and Burgess, Trish, *Riesling in Australia: the history, the regions, the legends and the producers*, Winetitles (2010)

Linn, Rob, *Yalumba and its People*, Openbook Publishers for Samuel Smith and Son Pty Ltd (1999)

MacDonald, Fiona, *Hill of Grace: 150 Years of Henschke Under Southern Skies*, Hardie Grant Books (2018)

McIntyre, Julie, *First vintage: wine in Colonial New South Wales*, UNSW Press (2012)

Mattinson, Cambell, *Why the French Hate Us*, Wine Front in conjunction with Hardie Grant Books (2007)

Robinson, Jancis, Harding, Julia and Vouillamoz, José, *Wine Grapes: A complete guide to 1,368 vine varieties including their origins and flavours*, Penguin/Ecco (2012)

Spain, Katie, with an introduction by James Tindley, *The Wine Producers: A Taste of McLaren Vale*, Bud Media (2021)

Spain, Katie, with an introduction by James Tindley, *The Wine Producers: A Taste of Barossa*, Bud Media (2021)

INDEX

Note: Producers are filed under surnames. Where family members with the same surname appear only in the producer description they are not indexed separately.